Deporting Black Britons

MANCHESTER
1824

Manchester University Press

For Kiana Amara Dixon, born 13 March 2020

Deporting Black Britons

Portraits of deportation to Jamaica

Luke de Noronha

Manchester University Press

Published by Manchester University Press
Altrincham Street, Manchester M1 7JA

www.manchesteruniversitypress.co.uk

British Library Cataloguing-in-Publication Data
A catalogue record for this book is available from the British Library

ISBN 978 1 5261 4399 0 hardback

First published 2020

Typeset in Kuenstler and Scala Sans
by R. J. Footring Ltd, Derby, UK
Printed in Great Britain by TJ International Ltd, Padstow

Contents

Pictures

Maps, tables and graphs

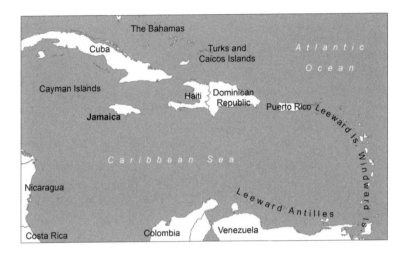

Map 1. *The Caribbean*

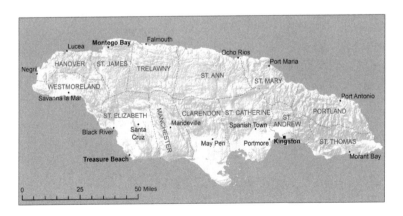

Map 2. *Jamaica*

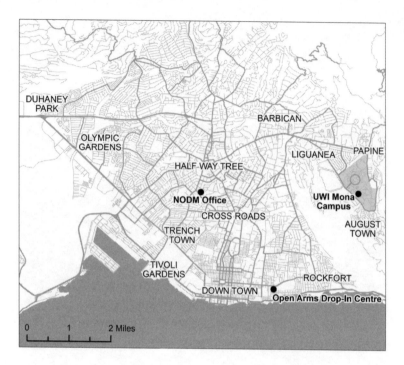

Map 3. *Kingston*

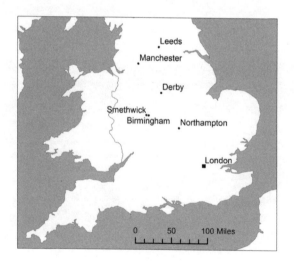

Map 4. *English cities and towns featured in the book*

Chapter 1

Introduction

A mile or so east of Kingston's downtown parade, where Victoria Avenue becomes Windward Road, there is a small dirt track that leads off the main road. Passers-by might not notice the faded sign reading 'Open Arms Drop in Centre', but most Jamaicans will be familiar with the area I am describing. Open Arms is just opposite Bellevue, Jamaica's only psychiatric hospital, and while Bellevue has a long history – first founded as the Jamaica Lunatic Asylum by the British in 1861 – Open Arms opened only in 2006. Open Arms now houses up to 70 homeless men, in two large dormitories and a handful of single rooms, and a significant proportion of the residents are 'deportees' from the UK and North America (I use scare quotes around 'deportee' throughout because the term has some pejorative connotations in the Jamaican context).[1]

I visited Open Arms several times, to meet men who had been deported from the UK. One afternoon as I was leaving the compound, unsatisfied with my interviews and troubled by my observations, I noticed a young man sitting in the shade, at some distance from everyone else, using what looked like a new iPhone. He was holding a portable wireless router and I made some inane comment about Jamaica's lack of data signal. He responded in a distinctly London accent and we had a brief conversation. His name was Devon, and he was wary about speaking with me. Anyway, he would not be in Jamaica for long, he explained. He had an ongoing immigration appeal in the UK, one that he needed to win so that he could return to his son and his family in London.[2] Devon, who was in his early twenties, explained that he had lived in the UK since he was seven years old. He did not think he could survive in Jamaica, and he told me that if he left Open Arms he would be killed. He sounded paranoid.

I saw Devon again on subsequent visits to Open Arms, but after a few months he was no longer living there. I do not know where he went, but the chance that he is back with his family in London is close to zero. Unfortunately, his story is not unique, not even unusual, and its themes became increasingly familiar as I got to know more deported people in Jamaica.

Open Arms is an unsettling place. On my last visit, in 2017, a group of local men arrived at the gates, threatening to kill two of the residents who had offended them, and promising to return with guns. This was not the first such encounter. On several occasions, men from Open Arms had been robbed of their phones, tablets and money just outside the gates, and the centre had been broken into on three occasions. Several people told me the story of an Open Arms resident who was killed just outside the centre two years earlier, a young man who had also been deported from the UK after spending most of his life there. Open Arms is clearly an extremely difficult place to live, especially for people who have just arrived from the UK, and yet it might be the best option a deported person has.

Open Arms has been partly funded by the UK government, through the aid budget, as part of the 'Rehabilitation and Reintegration Programme'.[3] In return for UK funding, beds at Open Arms are reserved for destitute 'deportees' expelled from the UK. The Home Office then regularly cites the existence of Open Arms to justify further deportations, referring to the homeless shelter in deportation decision letters under 'provisions on return'. In effect, the Home Office deports people to Jamaica even when it accepts that they have no family or social support on the island. To facilitate this process, the UK government funds small non-governmental organisations (NGOs) to provide 'reintegration services' which can be cited to justify further deportations (see Chapter 8).

However, the vast majority of people deported from the UK to Jamaica do not live in Open Arms on their return. Instead, most return to low-income neighbourhoods like those adjoining Open Arms, often to live with estranged family members. People who have lived in the UK since childhood – whom I provocatively describe as 'Black Britons' – usually have no idea how to navigate these neighbourhoods, and many live in fear of serious violence. For example, one young man I met, Omar, described his vivid and repeated nightmares about being 'shot in the head by gunmen', just like his father had been when he was a child. Ricardo, who features in Chapter 3, was concerned that he would be targeted in Montego Bay, where his brother had been murdered two years earlier. Others told me they had seen people killed 'in front of their eyes', while Chris, who features in Chapter 4, recounted the time when a police officer held a gun to his head in East Kingston.[4] This explains why so many deported people, like Devon, insist that they have to get out of Jamaica. Somehow they have to imagine that it might be possible for them to return to their homes and families in Britain.

I had travelled to Jamaica to meet people in this situation, people who experienced deportation as a kind of banishment. Whether I was prepared for it or not is another question, but I was interested in meeting people who had moved to the UK as children and been deported as adults.

This project began before the outbreak of the 'Windrush scandal' in 2018, when it was discovered that long-settled Caribbean migrants who had moved to the UK before 1973, and who therefore should not have been deportable, had been denied access to public services and in some cases been wrongfully deported because of the UK's 'hostile environment' immigration policies.[5] The treatment of the 'Windrush generation' caused public outrage, demonstrating that the settled status of 'Black Britons' remained revocable and raising a number of questions about race, citizenship and belonging in 'Brexit Britain'.[6] However, the deported people featured in this book were not from the 'Windrush generation' – they migrated to the UK much later, in the early 2000s and, most importantly, they were all deported following criminal conviction. Indeed, the 'Windrush generation' were explicitly contrasted with 'foreign criminals' in 2019 and 2020, when, in the wake of the 'Windrush scandal', the Home Office sought to reinstate deportations to Jamaica by deporting only those they defined as 'serious foreign criminals', on chartered mass deportation flights.[7]

My focus on people with criminal records, then, is deliberate. In my view, writing about 'foreign criminals' – those archetypal 'bad migrants' – requires more radical and interesting forms of critique. To understand the deportation of people with criminal records, we need to move beyond those liberal accounts that emphasise the victimhood and suffering of particular groups of migrants (e.g. 'genuine refugees' and 'victims of trafficking').[8] Indeed, it is by recognising the connections between punitive criminal justice policies and aggressive immigration restrictions – between cages and walls – that we can develop a more expansive account of state racism.[9] For this reason, *Deporting Black Britons* focuses on the deportation of 'foreign criminals', who in any case are the most likely to be deported despite having grown up in the UK.

Once in Jamaica, I was able to meet people who fit this description pretty much as soon as I landed: 'Black Britons' deported following criminal conviction who experienced deportation as banishment. However, despite meeting over 50 deported people during my time on the island, the book orbits around the stories of just four men – Jason, Ricardo, Chris and Denico – who

I came to know best, and who shared their memories and perspectives with me over four years. Importantly, the book's main focus is not on how these men survived in Jamaica post-deportation (more on this in Chapter 7), but on how and why they were deported in the first instance.[10] Chapters 2–5 offer individual life-story portraits of Jason, Ricardo, Chris and Denico, tracing their experiences of racism and criminalisation in the UK, as well as their legal journeys through the immigration system in Britain. Before engaging with their individual life stories, however, it is important to situate their expulsions in wider historical context.

What are the UK's laws and policies in relation to deportation? What broad social and political problems is deportation seen to respond to? How did we get to the point where deporting people from everything they know became both routine and unremarkable, and how can we best to situate deportation within a broader social and historical canvas? In short, why are 'Black Britons' being deported? Or, put differently, what is the preface to this book's opening scene? This chapter is organised around some tentative answers to this deceptively simple question: how did we get here?

Deportation nation[11]

For almost all of the twentieth century, deportation was seen as an exceptional form of immigration control in Britain, reserved primarily for 'enemy aliens' in times of war.[12] Since the Second World War, the term 'deportation' has carried echoes of Nazi genocide – memories that should still orient us in the struggle against racism and nationalism[13] – and this is part of what has made deportation controversial.[14] More recently, however, deportation, often rebranded as 'removal' or 'return', has become an increasingly routine and unremarkable element of immigration policy. Matthew Gibney refers to the staggering rise in deportations in the last three decades as the 'deportation turn'.[15] To understand how this came to be, we need to think about the various crises to which deportation is seen to respond.

Most obviously, deportations from the wealthy countries of the global North have increased partly in response to new migration dynamics. In Europe, since the late 1980s, more people have been migrating without official authorisation – unlike the post-war labour migrants and Commonwealth subjects before them.[16] These migrants have often claimed asylum as one route to settlement, which explains the focus on 'asylum seekers' within deportation policy.[17] As importantly, the overall number of people travelling internationally has increased significantly with the availability of affordable air travel, and this raises the spectre of uncontrolled and unregulated mobility. The increase in deportations is often explained by deporting states in these terms: as a response to clandestine mobilities, 'bogus asylum claims' and intensified border crossing in general.

However, while states like the UK might be wary about asylum, and remain particularly concerned about racialised migrants settling permanently, there has been a marked demand for temporary migrant labour in recent years, mainly at the bottom of the labour market.[18] Labour migrants are in demand for work particularly in hospitality and services in large cities – as well as within the agriculture, construction and health and social care sectors – and so immigration restrictions are, in practice, about managing competing interests, rather than actually 'expelling all the migrants'.[19] Indeed, in the last three decades it is the intensification of bordering, and not the intensification of migration, that has been historically unprecedented.[20] In this light, the person subject to deportation – the 'illegal immigrant' – is not a fixed type, and usually not a person who has crossed a border clandestinely, but rather an individual who may have been *illegalised,* for any number of reasons.[21] In other words, the law changes around people, and they are *made illegal*.[22] Migration itself is not a problem, or rather does not have any pre-determined social significance, until 'migrants' are defined in discourse and law, turned into juridical categories like the 'asylum seeker' and the 'illegal immigrant', and thereby subjected to legal and coercive state power.[23] Clearly, then, deportation is not a straightforward response to there being more 'illegal immigrants'. Instead, in the context of intensified bordering, demand for particular kinds of disposable labour and widespread nativist fears about changing demography, deportation has become a central tool in state attempts to order and restrict migration.[24]

Deportation therefore serves an important *symbolic* function, demonstrating to citizens that states are *in control*. Deportation confirms that citizens *belong* because, unlike unwanted 'migrants', they cannot be deported (although some British citizens can now have their citizenship stripped as a precursor to deportation).[25] Deportation as spectacle is crucial here, because most irregular and deportable migrants will not actually be deported (states do not have the capacity nor the desire to deport everyone who breaches immigration restrictions).[26] However, deportation is not only about this affirmation of citizenship through negation, it also operates as a tool of labour discipline. Critical border scholars have shown that the *condition of deportability* makes migrant labour especially disposable, and thus desirable to employers.[27] In her excellent book *Deported*, Tanya Golash-Boza argues that mass deportation from the US 'is part of the neoliberal cycle of global capitalism ... designed to relocate surplus labor to the periphery and to keep labor in the United States compliant'.[28] These arguments are compelling, but they do not map neatly onto the UK context.

Firstly, deportation from the UK does not exist on the same scale as in the US and so the claim that deportation involves the relocation of surplus labour seems a stretch. Equally, while illegalised labour is certainly desirable to some employers in the UK, it is not clear that the economy relies on it. In other words, demand for deportation and demand for disposable labour represent sometimes competing and confused interests. Racial anxieties and resentments surrounding 'migration' enforce their own logics and demands, which are never separate from but neither reducible to economic rationalities. My point here is that there is no simple, one-size-fits-all explanation for the UK's immigration policies. Deportation is neither a straightforward response to an increase in the number of 'illegal immigrants', nor is it a concocted trick designed to grant employers access to cheap and pliable labour (as Gargi Bhattacharyya puts it in her reflections on racial capitalism: 'No one maps out this programme and then enacts it').[29] The contradictions matter, and to reach a more sophisticated account of the 'deportation turn' we need to consider wider shifts in economy, society and state.[30]

Firstly, the 'deportation turn' has been accompanied by the retrenchment of the welfare state and a renewed emphasis on individual responsibility. Increasingly, the state is seen not to owe anyone anything, and people who are deemed unproductive have become the object of contempt.[31] Those who 'depend' on welfare have been defined as failed citizens, as have the 'criminals' who populate the UK's bloated prison estate.[32] The punitive turn within welfare, immigration and criminal justice policy are all connected, symptoms of the transition from welfare-based social democracy to neoliberal authoritarianism.[33] In this context, 'migrants', especially 'illegal immigrants' and 'asylum seekers', have been defined as undeserving outsiders who take from 'hardworking taxpayers' (in an important sense, this logic precipitated Brexit).[34] Deportation therefore targets 'unproductive and dangerous foreigners', producing the state as a meaningful actor working in the interests of decent, law-abiding citizens, regardless of what immigration controls actually do in practice.

Of course, since 9/11, deportation has also been legitimated by concerns over 'security'.[35] Widespread concerns about terrorism have intensified demands for the expulsion of ungrateful and dangerous 'migrants and minorities' more broadly, and fears surrounding terrorism, security and the 'enemy within' have made the confinement and expulsion of 'migrants' seem wholly legitimate (the 'war on terror' has even made it possible to denationalise and then deport British citizens).[36] Indeed, the figures of the 'terrorist', the 'migrant' and the 'criminal' seem to blur at the edges, and the anti-immigrant, law-and-order authoritarianism of both New Labour and Conservative governments has been licensed by this hydra-headed Other.[37] To summarise, in the context of austerity, anti-welfarism, punitive criminal justice, counter-terror and anti-immigrant fervour, deportation provides one answer to several questions about state authority and legitimacy in twenty-first-century Britain.

While this critical sketch of British politics might seem a long way from the lives of destitute 'deportees' in Jamaica, it is, in an important sense, the story of how they got there. Put in the broadest terms, twenty-first-century late capitalism is defined by the proliferation of borders and walls,[38] and 'the emergence of new logics of expulsion'.[39] Deportation from the UK to Jamaica should be situated in this context.

* * *

Deporting Black Britons examines the effects of immigration control on people's lives, without providing a close analysis of immigration law and policy itself. This is a book about how immigration control is lived, rather than a fine-grained account of the UK's immigration system. However, it is important to offer a broad account of the UK's deportation regime in this introductory chapter, and to explain some of the different types of expulsion and some relevant policy terms.[40]

Deportation represents the coercive negation of citizenship through forcible expulsion; it is the logical extension of migrant 'illegality' – 'the sovereign power to deport is an extension of the sovereign right to exclude'.[41] In practice, people are deported for a number of reasons and under different names, depending on the immigration policies of the deporting state. In UK law, 'deportation' is a specific term that applies to people whose removal from the country is deemed 'conducive to the public good'. Most often, this means people with criminal records. 'Removal', on the other hand, 'refers to a larger set of cases involving the removal of non-citizens who have either entered the country illegally or deceptively, stayed in the country longer than their visa permitted, or otherwise violated the conditions of their leave to remain in the UK'.[42] 'Refused asylum seekers' and 'overstayers' tend to be removed, while 'foreign criminals' are deported – although in practice many people move between statuses (e.g. people overstay, are criminalised *and* claim asylum).[43] In this book, however, I do not restrict the use of 'deportation' to its definition within UK policy. Instead, I use the term more broadly to refer to all cases of forced expulsion, in no small part because alternatives like 'removal' and 'return' are designed to obscure the violence of deportation.

The UK enforces the removal of non-citizens in different ways (I use the term 'non-citizens' rather than 'migrants' here because some people who are subject to immigration control were born in the UK, or moved as toddlers, and so it makes little sense to call them migrants). Some people are 'refused entry at port' and returned before they properly enter national territory (these removals are not included in the statistics presented below). In other cases, non-citizens living in the UK have their immigration applications rejected, and are then made illegal and told to leave the country or face detention and forced expulsion. Under current immigration policies, these illegalised non-citizens are denied access to employment, housing, healthcare and the ability to drive or open a bank account, and are thereby incentivised to leave 'voluntarily'. Many thousands leave each year on these terms and their removals are counted as 'voluntary returns' (there were 20,502 such returns in 2017). For thousands of others, removals are enforced, which means that they are deported via immigration detention, and escorted onto planes with force. In 2017, there were 12,321 such 'enforced removals'.

For those whose removal is enforced, a further distinction concerns whether they are deported on commercial flights or on specifically chartered mass deportation flights. Since 2001, the UK has used charter flights for deportation to particular countries. Initially, charter flights went to Kosovo and Albania – and there are still more charter flights to Albania than to any other country – but they have since flown to the Czech Republic, Afghanistan, Iraq, Jamaica, Nigeria, Ghana, Sri Lanka and Pakistan. Charter flights contain only 'deportees', escorts and the flight crew, and they leave in the early hours of the morning from undisclosed locations. They have therefore been described as the Home Office's 'most brutal and terrifying instrument'.[44] The violence of these charter flights was made publicly visible by 15 activists, known as the Stansted 15, who in March 2017 took direct action to ground a mass deportation flight scheduled to fly to Nigeria and Ghana (which led to a charge of terrorism offences, for which they were convicted).[45] There were four mass deportation flights to Jamaica between 2014 and 2019, although charter flights went much more regularly to Nigeria, Ghana, Pakistan and Albania over this period (in 2017, a total of 1,664 people were deported on charter flights). Importantly, however, the vast majority of 'enforced removals' still occur on commercial flights, where deported people are placed at the back of planes otherwise occupied by people going on holiday or visiting relatives.

As noted, it is only quite recently that deportation has become a routine component of immigration control in liberal democracies in the global North. Before the late 1980s, the total number of persons removed from the UK each year did not exceed 2,000. This number rose steadily throughout the 1990s, reaching roughly 7,000 by 1999. In the 2000s, this number spiked dramatically, peaking in 2004, when there were 21,425 enforced removals alone, with thousands more returning 'voluntarily' or 'assisted'. Since 2004, the number of enforced removals has been falling steadily, and in 2017 they were down to 12,049. Interestingly, the number of 'enforced returns' to Jamaica has been falling at a greater rate than the overall number.[46]

However, a note of caution is warranted here. The statistics on removals and deportations are slippery, because methods of data collection and categorisation change over time. In 2017, a total of 12,049 people were removed by force, but there were an additional 20,502 who left 'voluntarily', after being threatened with deportation (indeed, in 2017 more Jamaican returns were 'voluntary' than 'enforced'). Data on 'voluntary returns' have only been collected since 2014, and so it is not yet possible to track changes over a meaningful length of time. In this context, it is difficult to say whether deportations have been falling, or just changing form, and it is therefore important to view deportation in relation to the wider policies which illegalise and exclude non-citizens. The 'voluntary return' of people who have been denied access to employment, shelter, education and healthcare is of course far from voluntary, and it is worth noting that the collection of data on 'voluntary returns' corresponds neatly with the introduction of the UK's 'hostile environment' immigration policies – policies which were explicitly designed to increase the number and proportion of 'voluntary returns'.

The 'hostile environment' refers to the set of immigration policies introduced with the Immigration Act 2014 and intensified with the 2016 Act, which were designed to comprehensively exclude 'illegal immigrants' from all public services and to facilitate their detection through various data-sharing initiatives.[47] Landlords were required to confirm their tenants' 'right to rent'; employers could be fined up to £20,000 per worker for employing 'illegal migrants'; NHS staff were required to check people's right to access healthcare; university lecturers were supposed to monitor their students' attendance; schools were required to collect nationality information on their pupils; banks and the Driver and Vehicle Licensing Agency (DVLA) were required to share information with the Home Office.[48] All of this was designed to create, in the words of then Home Secretary Theresa May, a 'really hostile environment', so that 'illegal immigrants' would find it impossible to live in the UK, and thus would be encouraged to 'go home'.[49] Clearly, these policies will have impacted the number of 'voluntary returns'. Indeed, the intention of the 'hostile environment' was to incentivise people to enact their own expulsion by denying them access to the means of life.

The UK's 'hostile environment' came under intense scrutiny following the 'Windrush scandal' in spring 2018, when it was discovered that people who had moved to the UK before 1973, mainly from the Caribbean, were being caught up in the UK's 'hostile environment' immigration policies. Amelia Gentleman at The Guardian, along with a few others, began collecting stories of people who had lost their jobs, houses and access to healthcare because they had been illegalised – some had even been deported and were struggling back in the Caribbean.[50] The story picked up steam, and Home Secretary Amber Rudd was forced to resign. Quite quickly, a consensus emerged: the Windrush generation were citizens, members of the national 'we', and thus their treatment had been unacceptable and cruel. The Windrush generation were definitely not the 'illegal immigrants' that the policies were designed to target.[51] In this way, the harm done to 'Windrush migrants' was isolated from the treatment of more recent migrants who had been subject to the 'hostile environment' – people who were also illegalised, forced into destitution, detained and deported. That said, the scandal did provide some space for a broader conversation about the UK's draconian immigration policies, and for the first time in a long while deportation became controversial. Indeed, this explains the marked drop in 'enforced returns' in both 2017 and 2018.[52]

However, the concern for Windrush migrants was not without conditions. The 'Windrush generation' were constructed as 'good migrants/citizens' who had contributed, abided by the law and paid their taxes – even if they were now pensioners or in receipt of benefits – and this worked to distinguish them from un-deserving 'illegal immigrants'. This framing was made especially clear when Sajid Javid, the recently appointed Home Secretary, promised to assist all wrongfully deported Windrush migrants, *except those with criminal records*.[53] In effect, having a criminal record, however minor or from however long ago, was enough to nullify over 45 years of residence. Even in that rarest of moments in British politics, when there was widespread sympathy for one particular group of 'migrants', the deportation of those with criminal records remained perfectly proportionate. Never mind what they would be returned to – never mind the news stories we had just read about what they were being returned to – the mere mention of criminality was enough to set us back into default mode: 'send them back'. This reflects the almost total consensus on the need to deport 'foreign offenders', which the government would later rely on when deporting Jamaican 'foreign offenders' en masse in 2019 and 2020, despite the ongoing public outcry about the 'Windrush scandal'.[54] Fergus Shanahan, executive editor of the UK's most widely read daily newspaper, *The Sun*, laid out this perspective quite clearly back in 2006:

> Let's be clear, if someone comes to our country and abuses our hospitality by committing serious crimes, I don't give a toss what happens to them when they are thrown out. I'm willing to pay their airfare and for the bullet when they get home. We've got enough of our own villains without importing or releasing back into the com-munity the rapists, muggers and murderers of the world.[55]

It is significant that the men featured in this book were deported not simply as 'illegal immigrants' but as 'foreign criminals'.

Importantly, they were deported under laws created by New Labour to enforce the deportation of 'foreign national offenders'. To understand why the UK deports 'Black Britons', then, we need to travel further back, and perhaps the critical moment in this story is the 'foreign national prisoner crisis' of 2006.

'Foreign criminals' and racist criminal justice

The figure of the 'foreign criminal' first emerged in April 2006, when it was discovered that over 1,000 'foreign prisoners' had been released from prison without being considered for deportation.[56] An enormous political scandal ensued, and the mainstream press focused on the 'foreign killers, rapists and paedophiles' who were 'let loose' and 'roaming our streets'.[57] The Home Secretary, Charles Clarke, was sacked and the government promised to introduce new policies and laws to deal with 'foreign criminals'.

This 'foreign national prisoner crisis' surfaced amid more general 'moral panic' about the number of migrants, especially 'asylum seekers', who had been arriving in Britain over recent years. New Labour had been in power for nine years at this point, and while they had demonstrated their steadfast commitment to draconian immigration policies, punitive criminal justice, and anti-welfare politics over that period, they had not done enough to assuage the criticism of the Conservative opposition and the tabloid press. As such, when the 'foreign prisoner crisis' hit, it was made to represent not only Labour's lack of control over immigration, but also the government's soft touch approach to crime and welfare. The 'foreign criminal' emerged here as a kind of 'perfect villain', demonstrating Labour's total lack of control. Importantly for my purposes, while the 'foreign prisoner' scandal subsided after a few months, the figure of the 'foreign criminal' was born,[58] with far-reaching and ongoing consequences for policy and practice.[59]

Firstly, in response to the 'crisis', the government increased the resources allocated to its criminal casework directorate within the immigration service, expanding it to 35 times its original size in a matter of months.[60] 'Foreign offenders' were now routinely detained under immigration powers after they had served their prison terms, and they found it increasingly difficult to get released from prisons or immigration removal centres after serving their sentences (the UK has a system of indefinite immigration detention). The number of 'foreign criminals' deported increased fivefold, from about 1,000 in 2005 to around 5,400 in 2008,[61] and numbers have remained relatively stable in subsequent years, averaging over 5,000 in the four years following the scandal, and peaking at 6,171 in 2016.[62] The prison system has also been adapted to facilitate deportations – there are currently two 'foreign national only' prisons in the UK, and Home Office immigration staff are increasingly embedded within prisons more widely.[63] Since the scandal of 2006, then, 'foreign offenders' have increased as a proportion both of immigration detainees and of enforced removals, and thus the mushrooming of media stories on 'foreign criminals' has been mirrored in deportation practices.[64]

Changes to law and policy have facilitated the increase in deportations. New Labour's UK Borders Act 2007 introduced 'automatic deportation', which meant that the Home Office would automatically pursue the deportation of any 'foreign offender' who received a prison sentence of over 12 months. Since then, there has been a successive lowering of the threshold for 'criminality' in deportation cases. Individuals are increasingly being deported on the basis of minor and non-custodial convictions; many are defined as 'persistent offenders' despite not having received prison terms. The Home Office and the police initiated a joint policy called Operation Nexus in 2012, which allows 'Nexus officers' to build cases against non-citizens who have not been convicted in criminal courts, but whose removal is still deemed 'conducive to the public good' based on police intelligence. Individuals are thereby deported on suspicion,[65] and the fact that the UK now produces 'foreign criminals' without the crime is a sign of how punitive policy has become.[66]

As importantly, in the decade following the 'foreign prisoner crisis', appeal rights were cut, and legal aid was removed for deportation cases, so that most individuals facing deportation have been unable to find and fund legal representation. The UK also introduced a policy called 'deport first, appeal later' in 2014, to ensure that 'foreign criminals' could be deported first, and have their appeals heard from abroad. Unsurprisingly, out-of-country appeals were impossible to lodge effectively, and the policy was therefore ruled unlawful in June 2017.[67]

Even when 'foreign offenders' do get a chance to appeal from the UK, they have to demonstrate that their ties to the UK outweigh the strong 'public interest' in their removal. Many appeal their deportations on the basis of 'the right to respect for private and family life' – Article 8 of the European Convention on Human Rights – but the Immigration Rules make these claims extremely difficult to win. Relationships with British children and partners usually do not outweigh the 'public interest' in deportation,[68] and individuals have to prove that they have lived legally in the UK for most of their lives, are 'socially and culturally integrated' and that there would be 'very significant obstacles' to their integration into the country to which they are being deported.[69] Even where an individual meets this threshold, making the argument successfully is another matter, and for people who receive prison sentences of over four years the case is almost unwinnable. Some people facing deportation might claim asylum, but winning asylum cases is also incredibly difficult, especially for Jamaican nationals with criminal records.[70] Put simply, any foreign national who interacts with the criminal justice system will likely face deportation, and changes to the Immigration Rules and legislation have made appealing deportation increasingly difficult.[71] Of course, the 'strong public interest' in deporting anyone with a criminal record has marked implications for black men in Britain, given that the criminal justice system is institutionally racist.[72]

Overall, black people in Britain are more likely to live in poverty, to be unemployed and to have few qualifications – and, working with Census categories, 'Black-Caribbeans' face greater structural disadvantages than 'Black-Africans'. Black people in Britain face employment discrimination as well as high exclusion rates from school (affecting black boys in particular), and experience profound disproportionality in the criminal justice system.[73] Indeed, the racialisation of black people in Britain, and African-Caribbean populations in particular, has long focused on issues of crime and disorder. Racist 'common sense' surrounding 'black culture', the 'black family' and 'black crime' has remained remarkably consistent over the last six decades. In particular, the apparent criminality of 'black youth' has been explained in terms of pathological family structures, primarily in relation to 'absent fathers' and 'matrifocal families'.[74]

These tropes have found renewed articulation in relation to debates surrounding knife crime and gang violence, which have licensed new forms of policing and criminalisation targeting black men and boys.[75] Black people are stopped and searched by the police at around six times the rate of white people, and they are then more likely to be arrested, charged and given a prison sentence – most often for possession of drugs.[76] Importantly for the purposes of this book, the heavy policing of young black men now has deportation consequences, and it was clear that disproportionate policing practices precipitated the expulsions of the men I met in Jamaica. Many had been criminalised for possession or supply of drugs, carrying a bladed article or 'anti-social behaviour' – offences which inevitably reflect disproportionate policing practices. In the following chapters, I discuss processes of criminalisation and racism more substantively, but it is important to state at the outset that racist criminal justice practices propel 'Black Britons' towards deportation.

As is probably evident from the tone of the chapter so far, the emphasis in this book is not with interrogating why people commit crimes but rather with how and why they are *criminalised*. Of course, people exercise their own agency and make bad decisions; indeed, this is how deported people narrate their own lives. However, my critique is reserved for the state policies and practices which delimit agency and choice. Any reference to 'criminals' is used in scare quotes because the 'criminal' is not a human type but a juridical category, simply a person who has been criminalised in law (most people break the law, but processes of criminalisation are highly uneven).

The book does not attempt to moralise about why people sold drugs, committed robberies or got into fights, and it is hoped that by moving away from notions of moral and individual failure more critical and productive explanations will emerge. The argument presented in this book is that criminalisation and deportation should be viewed in historical context, as modes of racist exclusion. In this light, we can appreciate that while some Jamaican nationals might commit criminal offences, their forced expulsion from the UK to Jamaica forms part of longer arc of historical and racial injustice.

From *Empire Windrush* to Open Arms

The arrival of the *Empire Windrush* in 1948 has become central to the story Britain tells about itself. The boat, carrying 492 Caribbean British subjects, many of them former servicemen, is seen to have heralded the irresistible rise of multi-racial Britain.[77] However, when post-war migrants arrived from the Caribbean, the Indian subcontinent and Africa, they were immediately constructed as a problem.[78] Fears surrounding 'coloured migration' motivated restrictions on the movement of people from the Commonwealth, beginning with the Commonwealth Immigrants Act 1962. In subsequent immigration and nationality acts, the government further restricted 'coloured migration' by transforming the terms of political membership (the desired effect was never to restrict the mobility of those from the white dominions – that is, Australia, Canada, New Zealand). Britain was thereby transformed from an Empire and Commonwealth into a white island nation. Citizenship was increasingly defined by descent and thus 'race', and Commonwealth citizens were transformed into aliens.[79] The millions of people in the Commonwealth who had learnt English in British schools, recognised the queen as their sovereign and fought in two World Wars were, in quite a brief period of time, completely excised from the British polity.

The effect of this excision is that Jamaican nationals living in the UK today can be defined as 'illegal immigrants'. The reasons for them moving to and settling in the UK without official authorisation are afforded no real consideration. Those facing deportation to Jamaica are simply non-members who broke the rules, and that is all there is to it. This relies on the active forgetting of historical relations and entanglements, as though history were not relevant to contemporary patterns of migration and bordering. This forgetting is necessary to justify today's deportations to Jamaica.[80] In a cruel twist, when Jamaicans are deported 'back home', they often return with British accents, totally unfamiliar with life on the island, and many struggle to find basic security in a country with punishing levels of poverty, debt and everyday violence (see Chapter 7).

Contemporary Jamaican society is characterised by gross inequalities between rich and poor, as uptown people drive SUVs between shopping malls and their securely grilled houses, while people downtown live in severe poverty, in squatter communities with zinc-fence lanes and cramped tenement yards, amid the reality of 'turf war' and police violence, almost totally abandoned by both the state and labour market. Unsurprisingly, this uptown–downtown split maps closely onto racial and colour-based divisions on the island.[81] However, while Jamaica is renowned for its staggering homicide rate,[82] violence and poverty in Jamaica are a reflection of structural conditions and not 'defective cultures'. Since the 1980s, a brutal regime of enforced austerity has been enforced on Jamaica by the International Monetary Fund (IMF), and the country currently allocates around half of its yearly spend to debt repayments.[83] It is austerity and the constricted labour market which produce the conditions for violence, as Jamaica's urban poor increasingly rely on criminal modes of income generation – in relation to weapons, drugs, extortion and so on.[84]

Crucially, economic and social relations in Jamaica are still structured by the plantation, a point I elaborate in Chapter 7. If history does not pass, but instead accumulates,[85] then Jamaica's global marginality, its reliance on single-commodity exports and tourism, and its staggering debt profile cannot be disconnected from the history of slavery and colonialism.[86] In this light, the 'post' in 'postcolonialism' does not imply a clean break. As Wendy Brown notes, 'we use the term "post" only for a present whose past continues to capture and structure it'.[87] Because the economy is still structured by slavery, colonialism and debt, the Jamaican government is reliant on development funding and therefore courting the favour of wealthier states. In relation to the UK, this means complying with UK immigration policy in return for development funding, investment and the maintenance of cordial diplomatic relations. These unequal relations of development and dependency explain the existence of Open Arms Drop in Centre, the homeless shelter funded by the British government, through the aid budget, to house destitute and forcibly returned 'Black Britons'. Indeed, by tracing the journey from the *Empire Windrush* to Open Arms we can gain critical insights into the recent history of both Britain and Jamaica.

So far in this chapter, I have tried to situate the deportation of 'Black Britons' in historical context. This discussion should frame the life stories which follow. At this point, however, I want to describe the theoretical and political preoccupations which organise the subsequent chapters. In short, my over-arching concern is with better understanding the relationship between racism and immigration control, and it is worth taking some time to discuss how and why this remains the central question in the book.

Race, racism and immigration control in multi-status Britain

The dominant consensus in contemporary Britain seems to be that 'it is not racist to control immigration'. In this account, immigration policies are not racist because they do not make distinctions on the basis of 'race'. Racism, after all, refers to bigotry, intolerance and ideologies of biological superiority.[88] Political parties therefore consistently claim that their immigration policies are non-racist, because they are designed solely to protect and prioritise the interests of the British people.[89] However, neither 'the citizen' nor 'the migrant' are raceless figures. Only some 'migrants' become visible as 'migrants' – the Iraqi asylum seeker represents a grave threat, while the white Australian is scarcely visible. Meanwhile, even as some migrants do not really count as migrants, especially if they are wealthy and white, many black and brown British citizens are defined as second- or third- generation *migrants* still, made foreign despite formal membership. Without some conception of race, we have very little purchase on these issues. Nicholas De Genova's insights are instructive here:

> In the European context, the very figure of migration is always already racialized, and anti-racist struggles are inevitably concerned at least in part with the racial conditions of (non-European) migrants – even as dominant discourses of migration in Europe systematically disavow and dissimulate race as such.[90]

De Genova's point here is that, in Europe, the non-belonging of migrants is articulated through ideas about race, while racialised minorities are primarily defined by their 'migrantness'. In short, it is impossible to understand race and migration in isolation, and we need to better appreciate the 'racial dimension of the structural unease and the grids of intelligibility that inform the governing of immigration'.[91]

There is a broader and in fact more straightforward point to be made about the relationship between race and immigration control, though. Nation-states and the inequalities between them were formed through colonialism, which means that the bordering of these states inevitably has racial implications and effects. Race cannot be dispensed with so briskly when the principal target of immigration restrictions, the 'global poor', corresponds so closely with those 'formerly colonised' and those racialised as 'non-white'.[92] In this context, immigration controls are profoundly racial in their effects, even as race is disavowed – 'buried alive' to borrow David Goldberg's term.[93] However, this does not mean that racism is unchanging. As Stuart Hall reminds us, racism is always historically specific, and the challenge therefore is to theorise how racial distinctions and hierarchies are made and remade under particular conditions.[94] Borders are central to these processes of remaking, and *Deporting Black Britons* is therefore concerned with how immigration controls reconfigure racial distinctions and hierarchies in the present.

Several critical studies of immigration, racism and citizenship have developed precisely this argument. Mae Ngai, for example, in her important study of 'illegality' in the US, argues that restrictive immigration laws in the 1920s *produced* new categories of racial difference in the US, particularly in relation to Asians and Mexicans.[95] In the contemporary British context, Jon Fox, Laura Moroşanu and Eszter Szilassy examine the racialisation of Eastern Europeans, arguing that whiteness is 'the contingent outcome of immigration policy, practices, and processes',[96] while Les Back and Shamser Sinha have suggested that immigration controls produce 'new hierarchies of belonging', which reconfigure how racism manifests in contemporary London.[97] These scholars all argue that *race is produced by and through borders*, rather than existing in any stable way *a priori*.[98]

Importantly, then, it is not simply that immigration controls are enforced in racially discriminatory ways, but that the very terrain in which racial difference becomes meaningful is thoroughly structured by immigration restriction and the legal borders of citizenship.[99] This has significant implications for the struggle against racism, because as bordering practices change so does the very meaning of race and racism. This is especially relevant in a context in which borders are now everyday and everywhere:[100] 'transported to the middle of political space' and 'implosive, infinitely elastic, and, in effect, truly everywhere within the space of the nation-state'.[101] Borders get between people and follow them around, and this means that lines of difference and division – especially racial, national and cultural difference – are crosscut by migration and citizenship status.[102] To describe this terrain, I have found it useful to describe Britain as multi-status, and in fact this book is as much about racism in multi-status Britain as it is about deportation.[103]

By defining Britain as multi-status, I am firstly drawing attention to the fact that increasing numbers of the resident population in the UK are now non-citizens. Between 1993 and 2015, the number of non-citizens living in the UK increased from around 2 million to over 5 million (and the foreign-born population doubled from 3.8 million to over 8.7 million).[104] Crucially, non-EU citizens have been rendered increasingly temporary as the connection between migration, settlement and naturalisation has been unfastened – and a similar fate awaits (some) European nationals following the UK's departure from the EU. The British state now has the power to illegalise a greater number of people living within its borders, in more extensive and total ways, and this means that ethnic and racial differences are fractured and complicated by immigration status.[105]

If Britain is multi-status, then immigration control should be central to any account of racism and difference. Indeed, the prefix 'multi' has been used in several debates about race in Britain – the UK has variously been described as multi-ethnic, multi-cultural, multi-racial, multi-racist and characterised by emergent forms of multi-culture. Defining the UK as multi-status is therefore intended to centre immigration control within broader conversations about race, nationalism and culture (see Chapter 6 for a fuller account of multi-status Britain). Overall, the term 'multi-status' helps us to see new things about contemporary Britain, and in this book it helps me to describe people's friendship groups, family relationships and legal journeys.

More theoretically, the centring of status reminds us that immigration law is *productive*:

> While they are presented as filters, sorting people into desirable and non-desirable, skilled and unskilled, genuine and bogus, worker, wife, refugee, etc., national borders are better analyzed as moulds, as attempts to create certain types of subjects and subjectivities. Thus borders are productive and generative. They place people in new types of power relations with others and they impart particular kinds of subjectivities. Borders, then, are the mark of a particular kind of relationship, one based on deep divisions and inequalities between people who are given varying national statuses. It is important to recognize that this has far-reaching implications and is not simply restricted to the event of crossing a territorial border.[106]

Immigration controls not only produce racial distinctions and hierarchies, then, they are also productive of social meanings, identities and exclusions more broadly.[107] In later chapters, I question how immigration controls are implicated in the regulation of gender, sexuality and the family.[108] Indeed, the deportation of the men in this book was justified not only by reference to criminality and illegality, but also in relation to 'family life'. Each of the men appealed their deportation on the basis of connections to loved ones, and each was rejected on these terms, their relationships deemed insufficient to outweigh the 'public interest in deportation'.[109] In deportation appeals, some relationships are more legible than others, and legal determinations invariably mobilise race, gender and class-based stereotypes surrounding intimate and family relationships – particularly relevant for this book are ideas about 'absent fathers' and 'idle criminals'. Put simply, racism works through gender and sexuality to justify and enable deportation, and I discuss these processes further in Chapters 4 and 5.

Having presented some of the theoretical questions which frame the book, in what remains of this introduction I want to explore questions of methodology: explaining how the research was conducted; why I chose to speak to the people I did; and discussing some of the ethical and political questions that emerged in the process.

Ethnography, portraiture, power

Perhaps the first question worth discussing in relation to this book is 'Why Jamaica?', especially given that I am not Jamaican. Indeed, I had not visited the island before starting this project in 2015, and I decided to focus on the deportation of 'foreign criminals' before working out how and where I would meet people. All I knew was that I wanted to meet individuals after they had been deported, and I did not have the funds or resources to travel to more than one country (the research for this book was conducted for my PhD). In fact, the focus on Jamaica materialised only once I had contacted a local organisation in Kingston, the National Organization of Deported Migrants (NODM), and they had agreed to let me volunteer there.

In the first instance, then, I selected Jamaica because meeting deported people there seemed most feasible – the island is small and English speaking (although Jamaican English, or patois, is the main language) and a local organisation working with deported migrants agreed to host me. Further, even though Jamaica was not the easiest place to live, it felt more navigable to me than countries like Pakistan, Albania, Nigeria and Somalia – other countries that receive a sizeable number of 'deportees'. Importantly, while the book is focused on the deportation of Jamaican nationals, my hope is that the arguments will have a much wider resonance. Of course, the relationship between racism and immigration control takes on particular dynamics in relation to Jamaican nationals, especially in relation to the racist criminalisation of black young men in the UK, as well as with regard to the afterlives of slavery and empire in Jamaica (issues which I trace substantively in subsequent chapters). However, the theoretical and political implications of the arguments developed in this book should not be restricted to any one national or racial group.

I first travelled to Jamaica in September 2015, and began working with NODM straightaway. NODM is an organisation set up and run by deported migrants that provides assistance to people more recently deported from the UK and North America.[110] NODM has received almost all of its funding from the British government, which comes through the UK's aid budget as part of the same programme that supports Open Arms (see Chapter 8). Through this funding, NODM has been contracted to collect deported persons from Montego Bay airport, assist them with securing national documentation and help them to clear personal effects through Jamaican customs. The organisation also run workshops and offers other kinds of support where possible – although much of this additional support has relied on the initiative, commitment and tirelessness of Ossie, the now president of NODM.

Ossie was the face and the pulse of NODM during my time in Jamaica, and he was my main point of contact there between

2015 and 2019. During my initial trip to Jamaica, between September 2015 and January 2016, I spent the first few weeks mostly with Ossie at the NODM office. From there I arranged to meet deported people, firstly in Kingston and later all around the island (see Map 3). I met tens of deported people in those early weeks – including Jason, Ricardo, Chris and Denico – either at the NODM office, when following Ossie around Kingston, or after calling and arranging to meet people one-on-one. Ossie became a close friend and without him this book would not have been possible. He introduced me to deported persons, explained things to me and was always keen to 'reason' about politics more broadly. His insights are threaded throughout this book's pages.

In total, I spent just over eight months in Jamaica across four trips between 2015 and 2019. I met most of the people who feature in this study in Kingston, and tended to invite them up to the University of West Indies campus in Mona (UWI), where I was living. Deported people often felt unsafe and hypervisible where they lived, and so campus was a nice place to be: up at the edge of the city, shadowed by the Blue Mountains. Jason, Denico or Chris mostly came to meet me up at UWI, and we would walk around campus, go to the student bar or hang out in my flat, often watching football highlights. My interactions with Ricardo were slightly different because he lived in Montego Bay. I did not know anyone else in the city, and so most of my time there was spent with him, depending on whether he was working or not. When I returned to Jamaica in 2016 and 2017, Denico had moved to St Elizabeth, the sleepy parish in the south-west of the island, and so, with two of the four men living in the west of the island, more of my fieldwork was conducted out of Kingston, which I preferred (see Map 2). Whenever I was in Jamaica, though, whether in Kingston, Montego Bay or St Elizabeth, these four men were the people I spent most of my time with (with the exception, perhaps, of Ossie).

I did not intend to restrict my focus to these four men, however, and I met over 50 deported persons during my time in Jamaica. There were several others with whom I recorded long life-story interviews, maintained contact with over several years, and even drafted chapters for, but in the end I decided to restrict the portraits to just four. In part, this was because four stories already captured so much and because four felt like the right length, but it is also because I ended up with so much more material on Jason, Ricardo, Chris and Denico. I met them early on, and when I returned to the UK after my first trip to Jamaica I was able to stay in touch with them – primarily over WhatsApp, the messaging app on which we could send messages, pictures and voice notes (short recorded audio messages). Once I was back in the UK, I was also able meet some of their friends and family, which allowed me to continue researching and thinking about their life stories. This was especially important because the research process involved spending four months in Jamaica, before returning to the UK for nine months. And so, while there are many things that are especially interesting about the experiences and narratives of these four men, it is more accurate to say that the book orbits around them because they let me into their lives at the right time.

All four men are of a similar age, born between 1986 and 1992, and all left Jamaica as children, between the ages of 10 and 15. Each of them lived in the UK for around half their lives before being deported as young adults. Despite being part of a cohort, however, their stories diverge in important ways. Jason lived in London for around 14 years, and for most of that time he was homeless. Family rejection and immigration control compounded one another, and he could not find a route out of his illegality and enforced destitution. Ricardo, on the other hand, lived in Smethwick in the West Midlands, with his 'mum', in fact his step-auntie, who raised him with his cousins. He had a happy childhood and lots of friends, despite police surveillance and harassment from the age of 15. Chris was the only one of the four who had indefinite leave to remain (i.e. permanent residence), but after his first conviction for street robbery he could not naturalise, and he struggled to find work and to survive on meagre unemployment benefits. He sold drugs when his two children were 'on the way' and ended up being deported in 2013. Denico was also deported following a drugs conviction, but he had been an 'illegal immigrant' and so barred from seeking legal employment. He had moved to the UK when he was 13, but when his father regularised his stay with his new family, Denico was not included, and so he remained 'illegal'. He found some security when he met his partner Kendal, and they lived together with her two young daughters for around 18 months. However, at this point he was selling drugs to fund his immigration appeal, and this ultimately led to his deportation and separation from Kendal and the girls in August 2015.

Overall, then, the four men had very different experiences of criminalisation and illegalisation, but they all felt that their deportations were unjust because Britain was their home. Their friends, their families and most of their memories were in the UK, and they had nothing to return to in Jamaica. This is why the four men in this book might be referred to as 'Black Britons': they had attended British schools; they have British accents; and their reference points and cultural identifications are more British than Jamaican. Importantly, though, referring to the men as 'Black Britons' is not meant to recast them as 'really' British and not Jamaican. How these four men will relate to Britain and Jamaica is likely to change over time and with context, as with all identities.[111] By referring to them as 'Black Britons', then, my intention is simply to suggest that they are in many ways indistinguishable from black British citizens, and this points to some of the tensions between legal and lived forms of belonging in multi-status Britain – tensions which are brought into sharp relief by deportation.

To better understand these tensions, I travelled to meet the men's friends and family who remained in the UK. I visited Chris's mum several times, always at her house in West London. I met Ricardo's friends in the West Midlands and we talked about the police. I walked around the park where he had played football as a teenager and I spent time in his cousin's Jamaican restaurant. In East London, I played football with a group of homeless men and some of them remembered Jason from his time there. Two of them shared memories of Jason, the damage and vitality which defined his survival on the streets. South of Birmingham, I met Denico's partner Kendal and her mother Tracy, and they described how his deportation had affected them, especially Kendal's two young daughters. These friends and family members taught me that deportation is not suffered by individuals alone, even as it individualises. And, while deportation ruptures and separates, it is not 'the end'. While my relationships with family and friends were not as intensive as with Jason, Ricardo, Chris and Denico, our conversations have been essential to the overall shape and argument of the book.

* * *

In a book of this kind, it is important to reflect on my own 'positionality', especially in relation to race, class, gender and sexuality. I am a young man of a similar age to Jason, Ricardo, Chris and Denico, and we all grew up in major English cities and went to state schools at a similar time. This meant that we had a baseline of shared knowledge and experience from which to build – whether in relation to school, TV/film, celebrities and, most importantly, football. My maleness is clearly relevant here, and given that I am a straight-presenting man, a certain unquestioned heterosexuality permeated our relationships. I would speak about my partner with the four men, and they would ask how she was doing. Heterosexuality and maleness were part of what made me similar, and perhaps unthreatening, to Jason,

Ricardo, Chris and Denico. Assumed norms around gender and sexuality underwrote our rapport, the ease with which we got to know one another, and allowed for a certain kind of intimacy which that sameness can make possible. And yet there are obvious dangers in relying on maleness and heterosexuality to build rapport, when both are sites of such profound violence.[112] While I might claim that I did not to encourage machismo, and that I challenged certain sexist practices when I encountered them, there is no denying that our hanging out necessarily entailed certain gendered performances and complicities.

In fact, my focus solely on men was not intended, and I did meet and interview several deported women. However, I did not become as close to the women I met, nor spend anywhere near as much time with them as I was able to with the men featured in this book. Equally, many of the women I interviewed were older and did not have criminal records – my focus on criminality meant that there were more men who fit my target sample (although see the discussion of Michelle's story in Chapter 5). Despite my focus on deported men, however, I do incorporate gender into the analysis (however incompletely). Of course, gender is pertinent not only for women, and the men in this book experienced racialisation, criminalisation and illegalisation in profoundly gendered ways.[113] As Gail Lewis argues, 'racialization is a compound process that gathers into itself and is inseparable from discourses of gender and sexuality', and I try to recognise this inseparability of race from gender and sexuality in discussions throughout the book.[114] I also feature the perspectives of mothers, (ex)partners and female friends across the chapters (although the book would certainly benefit from more of their insights).

In terms of positionality, it is also relevant that I am mixed race (Indian/White British). When I asked Ricardo if it would have made a difference if I was white, he said 'Yeah, it definitely made a difference that you were mixed innit; if you were white I wouldn't feel comfortable telling you my story so deep'. I prodded him further on this, and he refined his answer somewhat: 'Okay, it's just like, if you were a white person it might have taken longer to gain that trust, because what I spoke to you about was very emotional, stuff that I don't talk about like that'. On the other hand, when I asked Denico if my 'race' made a difference to our relationship he replied: 'Not really. It's how you put yourself across really. That's how I decided to open up and get involved' (indeed, Denico read me as 'maybe Italian or something' when we first met). Of course, the research would have played out differently if I were black and/or Caribbean, although it is difficult to say exactly how. That said, I am cautious about what can be inferred from either racial proximity or difference. There is always more going on, something in excess of racial categories, and positionality should be about more than listing categories of identity.

Let me be clear, I am not suggesting that there are no relevant differences between me and the four men, nor that my ability to connect on a 'human level' flattened out imbalances of power. I am not Jamaican, I am not black and I did not grow up in poverty. Perhaps more importantly, I am a university researcher, I am writing this book (which represents an immense imbalance of power) and I have a British passport, which means I can move back and forth between the UK and Jamaica. However, having known and cared about these four men for some time now, my view is that understanding is possible through ethical care and political commitment. This kind of research presents as many opportunities for understanding and solidarity as it does for exploitation and violence – and this is as much about what happens outside the pages of this book as within them. In any case, hopefully something of my friendships with Jason, Ricardo, Chris and Denico comes through in the pages which follow, not overplayed or self-righteous, but as the necessary ground for a mode of research in which 'showing the people' is never an end in itself but only a beginning, a very small contribution to the collective struggle against racism and expulsions.

* * *

Deporting Black Britons is an ethnography, and ethnography can be defined most simply as 'the close observation of particular lives in particular places'.[115] Ethnography relies on 'deep hanging out', informal conversations and intensive relationships developed over time.[116] For me, ethnography meant getting to know people, rather than conducting one-off interviews. It meant spending the day together, running errands, chatting, without necessarily thinking instrumentally about informal conversations as data – even as they were, in aggregate, the source of my deepest understanding. Ethnography meant becoming part of people's lives in enduring, committed and sometimes ethically complicated ways (as when Jason told me I was the best friend he had in Jamaica; or when people asked me to send money). In this project, ethnography blurs the border between research and everyday life, not because I was trying to 'go native' or to pretend not to be doing research, but because if you spend enough time with people, then 'the research' becomes part of your 'real life'.

For me, an ethnographic engagement amounts to friendship, with all the complexity and messiness implied. Ethnography means committing more of your time and more of yourself to research encounters because you think that is the best way to research a given topic ethically and responsibly. Clearly, in the case of deportation, there are many reasons why people might take time to open up, and perhaps the most compelling reason to engage ethnographically is because people simply will not tell you the most important things otherwise. In this ethnography I am definitively not concerned with representing 'a culture', as in many anthropological studies. Instead, I use ethnographic and life-story methods to critique the UK's immigration system.[117] The end result is a series of four ethnographic portraits, followed by three slightly more theoretical chapters on citizenship, race and mobility.

Structuring the chapters as individual portraits allows for something richer than I could envisage with chapters organised thematically. When planning this book I had read several ethnographies of deportation and most of them were organised thematically and therefore chronologically – moving from initial migration, to experiences in school and at home, to criminalisation and prison, and then to deportation and post-deportation.[118] When reading these texts I often found it difficult to recognise and clearly remember different deported people from one chapter to the next. As Mitch Duneier argues:

> If you are going to get at the humanity of people, you can't just have a bunch of disembodied thoughts that come out of subjects' mouths in interviews without ever developing characters and trying to show people as full human beings. In order to do that it is useful to have a character that lives in a text.[119]

In *Deporting Black Britons* I want to develop characters, and to write in a way that makes remembering who is who easier.[120] Put simply, I want the stories to stick. Admittedly, structuring the next four chapters as individual portraits means that there are some missed opportunities for comparison. However, I hope that the engagement with each biography is more immersive this way, allowing the reader to become familiar with and to recognise Jason, Ricardo, Chris and Denico. Indeed, the four men are all invested in this book project, and they were motivated to tell me their stories in the hope that other people would not have to go through what they did. Like me, they hope the book will be read and that it will make a difference, however small.

Chapter outline

In Chapters 2–5, I present the four ethnographic portraits, which focus primarily on processes of criminalisation, illegalisation and meanings and experiences of racism in each of the men's lives. These four chapters question how and why each of the men was deported, developing several arguments about immigration controls from the perspective of their biographies. In Chapter 6, I turn to family and friends, using the findings from my research encounters in the UK to map out some of the hierarchies of both citizenship and non-citizenship in multi-status Britain. The book then moves away from Britain and approaches questions of race, citizenship and mobility in and from Jamaica. In Chapter 7, I develop critical theorisations of citizenship from the perspective of the 'deportee', arguing that citizenship is the global regime for the management of unequal populations. In Chapter 8, I examine the wider inter-state relations within which deportation is organised, and interrogate contemporary meanings of development in relation to the wider government of mobility. The Conclusion then ties together some of the key arguments from the preceding chapters, offering some final reflections and intimations of hope.

A note on format

Deporting Black Britons offers intimate and personal accounts, and not all of the people featured in the book want to be identifiable. Two of the four men featured in Chapters 2–5 are anonymised, and I have avoided using pictures of faces unless people agreed. Moreover, I have used pseudonyms for all family and friends, including in directly quoted documents and reported speech, and have changed most place names in the UK. Additionally, in some of the quotes italic type is used to add emphasis, either because the individual emphasised these points in their speech, or because I want to highlight passages that are of particular relevance to my argument.

The book also tries to appeal to both academic and non-academic readers, which has been difficult. For the academic reader, it means that much of the book's 'intellectual contribution' remains implicit. Very few words are committed to situating the argument in relation to wider intellectual debates, even when I am trying to intervene in specific academic conversations. Conversely, for the general reader there will be places where the book takes a notably theoretical turn. However, I hope that these sections are still interesting and that their political significance is made clear. The endnotes offer further reading and signposting for those interested, and they allow the text itself to be less weighed down with academic positioning and posturing. In any case, the binary between academic and non-academic is perhaps unhelpful, partly an effect of the university's institutional imperative to produce and sanction authorised knowledge. In the end, I am concerned only with helping us see the problem more clearly, so that we might challenge it more effectively.

Chapter 2

Jason

Jason was the first deported person from the UK I met in Jamaica. It was my second day on the island, in September 2015, and I was following Ossie from the National Organization of Deported Migrants (NODM) around. He had invited deported persons to the Salvation Army facility in downtown Kingston, where they could have their pictures taken for their national identity card applications. I sat quietly in the corner, my legs sticking to the old leather seat I perched on, while three staff from NODM stood puzzling over a printer. A few people were coming and going, waiting to have their pictures taken, when Jason bounded in at some pace. He spoke with a distinctly East London accent, frenetic and loud, and announced that he was ready for his photo. Ossie told him to 'hold on a minute', and so he stopped to wipe his face and change his t-shirt.

I went over and introduced myself and my accent clearly took him by surprise. 'I'm from Manchester, yes', I explained. He was slightly manic, and told me about a girl from Manchester he had dated when he was in England. He then brandished his Sondico trainers, a budget sports brand in the UK, and said 'You know about Sondico innit?!' He was full of life, charming and intense. After he had his picture taken, we sat and talked about his situation in Jamaica, and I tried to explain my reasons for coming to the island. I felt like he understood my project, but then he also wanted to tell me about business opportunities in Ocho Rios, from which he was sure I could 'make millions'.

'Do you smoke?', he asked after a few minutes, looking a little restless and keen to get outside, before leading us out into the bright hot midday clamour of Kingston's downtown parade, in search of a cold drink and a cigarette. Jason had a nice way of interacting with people around downtown parade – open, bold and joyful, even if his patois was unconvincing – and he seemed to enjoy showing me around. After our cigarette we went back into the Salvation Army building, where Jason spoke more about his life and his family in the UK:

> JASON: You know some of them Christmases there, I've slept out in the cold. Some of them Christmases there, I've been behind bars, you know. Some of them Christmases there, I didn't even get to see family, because I had to walk from London to Barking, yeah, to meet my family, and they lived at a different address you know, so, it was really, really upsetting. But I really do miss the festives, and the people, the people are very nice. Genuine people out there.

Jason had moved to the UK when he was 15 and had spent half his life in London. For most of that time, he had been homeless. He was an 'illegal immigrant' with 'no recourse to public funds', and so he could not work legally or access housing services and welfare benefits.[1] In this context, Jason would spend long nights loitering around London's West End, trying to make conversation with tourists, offering to help them source drugs and event tickets, or sometimes just seeking warmth and conversation in brightly lit games centres. His life in the UK was hard, and he described cold nights walking the streets, sleeping on buses, repeated encounters with the police, fears of deportation, and family rejection – from his mother in particular. That said, Jason never expressed any regret; whatever had happened, he was 'glad to have experienced the UK'.

In Kingston, Jason was still homeless and destitute – although this time with some consistent shelter in Open Arms. He had no money to move around the city, and he was not sleeping or eating very much for all the time that I knew him. Still, he retained a brightness and vitality that was both infectious and exhausting. He was always very enthusiastic about spending time with me, and he rang me more than I rang him, whether I was in England or Jamaica – at least when he had a working phone. While I was on the island, we mostly met up at the University of West Indies campus where I was living. With its slower tempo, campus afforded Jason a welcome break from downtown. Given how much time we spent together, especially in the first few weeks of autumn 2015, I had significantly more field notes for Jason than for anyone else on my first trip. We also recorded long life-story interviews which complement the many informal conversations we had.

Despite his liveliness, Jason had clearly suffered from many years of destitution, homelessness and abandonment, and I cannot write about him without emphasising *both* the damage and the vitality.[2] However, what is most striking about Jason's biography is that his early years were filled with such promise. As a boy in Jamaica, he attended prestigious schools and excelled in sports and athletics, and it was only after moving to Britain that he became socially marginalised. In this light, Jason's life story is a kind of tragedy. However, in the pages that follow I emphasise that this tragedy is not reducible to family rejection and bad luck, but must be interpreted in relation to the structuring force of immigration control. While people tend to narrate their life stories in terms of personalities and passions, this book situates individual and family biographies in relation to the law and state violence – connecting 'private troubles' to 'public issues'.[3]

School days

'I'd really like to see the new James Bond film', Jason said one afternoon, six weeks on from when we first met. We went to see

Spectre in the cinema uptown on Hope Road, and Jason offered commentary throughout – about his suit being Armani, her dress being Chanel, maintaining that the Ferrari was better than the Aston Martin, and then lighting up when the camera panned across central London: 'I used to be there, every morning', he explained. When the film finished, we piled out with the other cinema-goers, most of whom were getting into their SUVs to drive further up the hill. Jason and I stood in the car park, de-briefing in the sticky evening heat. I was thinking about taking a route taxi back up to campus when Jason said: 'Let's go and see my old primary school!'[4]

We crossed the road from the uptown mall and cinema, and reached St Peter and Paul, a fee-paying Catholic prep school, within two minutes. When we reached the front gates Jason persuaded the kind-faced security guard to let us look around: 'Just five minutes suh, I just want to show my friend my old school'. Once we were inside, he talked about running from here down to there every day, and pointed out the monkey bars he used to play on. He explained that his former classmates were now in America and Canada, 'Earning good money', and he reminded me, again, that one classmate had gone on to become Miss Jamaica. As we left the schoolyard he said, 'They'd like me to visit you know; in fact, I think they're waiting for me to come and say hi down here'.

One year later, Jason invited me to his former high school to watch the football team play. St George's is famed for its sporting success, and Jason had told me many times about his time there as star striker on the fifth-form football team. We watched the game, and Jason was visibly energised: shouting words of encouragement from the side-line, fist bumping and saying 'yes ma boss' and 'guidance' to everyone who walked by, as is his way. We were both excited because St George's won 6–0 in an impressive performance, but there was also a certain sadness about the whole scene. Jason was not that teenager any

Pictures 2.1 and 2.2. *Jason and classmates at St Peter and Paul prep school*

more, and neither was he recognisable as a former student of the school.

At one point, he felt like someone was laughing at him and exclaimed: 'I've got a journalist here from England who is talking to me'. Someone then said something about him being 'a deportee' and, frustrated, he turned to me and said: 'My friends from George's are all in the US. I wish they were here to see this.' In fact, Jason does not have any ongoing contact with his former schoolmates. Sometimes he would use my laptop to send messages to people on Facebook who had not responded since his last one. That one-way stream of communication captures something important about Jason's life: he is always reaching for connection and he does not like to think of his life as one he lives alone.

Jason taking me to visit his old schools demonstrates his desire to write himself back into these places.[5] This was important to Jason because his life had been defined by such rupture. The two schools were places where Jason's life had been hopeful, respectable and 'on the up', and visiting them all these years later, when Jason was a homeless 'deportee', and visibly so, seemed to capture the tragedy of his life. But Jason did not describe things this way: he took me there because it was interesting, important and fun. He wanted to remember and return, not to ruminate on what might have been. Ultimately, Jason wanted me to understand and then to tell his story in its fullest.

JD bags on the roof and sleeping on the N25

Jason and I had spent many hours together before I began recording any interviews. I had a good sense of his biography from our informal conversations, but Jason would often get lost in elaborate, dream-like narrations of particular encounters, sometimes evidently fanciful ones, and I thought recording his life-story might help me get a better grasp of some dates and details. I suggested that we record in Open Arms, where he was living, but after a few false starts and interruptions we decided to move to my flat. Once back at campus, we recorded for over four hours, and Jason provided me with a clearer, although still jumbled, picture of his life.

Jason was born in October 1984 in Kingston. His mother was young and so he was raised by his grandmother – as is fairly common in Jamaica. Jason's grandmother raised him for the first four years of his life, until she moved to England in early 1989.[6] Not long after, Jason's mother moved to England, and so he was raised by his aunties in Kingston, along with his younger brother Kevin and cousins. When he was 15, however, it was decided that Jason and Kevin would move to London to live with their mother, despite not having seen her for over 10 years. For the wider family, the option to 'go foreign' was viewed as 'the dream ticket', and so in August 2000 Jason and Kevin, aged 15 and 13, were put on a flight from Kingston to London Heathrow to settle with their mother (although the official version was that they were just visiting their grandmother for a few weeks).[7] This was the first time Jason had ever been on a plane; indeed, it would be the only commercial flight he would take:

JASON: Upon arrival it was my grandmother and my aunt that was waiting there. Then, just going around the corner, my mum with her husband was there. It was really nice to see my mum. I gave her a hug, didn't know this was my stepdad, I shaked his hand.

LUKE: Did you recognise her?

JASON: I, I, I've never seen her.

LUKE: Since you were two, of course.

JASON: Yeah, so I –

LUKE: Did you speak to her a lot on the phone when you were in Jamaica?

JASON: No.

LUKE: Not at all?

JASON: Not at all.... So, from then on now, when we were going back to Hackney, my stepdad said something, and he said, to my younger brothers and sisters, Talia, Sandra, Michael and that: 'Oh yeah, this is not your brother, these brothers are not your brother'.

Jason's relationship with his stepdad was tense from the beginning; Jason was accused of 'stealing things from the house' and 'looking for women'. He also struggled at school: 'The Asians didn't like me; you know they didn't wanna talk to me because I was black'. After just two months at a school in Ilford, London, Jason got into a fight and was expelled.[8] His mother told him to move out of the house:

JASON: I had my possessions in 12 JD bags [drawstring sports bags], and she kicked me out the house. I put them on top of a roof, of somebody's house. Because I didn't have no friends, where am I supposed to go, yeah? The people dem what I know from school couldn't help me. And I didn't want them to see me in that state, that position, so literally, I would stay outside of her house, until night come, and I wouldn't even eat nothing, yeah, and my lips are white, white like the wall, yeah, and I think it was a way of showing me as a mum, as a mother, it's time to do your own thing. But I needed her help. I needed her help big time, because, how am I supposed to go out there and do something when I don't have no ID? How am I supposed to go and get a job? How am I supposed to go and do this and do that? I thought to myself, okay then, let me try and do a newspaper round. I was sleeping on the bus.

Jason lost those JD bags on the roof, and with them some medals and certificates from St George's, which visibly upset him still. He was still attending college on and off at this time, and so he should not have been completely invisible to those who might have intervened, but for whatever reason he was not picked up by social services. And so, after just a few months in the UK, aged 16, Jason was homeless, and sleeping on the N25 night bus between Ilford and central London.[9]

After around two months, Jason's mother and stepfather agreed to let him back into their house on the condition that he help collect the younger children from school. This arrangement worked for a few weeks, until Jason was arrested on the bus while taking his brother Kevin to the cinema. He was accused of stealing a laptop, which he knew nothing about, and his mother's house was then searched by the police while he was held in the station. Jason's mother was furious, and he was kicked out again, this time permanently. Back on the streets, Jason began making friends with people he thought might provide him some support, companionship and shelter. He befriended 'Fish', a white boy around his age who lived in Essex, and they sold weed together. Jason would sometimes stay on his floor, under the bed, until he was discovered one morning by Fish's shrieking mother.

In and out of police stations

A year after Jason arrived in the UK, his aunties Valerie and Wendy both moved to London. They had been his primary carers in Jamaica, raising him from the age of 4 until 15, and in 2017 I met them both in Valerie's office, in the primary school where she worked as headteacher in West London:

> VALERIE: To be honest, when I first came to England and saw Jason a year later, I said 'I should never have sent them here' – that's how I felt. I was so angry. I said 'they should never have come, I

should never have...', I felt like ... first of all the shock when we actually saw him: he didn't even look like the Jason that we sent here.

According to Valerie and Wendy, Jason's 'new lifestyle' involved smoking and drinking, and he was therefore no longer the well-mannered boy they had raised. They did let him live with them at points, but they were also finding their own feet in London and Jason was unable to abide by their rules and curfews. Jason was also unable to convince his mother to let him stay with her, and in some ways he had become accustomed to a life on the streets. And so, while Jason sometimes found temporary shelter – with his aunties, in a flat he rented, with friends, or in squats – his living situation was never secure, and he spent many months sleeping on buses, staying up in the West End all night, and sometimes sleeping rough:

> JASON: Yeah. I literally slept in the cold on the streets one time, in ice. In ice my friend, you know. I padded up in somebody's doorway, at the back of their house in, erm, Barking, near the bus station, yeah. Barking bus station, and I padded up behind there and just had a sleep you know.

In the context of Jason's destitution and homelessness, he had repeated run-ins with the police and spent many nights in police cells. Usually, he was arrested for minor infractions, including being drunk and disorderly, and he regularly received tickets for unpaid travel fares – for which the fine letters piled up at Valerie's address. Jason also spent some time in prison, having been charged with several offences over the years – including assault, theft and damage to property. For example, one summer afternoon after playing football in the park, Jason took a bottle of Lucozade from a supermarket without paying, he said because the water fountain was broken. He was then confronted by the security guard and a scuffle ensued, which led to him being charged with common assault. On another occasion, he was arrested after arguing with bouncers outside a nightclub. When the police arrived, they found cocaine on his person, which he said he was holding for his friend.

In general, Jason's experiences of criminalisation involved being charged with some relatively minor offence, then skipping bail because he had no fixed address and no legal migration status, before later being arrested for something else and having those previous charges raised against him. This was how he ended up spending time in prison: for accumulated minor offences and breach of bail. As he put it: 'The problem with my life was I've been in and out of police stations'; 'my life was more like being in handcuffs'. Importantly, Jason was hypervisible to the police because he was 'hustling' around the West End and often sleeping rough. In this context, he was regularly stopped by the police, and sometimes found to be doing or carrying something illegal. Of course, these experiences of criminalisation are not unique.

According to the Prison Reform Trust, 69% of prisoners in 2018 had been charged with non-violent offences, and almost half of the people sent to prison that year were sentenced to serve six months or less. Strikingly, more than one in five of these short-term prisoners were homeless. Further, 11% of prisoners are held on remand – that is before being tried – and black men are 26% more likely to be remanded in custody than white men.[10] In this light, the circular character of Jason's time in and out of police stations and prisons is part of a wider pattern, in which the criminal justice system punishes the poor, and the racialised poor in particular, targeting, in the words of Vickie Cooper and Joe Sim, 'the detritus and the damned'.[11] Jason's experiences therefore reflect both the criminalisation of homelessness and the criminalisation of (illegal) immigration.[12] One implicated the other for Jason, a reminder that there is much to be gained from thinking about class, 'race' and migration together in multi-status Britain.

The profound exertion required to survive homelessness, il-legality and criminalisation over such a protracted period clearly took a toll on Jason, and he began drinking more heavily in 2012. His arrests became more frequent and he could not see a way out. Increasingly, he felt that the immigration authorities would catch up with him. It was during this particularly difficult period, in late 2013, that Jason decided to take a trip to Wales with a Nigerian friend, to get away from London for a few days. However, after a fight with some locals outside a pub, Jason and his friend were arrested. At that time, the police and immigration authorities were beginning to share information in new ways, and Jason's details were run through the immigration database by the police.[13] The police force in South Wales then held him under immigration powers before sending him to an immigra-tion removal centre on the south coast of England (Haslar, which is now closed).[14] Jason was detained there for seven months:

> JASON: Yeah, it felt like another prison, basically. You would see ducks outside, and you're in a cage [laughs], so you'd wonder to yourself, if the ducks were meant to be in the cage and you outside, you know? And it was a big irony, because you'd see ducks fly off, or fly out, and they can go into the sea, because we were just near to the sea.

Jason's attempts to appeal his deportation from inside detention were fruitless. He had no decent legal representation, and his case would have been near impossible to win even if he had. Even though he had lived in London for nearly 15 years, he had no partner, no children, and had been largely abandoned by his family. He had been 'illegal' throughout and so he had no formal employment history. He could not evidence the ways in which he was 'integrated' or had 'contributed', and his criminal record certainly worked against him (see Chapters 4 and 5 for more on immigration appeals). And so, after seven long months in deten-tion, Jason was deported on a mass deportation charter flight from London to Kingston in November 2014.[15] His second flight.

After three hours recording these first interviews, Jason and I both needed a break. We left my flat and walked down to the Mona Bowl to watch the athletes train. Some were sprinting, dragging wheels behind them, others were stretching, some chatting. At this time of day, with the sunlight fading, the Mona Bowl is a beautifully serene place to be, dusk shadows slowly walking down the Blue Mountains towards the field. I was reminded that had Jason stayed in Jamaica, he might have attended the University of West Indies, and perhaps would have trained on this very field. Valerie and Wendy told me that Jason 'could have been a Ronaldo or a Usain Bolt', and they had kept a cutting from a newspaper in which Jason was crossing the finish line ahead of Jamaican sprinting champion Asafa Powell in a 100-metre school race (Asafa Powell holds the fourth fastest time in the 100-metre sprint at the time of writing).

As we sat watching the athletes, I asked Jason: 'Did you not want to come back to Jamaica when you found England difficult?' 'Of course I did', he replied. 'When I told my mum that I wanted to go back to Jamaica before the six-month visa expired, she said, "Are you mad?", took my passport away from me, and dashed it in the bin.' The fact that Jason's mother 'dashed' his passport in the bin highlights that family rejection was knotted up with state controls on movement – the passport, the visa, the border. Jason's mother did not allow him to move back to Jamaica, but neither would he be allowed to remain in Britain legally. It could have been otherwise. If Jason had been granted settled status as soon as he landed, or if the UK did not exclude 'illegal immigrants' from social rights, then he would at least have had access to housing and welfare benefits, and he might have stood a better chance of building his own life, despite difficult family circumstances.

Instead, when Jason was homeless and trapped in illegality, his mother, aunties and his cousins were on the path to British citizenship. Jason's rejection from family, then, was always inseparable from his exclusion from British citizenship, and this is an important theme throughout the book. While family troubles are central to the stories of criminalised and deported people, immigration controls shape how family dynamics play out, adding weight and consequence to family crises. Of course, Jason's destitution and illegality might have been avoided if he and his family had acted differently, but for as long as immigration controls function to illegalise, exclude and expel, some people will find themselves in these circumstances. Therefore, while there might be unique personalities, passions and contingencies that shape each biography, this book is concerned with how immigration controls fundamentally structure individual and family stories.[16]

What Jason's story also makes clear is that deportation begins long before anyone gets on a plane.[17] As a result, the study of deportation is not simply about the total exclusion of 'migrants' *from* British society, but also about how immigration controls produce inequalities and hierarchies *within* British society.[18] Immigration controls shape and produce inequalities in Britain – particularly in terms of race, class and gender divisions – and this is a central thread throughout the book. For example, Jason's experiences of homelessness and destitution suggest that processes of illegalisation operate as modes of class division and neoliberal statecraft.

Neoliberal statecraft and the figure of the 'illegal immigrant'

Jason's life in the UK was difficult, but it was not without joy or friendship. Jason often spoke about his friends in London, particularly those he played football with each week at a church mission in East London. He had lost the phone numbers of people he knew there, but he told me to go down to the mission myself: 'You have to meet those guys and say hello from me'. A few months later, when I was back in the UK, I started playing football every Wednesday morning with the group, and I stayed for lunch each week over the course of two months.

They were, unsurprisingly, a profoundly multi-ethnic group of homeless (and formerly homeless) men, but they were also multi-status – that is, some were ineligible for housing support and welfare benefits, and some were vulnerable to deportation. I met a few people who remembered Jason, and I interviewed Remy, a young black British man in his late twenties, in a pub in Bethnal Green:

> REMY: What should I say mate? He used to go down West End trying to sell fake drugs to people. Just trying every little piece of dodginess he can ... someone told me that he went out and was trying to sell Charlie [cocaine] out of knocked-up paracetamol. Sometimes he might have had the real thing, but most of the times he was just going out and trying to make a quick buck off a tourist.

As Remy explained, while Jason had 'the gift of the gab', and sometimes found ways to make money from tourists, he was also incapable of spending money sensibly. Jason often spoke about splashing money on nights out, or simply giving money away to people he was around. He also spent lots of time in 'bookies' (bookmaker shops where he would place bets and gamble on machines):

> JASON: I didn't get to travel around the country as much as I wanted to in them four years, because more of it was survival based. More of it was like, I was in the bookies every day, Paddy Power, to double up, you nar mean? Because, you know, you don't think 100 pound would last you when you don't have nowhere to live, you nar mean, come on, let's be fair Luke. It's not gonna last, you know that, no matter how high the value of the money is over here, but 100 pound is 16 grand over here, but 100 pound, is 100 pound over in England. So it's not gonna last. You have to double it!

Nathan was another young man from football who remembered Jason well, a white South African skateboarder who had spent lots of time with him over a period of a few months. He described their time on the streets:

> NATHAN: Leaving Jason, to stay at my mate's, I felt like I was abandoning him. You know, because we were both going through it together, you know what I mean? And then he's like: 'Ah yeah, I'm just gonna go down to the West End and see if I can get lucky'. And there's times we went down there, and he'd hang out in a sort of games centre you know, sort of hang out there, and then talk to randomers and see if he could get any change, just to kind of occupy himself, or just a place to chill when it rains, just to sit there really.

Nathan described forms of solidarity and care between homeless people, many of them migrants, but the mutual support could not overshadow the profound sadness in his memories of Jason:

> NATHAN: I mean his legs. I remember one time he was so fucked, he couldn't even walk properly, just because he'd been on the road for like, so long, he couldn't even play football, so what he did was, like, where we have lunch, he'd just go there, and sleep. And Martin [the church leader] would let him sleep.

While Nathan experienced homelessness with Jason, at some point he was able to access housing support. Nathan is a dual national (British and South African), and his British passport entitled him to social rights – to housing and welfare – however precarious and hollowed out they might have been.[19] He could also work legally, without fear of detention and deportation. Indeed, both Remy and Nathan were British citizens and therefore when they emphasised the ways in which Jason had it harder than them, they were identifying the difference that citizenship makes.

This does not mean that they had it easy; clearly they did not. Rates of homelessness have increased dramatically since 2010 – the number of 'rough sleepers' more than doubled between 2010 and 2017 – and 'undeserving' British citizens are increasingly abandoned by the welfare arm of the state and punished by the coercive arm.[20] This mode of government is what Loïc

Wacquant describes as 'neoliberal statecraft'.[21] However, what is true for homeless British citizens – that the state is simultaneously abandoning and punitive – is augmented for non-citizens, who have 'no recourse to public funds' (total abandonment) and who live under the constant threat of deportation. In this way, 'illegal immigrants' like Jason encounter the neoliberal state at its most severe.[22]

The point here is not simply that 'illegal immigrants' have it worse. The need to exclude 'migrants' also justifies wider forms of disentitlement which impact citizens.[23] Indeed, the exclusionary logic of immigration controls has been central to wider arguments for austerity: there is not enough to go around; migrants do not belong; and thus we need to exclude them from access to public services and welfare benefits. These policies of exclusion ostensibly protect the British people, but of course it is not only migrants who are excluded.[24] Tightening eligibility criteria and policing welfare claimants does not affect 'migrants' alone, and nor is it intended to.[25] As Bridget Anderson argues, the nation is defined as a 'community of value' not only through the exclusion of non-citizens (who do not belong because they are foreign), but also through the exclusion of failed citizens (who do not belong because they are criminal or idle). The undeservingness of migrants, then, is intimately connected to the undeservingness of 'welfare scroungers' and 'criminals', who fail to demonstrate 'good citizenship'. All of these failed and excluded non-members can be contrasted with law-abiding and hardworking 'taxpayers'.[26]

Anderson's larger argument here is that immigration controls are as much about 'us' as about 'them'.[27] For example, when 'migrants' are required to prove their 'right to work' and their 'right to rent', this has significant implications for British citizens, who become aware of their own 'rights' every time they too are required to show their passports to employers and landlords. In fact, in the context of the housing crisis and increased job precarity, it appears that the right to work and to rent only mean anything because migrants are denied these 'rights'.[28] In this way, immigration controls tell citizens that they are included, that they have rights and that they belong, even as 'citizenship is being evacuated of much of its social content'.[29] Anderson therefore argues that immigration controls produce a kind of *fantasy citizenship*, and it is worth quoting her at length here:

> The widening engagement of citizens in [immigration] enforcement, calls for British jobs for British workers, claims to protect welfare benefits from the depredations of migrants, all contribute to the production of fantasy citizenship, imagining that citizenship, if you have it, means equality – the fantasy citizenship of real inclusion, that promises, once you have permanent residence or citizenship, everything will be alright. But it will not. Fantasy citizenship makes migrants exceptions and discourages a politics and an analysis that finds commonalities between migrants and differentiated citizens, even as it makes this analysis more urgent. Fantasy citizenship reifies an axis of difference, implicates citizens in the making of that difference, promises to protect citizens from that difference, as if that difference were the only one that matters, as if this is enough and everyone should be grateful for it.[30]

To resist the exclusionary logic of immigration control, Anderson argues that we need to find new ways of articulating the commonalities between migrants and differentiated citizens, and, returning to Jason's life on the streets of London, it is clear that such commonalities often emerge organically among homeless people. For Nathan and Remy, Jason's fate was tied up with their own, even as his non-citizenship trapped him in homelessness indefinitely. More broadly, for the homeless men who play football each week in East London, immigration and citizenship status are not necessarily sources of social differentiation, even as they determine who can join the housing waiting list and who instead might face deportation. These everyday realities in multi-status Britain – in which immigration status determines access to housing, work and welfare – should

Pictures 2.3 and 2.4. *Jason writing in the scrapbook I gave him; Jason up at University of the West Indies campus (2016)*

remind us that class analysis needs to incorporate and critique immigration controls.[31]

This is especially important when so much of what goes as 'class politics' is saturated in nativism. The emphasis on the 'left behind white working class' obscures the commonalities between marginalised citizens and illegalised migrants.[32] Obviously, class oppression is not solely the preserve of 'white natives', and anti-racists have long analysed the relationship between race and class.[33] However, in multi-status Britain it is increasingly important that we factor immigration control into this understanding. As I have argued, 'illegal immigrants' experience the abandoning and punitive neoliberal state at its most severe, and one effect of deportability is to render migrant labour especially disposable (see Chapter 5).[34] More broadly, the need to exclude 'migrants' operates at the discursive level to justify austerity and disentitlement. In some ways, this is simply another example of how racism – as the production of group difference and hierarchy – divides the working classes, but my focus here is specifically on the role of immigration control.[35]

In short, to understand racism, class division and neoliberal statecraft in contemporary Britain, we need to think more carefully about immigration control. In fact, for Jason this connection between 'race', class and status was lived, and this became clear when he described his experiences of racist violence in London.

Race, class and status

Jason often spoke about his experiences of racism in England, sometimes referring to the police, at other times to racist violence in the streets. He spoke about being chased by white men, about people shouting racist abuse at him from pub gardens, and about a group of white youths attacking him in a chip shop in Essex. He explained these incidents of racist violence in terms of him being black, but also in terms of his poverty, or the fact that he looked poor:

> JASON: We had a punch-up in the bookies, you nar mean. And everybody saw what happened and knew that it was the employee's fault, yeah. But when the police came they arrested me, yeah. You know, it was like, oh, this guy looks a bit dodgy. Because I look like a person who's on the streets, you have a chipped tooth, you have a little cut on your face, people straight away think, 'Oh you're a thug'. I look like a person who I don't know what I'm talking about. I look like I'm an eediot.

From Jason's descriptions of racist events, and his sense of how he was perceived, it is clear that racism and poverty were experienced through one another. It was having a chipped tooth that made Jason look like 'a thug', just as it was looking like he lived on the street that got him arrested. Notably, Jason told me that the police were racist, always watching and harassing him, but he always related this to his hypervisibility as someone who was street homeless:

> JASON: It was really hard because you're trying to not get in trouble, but once you're on the street you're going to get in trouble. Understand? It's not somebody driving by and saying, oh, he's going about his business. It's the police: 'Who is that? I see him last week, I see him again this week'. Yes. And that's what was happening.

Picture 2.5. *Travel tickets Jason had retained from London*

Jason's illegality was paramount here, because it trapped him in destitution. In fact, he made this connection himself when he moved, in his own rather fluid way, from discussing racist violence to his lack of immigration status:

> JASON: Some of the areas that I went to in Romford like Collier Row, and erm, Howard Hill, is very racial. So for you to go down there as a black person, you're not accepted, you nar mean? It was really worrying in a state that you're living in the year 2000 and there's people out there still like that, you nar mean? That wouldn't mind headbutting others in the head, or burning down somebody's fuckin' house because there's Chinese living in there, or Nigerians living in there, you nar mean? So, all round I faced a lot of difficulties pursuing that effect. But in terms of effect where I wanted to do me, that was much harder. Because I didn't have no right abode, address, yeah, I didn't have no ID, specialising me to move about somewhere you know, and it was harder for me to get things, like job centre, post office ID, you know? So I've said to myself, erm, let me try and do something, but I was on the street.

When Jason connects acts of racist violence in a 'very racial' area to his own experiences of illegality, he reveals the connections he makes between different modes of exclusion. Jason's experiences of popular and police racism were related to his homelessness, which in turn was produced by illegalisation. Following Jason's own meandering narrative here, we can observe that his main issue was not having ID, and his rightlessness and abjection flowed from that, which then rendered him more vulnerable to certain kinds of street and police violence. We should take Jason seriously here, and recognise that immigration and citizenship status often determine how racism gets into people's lives.[36] This argument is central to *Deporting Black Britons*, and the next chapter, which focuses on Ricardo's story, develops a more substantive analysis of how racism is structured and shaped by immigration control.

Conclusion

During the time I was getting to know Jason, between 2015 and 2017, he was staying at Open Arms Drop in Centre. He spoke about condescending and punitive treatment from the management, regular altercations with other residents, and rats and bed bugs in his room, but he refused to let Open Arms become the place of his internment. For many of the residents, Open Arms did become a kind of prison, because the world outside was so unknown and threatening (see Chapter 8), but Jason did not see it that way. He spent his days walking around downtown, talking to people and reading the newspapers in the national library. He made space for himself in Kingston, just as he had in London, and while this ability to survive should not be romanticised, it is impossible not to recognise.

When I returned to Jamaica in 2017, however, Jason had been kicked out of Open Arms, and was spending his days by the court house downtown, with a group of men, some of them 'deportees', who hung out on the street corner. He was sleeping by the court house as well, but some locals had threatened to drop large rocks on his head when he was asleep. He did not feel safe there, and he told me several times about his friend, Donovan, a 'deportee' from the US, who had been murdered a few weeks earlier, violently stabbed by a local man who, according to Jason, did not like 'homeless, deported and mental people'.

For all the time I had known Jason he had no money and he was hungry, but in summer 2017 he was profoundly distressed. He was unable to shower and so when I saw him he felt conscious that he smelled bad. His vitality was waning, and he was not as loud as before. On my last night in Jamaica in 2017, he showed up at the gates of the university campus, desperate to borrow a few hundred Jamaican dollars to pay back some debt he had incurred. As I paid him into a taxi downtown, the last thing he said to me was: 'Listen, if you hear in the next year that I'm dead, please don't come to my funeral'.

Jason's circumstances in Jamaica were bleak, and his biography is a kind of tragedy. However, this chapter is not designed simply to evoke sadness. There is much that can be learnt from Jason's experiences and narratives, and I begin with Jason because these arguments help frame the book. Firstly, even though Jason's story is tragic, it could have been otherwise. It is therefore important to explain deportation not only in terms of family troubles and bad luck, but in relation to the fundamental role of illegalisation in structuring these painful life stories.

Jason's story reminds us that deportation begins long before anyone gets on a plane, and thus *Deporting Black Britons* is about how immigration controls are implicated in the production of inequality, difference and hierarchy *within Britain*. As Bridget Anderson puts it, 'it is necessary to move beyond the taken-for-grantedness of immigration controls which views them as neutral sorting mechanisms, and consider them as a factor in shaping actions and processes, productive of certain types of relations'.[37] As I have argued in this chapter, immigration controls produce class inequalities (by excluding 'illegal

Pictures 2.6 and 2.7. *Jason by court house with friends (2017); Jason and me in Hope Gardens (2016)*

immigrants' from the means of life), while also justifying wider forms of disentitlement and austerity that impact citizens (via the exclusionary logic of immigration control). Therefore, a critique of immigration controls should be central to class politics. Finally, in this chapter I have shown that Jason's experiences of racism were lived in relation to his homelessness, which was in turn produced by his illegalisation. This reminds us that immigration controls determine how racism gets into people's lives, and the next chapter develops and expands on this argument when discussing Ricardo's story.

Coda

One day in October 2015, Jason wanted us to go to Port Royal, the former capital that was destroyed in the great earthquake of 1692. We met in the morning at Kingston's downtown parade and travelled there on one of Jamaica's yellow public buses. There was very little to see in Port Royal and so I suggested we find a way down to the shore. We traipsed through bushes and litter to reach the sea, and I sat on the scraggy beach while Jason threw stones into the water. I was enjoying the fresh air and sounds of the coast, watching a cargo ship fade beyond the horizon. Jason was looking for old coins, his words meandering along the borders of sense and nonsense. He explained that the queen was planning to come back to Jamaica to reclaim all the treasure that sank with the earthquake over 300 years ago, just out from where he threw stones.

It was a fitting place to think about Jason, a lonely place, a kind of out-of-time place, a beach without visitors. But there was also breeze and life. He spoke, as he often did, of his family. Jason always spoke kind words about his mother, despite their turbulent relationship. His aunties were another source of praise: 'She is just so distinguished, you know, on every level. Her name is Valerie, but I think she is an Angel if you ask me.' Jason was also always very kind to me, and wanted to know about my family, friends and partner. He would call me to check up on me and tell me to 'drink lots of water'. He asked after my parents, and bought a Christmas CD for me to take back to them in both 2016 and 2017. Once, after noticing my Nivea shower gel, he bought me Nivea aftershave balm from downtown as a gift. Jason was always reaching for connection, and ultimately for family. While at times this was uncomfortable, like when he told me I was his only real friend in Jamaica, I also felt the most useful thing I could do was to recognise that need for connection. Jason was desperate to 'write [himself] back into people's lives', and I hope this portrait contributes to his long-fought struggle against his abandonment.[38] In no small part, I begin with Jason because I want to foreground the damage and the vitality in the lives of the deported people I have come to know, and no one evokes this more than Jason.

In the end, Jason was very enthusiastic about this project and keen to have his story written in a book that people might read. Jason does not want to be forgotten by those he cares about, and I want to conclude with the words of people who prove that he is not:

NATHAN (friend from football): He's got a really infectious laugh. A bit confused at times. But just generally a good person in a really shit circumstance. In a horrible circumstance.

REMY (friend from football): If Jason's there and he's sad cos he's had one of them bad days, or even if he's not there, everyone might not be speaking as much, and might go in their own way, but he was one of the people that actually brought people together.

VALERIE (auntie): If you talk to my mother, my mother has dementia, every single day she says 'Have you heard from Jason? How's Jason?' She asks every single day, because for her, Jason is her favourite grandchild, her absolute favourite grandchild. And she would do anything for him.

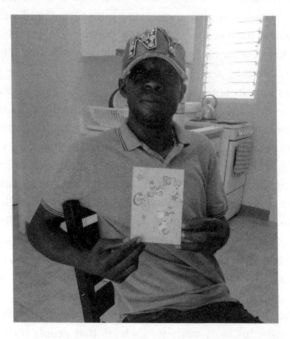

Picture 2.8. *Jason with a card from his Grandma, which he received in Jamaica as a child. He kept the card safe for all his time in the UK, and managed to bring it back with him when he was deported – one of his few treasured possessions. In my flat, University of the West Indies campus (2016)*

Chapter 3

Ricardo

In October 2015, I travelled to Jamaica's second city, Montego Bay (known locally as Mobay), on one of the many coaster buses that leave daily from downtown Kingston. After being squeezed into a three-seat row with four others and their luggage, I arrived feeling weary. I dropped my bags and called Ricardo for only the second time, and he told me to head to Nyam and Jam, a local restaurant in the town centre where we would get 'box food'. We offered descriptions of ourselves, and I was looking out for 'a big guy in a white t-shirt'. I noticed him as soon as he walked in, wearing a bright white Nike t-shirt, cap backwards and squeaky clean trainers – broad, sharp and handsome. He was late; I was halfway through my fried chicken, and so our first handshake was greasier than I might have hoped. When I finished my food, I bought Ricardo some, and he suggested we walk down to a bar called Pier One.

We sat outside the bar, on a rock by the water, while Ricardo finished his food, talking in the early-evening blue dark. I immediately felt comfortable around him and conversation was easy. Ricardo retained an overwhelming calm, a pleasant slowness about things. He laughed often, usually a kind of chuckle, often repeating what I had said as his smile broke into a short laugh. He is not a person who mocks or jibes; he is kind rather than quick-witted, gentle rather than dominating. Already, I had the sense that we would get to know one another well.

Ricardo grew up in Smethwick, a town in the West Midlands that in 1964 had been host to 'the most racist election campaign ever fought in Britain'.[1] He did not know about that election, a flashpoint in Britain's history surrounding race and immigration, even as, in a way, he lived with its consequences. Ricardo explained that Smethwick was his home and that everything and everyone was there. He told me how hard it had been since he returned to Jamaica, almost exactly one year earlier. He did not feel safe, in no small part because his older brother had been murdered in Mobay two years before: 'They shot my brother Delon, shot him like twelve times. That was while I was in prison in England ... yeah'. We sat in silence for a minute. I was not sure exactly what to say. Ricardo did not explain it at the time, but his brother Delon had also lived in the UK for most of his life and he was killed just two years after being deported, aged 22. We sat for a moment longer, looking at the sea, before Ricardo stood up, put his polystyrene box in the bin and said 'Come, let's go in'.

Pier One is a popular bar, frequented by a mix of tourists and locals. The colourful, laminated menus offer seafood, chicken and cocktails, all priced in US dollars. Pier One became a kind of 'base camp' for us in Mobay. If we were not sure what to do, we would go there and buy a drink so that we could sit at a table by the sea, at different times of day, the bar sometimes empty, sometimes full, and talk. On that first night I bought us a drink, and Ricardo got talking about the police in Smethwick and nearby West Bromwich.

RICARDO: I was arrested over 100 times and always NFA'd [no further action], never charged. The police used to just come on the park, and everybody would run. They used to hassle me differently fam, always arresting me for no reason ... listen, it used to happen so often. Once I was interviewed by the BBC, for a programme on anti-social behaviour. I think my auntie complained and that's why.

Picture 3.1. *Ricardo on the roof of my rented apartment, Montego Bay (2016)*

I was never able to find out which TV programme Ricardo featured on, but I too think his experiences with the police are worth documenting. I made several trips to the West Midlands to meet Ricardo's friends and his cousin, and they shared their own stories about aggressive and racist policing with me. The fact that these experiences precipitated Ricardo's deportation points to the connection between racist policing and immigration control. In this chapter, then, I build on the accounts of Ricardo and his friends to reflect on the dynamics of police racism in multi-status Britain. The chapter begins, however, in Mobay, where Ricardo and I got to know one another.

Remembering Smethwick from Mobay

The heart of Montego Bay (Mobay) is its bustling town centre: it is white hot, dirty and dusty, busy with people moving in every direction, with never enough pavement to accommodate the traffic. The tourist side of Mobay, the 'hip strip', begins a mile or so west of the town centre, and it is less busy and more colourful, with the gimmicks of a slightly dated package tourism. The roadside is well paved, lined with innumerable gift shops, their owners sat outside coaxing tourists inside to consume the image Jamaica sells of itself: Bob Marley; marijuana; red, gold and green; sun, sea and sex.[2] Exclusive hotels and resorts then run for miles east along the coast, each with its own zoned off private beach – penned paradise.[3] Most of Mobay's local residents, however, live in the hills that rise up sharply as you head inland away from the prized northern coastline.

Very few tourists venture into the town centre (and certainly not into the hills). There were over 250 murders in the parish of St James in 2016, the overwhelming majority of them in Mobay, a city with a population of 110,000.[4] In 2017 the murder rate spiked again, with 335 murders in the parish.[5] While most of these murders occur in low-income neighbourhoods in the hills, like Norwood where Ricardo lived with his uncle, there were several killings in the town centre, sometimes in broad daylight. On one occasion, when I had just returned to Kingston from Mobay, Ricardo texted me to say that two people had been shot in their car that afternoon, just outside Juici Patties where we met for breakfast each morning.

When I was in Mobay in 2015, I spent most of my time with Ricardo. We moved between the town and the tourist strip, and he liked the tourist side of Mobay more than I did. He liked 'seeing people enjoy themselves'; 'it makes me feel just normal', he explained. In the evenings, we would hang out in the self-contained apartment I was renting, a dingy but spacious bottom-floor flat in a large house built with remittance money from Canada. We recorded long interviews into the night, recording for over 10 hours over three or four evenings in October 2015. I would cook mackerel and rice, and Ricardo would flick through the disappointing cable channels, looking for football but mainly watching adverts. Listening to our recordings transports me back to those evenings: our slow conversation, the loudness of the crickets, the rude interruption of dogs barking by the securely grilled windows, and Ricardo telling me the story of his life.

Ricardo moved to the UK in 2002, when he was 10 years old, to live with his father, leaving his mother and younger brothers in Mobay. He followed his older brother Delon, who had moved to the UK a couple of years before. I asked Ricardo why he thought his parents decided he should move when they did. 'I don't know, you'd have to ask them', he replied, as if slightly annoyed by the question. Once in the UK, Ricardo lived with his dad for two years in Birmingham, before moving in with his two cousins in Smethwick:

> RICARDO: I used to always go to my auntie's on the weekend, like, from Friday and come back Sunday. And I just, dunno, I just liked it. It was just different innit. The park is there; you can just go and play football. And I just, I would rather just stay there instead of stay with my dad. So, I started to stay there, that become my home … How I got on with my auntie was good; how I got on with my dad wasn't.

Ricardo's auntie, who he sometimes referred to as 'mum', was in fact his cousins' step-mother. She had separated from Ricardo's uncle, but continued to raise her two stepsons, and subsequently Ricardo and Delon too. She was a black British citizen, who raised four boys of a similar age, all non-citizens, none of whom were her biological children. She also had three of her own children younger than the boys, as well as a daughter who was older. In the end, she did not want to meet with me, but Ricardo spoke warmly about her, as the 'mum' who had 'grown' him.

When Ricardo returned to Mobay, he was actually reunited with his biological mother. But they remained distant:

> RICARDO: It's not like a mum and son relationship. We just ain't got nothing to talk about. I don't know, it's weird. It's just, I don't like talkin' about it. It's not a mum and son relationship no more … you just feel like a stranger because you got nothing to talk about. The most we can talk about is like my dad innit. Because,

you nar mean, I don't like him, she don't like him [*laughing*]. So that's the only thing probably.

In the end, Ricardo said he did not need family connection. He had never got along with his dad and he did not want anything to do with his biological mother (he said this had something to do with Delon's death, but he did not want to talk about it). It was his girlfriend, Tinesha, who kept him going: 'What would I do without her?' he asked one afternoon. Tinesha supported him with money and job applications when times were tough, and when I was visiting in 2015 and 2016 they would meet in the town most evenings. They would snatch an hour or two together at dusk, when Tinesha returned by coach from the call centre where she worked, before Ricardo and I went off to Pier One or to my flat.[6]

Arrests, NFAs and the broken front door

Ricardo would not have expended as much time talking about the police had I not prompted him. He did not like to dwell on that aspect of his past and his descriptions of his teenage years were not defined solely by police harassment. He reminisced fondly about football on the park, playing computer games and sleepovers with friends. His closest friends would often stay at his house all weekend, especially Josh and Michael:

> RICARDO: We growed up together and stuff. Josh and Michael used to be at my house 24/7 – they never even used to go home. They used to just live on the couch, like literally live on the couch, because in my room I used to have a fold-out bed, a sofa bed thing, and Michael would sleep on that, and Josh used to just sleep on the floor, like, they don't wanna go home. Even when Michael had his own flat, he was hardly there.

The teenage excitement and intense closeness of friendships felt familiar to me, but somehow these memories were more vivid and accessible to Ricardo – perhaps because he had been in prison for much of the time since. In any case, it is important to

recognise that Ricardo had many positive memories of Smethwick and West Bromwich, and the police could not prevent him
from having fun or maintaining friendships. Ricardo did not
want police harassment to completely define his teenage years,
nor the stories he told about them. For my purposes, however,
Ricardo's experiences with the police were so extreme, and so
central to the questions that had led me to Jamaica, that I kept
asking him to return to them. I encouraged him to remember
that grey town in the West Midlands, and to transport me back
to his life there as a 16-year-old, when, clad in 'black garms', he
had to figure out how to see his friends without getting arrested
and spending the weekend in a police cell.

Ricardo explained that the police first became a part of his life
when he was 15:

> RICARDO: We was playing football in the cage now [the small enclosed
> pitch]. And you know how we are, we're young and that, you
> know what I mean? We seen the cars coming in, speeding up to
> the cage. So, like, first it only takes one person to run, and other
> persons start running and then everyone starts running, like. And
> you're thinking, why you running, you ain't did nothing anyway?
> So why we running?

The boys ran uphill, away from the police car, splitting into
two groups, one splintering left, the other right, but one boy,
Damien, ran straight on. Ricardo watched, hidden behind a tree,
as the police put his 13-year-old friend in their car. Expecting
him to be released any minute, Ricardo stayed out of view, but
the police car drove off with Damien in the back. A couple of
hours later, Damien returned, explaining that the police had
dropped him off in Aston, four miles away, and said: 'Now
you're gonna know how it feels to get robbed' (Damien was also
a Jamaican national and he was deported in 2018).

After that first chase from the police, Ricardo explained that
he was 'just always getting arrested for robberies'. He began to
feel that he could not leave his house without being harassed by

the police. To be clear, Ricardo had not committed any robberies, and yet was repeatedly arrested and always released without charge. Often, the police would show him some CCTV footage, claiming that the person on screen had his clothes, trainers or body comportment. Ricardo said some of these accusations were laughable, when the person on camera looked nothing like him and was committing an offence somewhere he had never been.

By the time Ricardo was 17, he started staying in his house to avoid the police. His family moved from Smethwick to West Bromwich, and his auntie hoped this might mean less hassle from the police. However, on their first night in their new home the police came in force to arrest Ricardo on suspicion of committing 'nine separate robberies' – a story Ricardo returned to many times in our conversations. The accusation had no merit, and he was soon released without charge, but Ricardo said 'they knew what they were doing':

> RICARDO: I'm thinking, you know how bad it looks, that family just moved in, black family, most people on the road is white, we're the only black people on the road, there's Asians but we're the only black people ... and when we've just moved in, you nar mean, the next day that much police is at the house. Imagine what people must've thought.

Because Ricardo was 'known to the police for robberies', despite never having been charged with an offence, he was assigned a personal officer, PC Marsden – a name neither he nor his friends had forgotten. PC Marsden would come and check on Ricardo, daily, to record whether he was in and what he was wearing: 'Most of the time I'd just go down in my boxers and my socks, because they write down what you're wearing, because of the matching description bit', he explained. When Ricardo did leave his house, PC Marsden would often be waiting for him and his friends: 'He's always on the bike, bicycle. He would just ride around and wait for us to come out, and follow us and just say: "Where you guys goin', you going to rob someone today?"'

Ricardo was still angry when I asked him to rehearse these encounters. He described one morning when, after taking his younger brother to school (i.e. his step-auntie's son), he went to McDonald's for breakfast. On his way home, a police car pulled up beside him and an officer said, 'Did you enjoy your donuts Mr Thompson … you were hungry too, went back for seconds didn't you?' As Ricardo explained, 'They were letting me know that they were watching me, innit'. More generally, the police would follow him back from college, and he was surveilled pretty much whenever he left his house. He explained that Friday nights were the worst, because if he was arrested then, the police could hold him over the weekend without charging him. Several of his friends described the same practice.

Ricardo had not been charged with any criminal offences at this point. He had been cautioned by the police for what he described as 'running through a shopping centre after school' and 'doing some graffiti', but he had not received any convictions. However, because of this apparent 'anti-social behaviour', and his repeated arrests for robbery, his movements and associations were restricted. The terms of his anti-social behaviour order (ASBO) stated that he could not go to certain areas, especially places where he had been arrested, like West Bromwich town centre.[7] There were also buses he could not take because the route went through areas he was banned from, and the police gave him a map which highlighted the areas he could and could not enter, the streets he could and could not walk down. If Ricardo did enter these areas, or associate with certain friends, then he could be charged with breach of ASBO – which is a criminal offence and can carry a custodial sentence. Ricardo's ASBO was a civil order that was therefore issued without trial, and yet its breach carried criminal sanctions.[8]

In this light, Ricardo's criminalisation relied on *pre-criminal* forms of social control.[9] He was banned from certain areas because he had been arrested there, and he was barred from associating with certain friends because they had been arrested together. The fact of Ricardo's repeated arrest indicated his wrongdoing and therefore licensed restrictions on his movements and associations. This is despite the fact that after over 100 arrests he had never been charged, let alone convicted of an offence. This is what heavy and disproportionate policing in the UK looks like: the reversal of the presumption of innocence and the evasion of due process. The police also set up a camera directly outside Ricardo's house, which faced the front door, apparently to deal with 'anti-social behaviour', and Ricardo and his friends told me that the police used to 'kick the front door in' when looking for his brother Delon, and so 'the door was always broken', the lock unable to catch.

Ricardo's experiences of policing were extraordinary. He was harassed almost whenever he left the house, arrested countless times and detained without charge in police stations. He was denied access to public space, to freedom of association and to the presumption of innocence. As a teenager who had not been charged with a criminal offence, he had a personal officer visit him at home, every day, to the house with a broken door and the CCTV camera looming. Clearly, such intense, heavy policing makes some people especially vulnerable to deportation power.

Indeed, most 'deportees' I met in Jamaica spoke to me about racist policing practices. This does not mean they were not engaged in criminal acts, only that they were more likely to be caught, arrested, charged and convicted because they were black.[10] These processes were clearly at play in relation to Ricardo's arrest and subsequent conviction, when, as an 18-year-old, he joined in with a group of people committing a burglary.

> RICARDO: They said 'You don't have to come in, just stay here and just watch out innit, you just stand by the door' … Obviously you're nervous, you're scared. Then the police came, everyone ran, and all I could hear was: 'Mr Thompson, Mr Thompson, stay there. We know it's you Mr Thompson.' I was thinking ahh! A helicopter came and everything. They weren't chasing

no one else, you know. If they had chased everyone else they would've probably got everyone. But they just clinged on to me. I can remember seeing one police officer there that came round to where my auntie lived, my mum, round by there before. And I can remember when I was on the floor he was making the dog like, you know what I mean like bark in my face like that.

While Ricardo was indeed guilty of burglary – or, more precisely, of standing by the backdoor while others went inside to commit a burglary – the reason he was apprehended, and not the men who had orchestrated the offence, was that the police knew and recognised him. In court, Ricardo remembers two familiar police officers waving and smiling at him mockingly as he was sent down. 'They were saying, like, we finally got you', Ricardo explained. The officers were celebrating the years he would spend in prison. Ricardo was convicted of aggravated burglary and sentenced to six years in prison. After just under three years inside, he was deported in November 2014, on the same mass deportation charter flight as Jason.

Explaining police racism: 'It was just, like, normal'

From my perspective, Ricardo's experiences of intense and aggressive policing were evidence of racist criminal justice in action. As I explain to Ricardo on one of the recordings, 'Black men are over six times more likely to be stopped by the police, and they are then more likely to be arrested, charged, convicted, and locked up'. Ricardo says 'yeah' here and there, seemingly unimpressed. I am trying to situate his experiences within my understanding of racial disproportionality in the criminal justice system. To me, Ricardo was a victim of police racism: the black man, or boy, behind the statistics. And yet to describe Ricardo as a 'black man' facing 'police racism' is a form of abstraction. Abstractions are important, allowing us to move from the specific to the general, but there is also something more locally specific going on, and Ricardo knew that better than I did.

LUKE: But why do you think the police bothered you so much?

RICARDO: They're saying because of my brothers, basically innit. They think I'm following in their footsteps. So, basically, because of what they do and what they've been arrested for in the past, they think, okay, he's young, you know what I mean, he growed up in the same household as them.

LUKE: And where do you think racism comes into this?

RICARDO: All my friends, they got the same. I had white friends [mostly Albanian], I had Asian friends, they all got the same. It was just –

LUKE: But they can't have been arrested as much as you?

RICARDO: I mean, the black – nah, not the same as me but they all got like arrests as well innit. So, police used to knock on their doors with the same procedure so, like, I didn't feel like it was just me.

LUKE: So you think it's not just about race, you think it's about the area or...?

RICARDO: And the way we dress and all them stuff innit. I would say, 'Yo, I'm not changing my style of dress. For what? For what reason?' You know what I mean? I'm not gonna start wearing light colours. Even my mum, my auntie, used to say, 'Please just wear something grey today', you know what I mean like, and I'd say 'Look, listen, there's no point me changing', making them make me decide, you know what I mean, make them decide what I should wear and what I shouldn't wear, so I used to just wear what I want.

LUKE: Which is black?

RICARDO: Which is black.

LUKE: Yeah, I understand that. Were you happy? When you were between the ages of 15 and before you got arrested?

RICARDO: Yeah. I was happy. I didn't let stuff take me down like that. I didn't, like I wasn't, make it drag me down. It's always been there in the back of your head like, because you was young you just wanna, you know what I mean, everything's going fast, you don't have time like now to think about stuff like that.

LUKE: I guess you're so young as well; it's just that's what the world is like.

RICARDO: Yeah. So, it was just, like, normal. The only reason I'm talking about it now is because you're asking me. I don't really think about all that.

For Ricardo, as for Jason, race was lived through class, age, gender and place and, as such, racism was both unremarkable (i.e. just part of life) and hard to isolate and name. Ricardo explained that his best friend, Josh, had had similar experiences, and he was 'half Pakistani, half white'. He said that his Albanian and Asian friends also faced police harassment. This might be why Ricardo drew attention to 'the area' he lived in, 'the garms' he wore and his brothers' police history, and why he seemed somewhat unimpressed by my statistics on racial dispropor- tionality. That said, most of Ricardo's friends were racialised as black, and several of them were unequivocal when describing police harassment in terms of racism: 'All of this is because man are black', Ricardo's friend Marcus told me, before recounting times when the police actively abused him using racist language. Ricardo's discomfort around discussing race and racism, then, might not be because he thought being black had nothing to do with it, but instead a reflection of how painful he found it to talk about these things:

> RICARDO: I don't like talking about race and stuff like that. I just try not to make it brainwash me. Basically I don't want to fall to their level and be racist back towards them ... it's a powerful thing you know. Because they build it into us from when we was young. But it's something that I don't wanna feel. I don't think everyone is the same. Not all white people are the same. Not all black people. And being racist just creates problems. That's why I don't wanna fall to their level, even though sometimes it's so powerful you can't control the way you feel.

Importantly, Ricardo *did* think the police were racist, and he often reminded me that all the officers were white (except one South Asian officer). However, he was also resistant to neatly separating out the experiences of his friends along racial lines when so many of their experiences were shared. As Ricardo explained, his mixed, Asian and Albanian friends lived in the same neighbourhoods, attended the same schools and were criminalised in very similar ways. This is not to argue that 'race' is insignificant and that this is *really* a question of class, age and place. The treatment Ricardo faced often seemed more severe than that faced by his mixed, Asian or Albanian friends (all of whom were racialised as not properly British), and thus being racialised as black can still make the world of difference.[11] However, there is also something more complex and locally specific going on in the racist encounters Ricardo describes, something that cannot be captured by statistics on racial disproportionality, or with reference to 'implicit racial bias'. After all, Ricardo's encounters with the police were repeated and intimate; the officers knew his name, where he lived and the criminal histories of his siblings.[12] On reflection, what Ricardo was teaching me was that local specificities mattered, and that racism is not lived as abstraction.[13]

Picking on dark-skinned people: immigration control and the production of race

In April 2016, I rented a room in Smethwick for a week, not far from where Ricardo had lived until he was 16. I walked around the neighbourhood, trying to get a sense for the kind of place it was, but without a tour guide I was not sure exactly what to look for. The high street was bustling with Caribbean food stores, a large Pakistani supermarket, a KFC and countless other chicken shops. It looked like other low-income multicultural high streets in the West Midlands, Manchester and London. I went to the park that Ricardo had spoken about, but walking around did not afford me any fresh insights into Ricardo's time there. I stopped at the football cage where Ricardo played most evenings, and where the police first gave him chase. I looked at it for a while, empty in the late winter sunshine. I took some inane pictures to show Ricardo later, and then left, unsatisfied.

I returned to the high street and called Ricardo on WhatsApp. He was in his uncle's yard in Norwood, Mobay, doing his laundry on his day off work. I described where I was and he laughed when I named a few of the shops and explained my view of KFC. I was still vaguely hoping that his two best friends, Josh and Michael, might meet me, but when I asked him on the phone he said they definitely would not. He did say that his friend Melissa would be a good person to interview though: 'There's one girl, like she's, she's a lesbian, she's like my best friend, you know what I mean like, my best friend from when we was young'.

Melissa had lived on the same road as Ricardo in Smethwick from 10 years old and they went to school together. When I was in the West Midlands, I tried to meet with her several times, but she was clearly unsure about meeting me, especially on her own. As in Jamaica, it was more difficult for me to meet and interview women, especially those around my own age. On my third trip to the West Midlands, though, I did manage to meet with Melissa, in a large Wetherspoon's pub in Bearwood, Smethwick. Once we worked through the awkward first few minutes, I asked her some questions about her friendship with Ricardo, and she spoke with real affection about him, explaining that she planned to visit him in Jamaica later that year (Melissa's father was Jamaican and so she had family there). Where Ricardo's male friends defined him as 'real', 'a true friend who was no snake', Melissa described him as a 'lovely boy', as 'caring' and 'considerate', and she gave a particularly vivid account of their childhood together: the carefree, light and fun times, the silliness and the games that were punctured by police harassment long before they reached adulthood:

MELISSA: Like, imagine kids going cinema on the weekend, you know, getting pocket money off your dad, or, your mum's come down and said you lot need to be quiet, you know. We're all in Ricardo's room playing PlayStation, on the SingStar, his little siblings as well remember. We used to camp in his garden, too, with a pop-up tent. And Matthew had asthma, and his mum would be like 'No, get in, you can't be out here, get in!' I remember it all … and then it just got ruined; the police are outside, circling, like a torch or something would come through the window.

LUKE: So when did that happen, when did it move from, like, kids just playing, or was it at the same time?

MELISSA: Say year 9. Year 9, year 8 [aged 13–14].

LUKE: Then it starts to...?

MELISSA: Yeah, cos then you're bigger now aren't you? You're bigger, so police would think –

LUKE: That's really sad though, to think that you get forced by the police from being a kid having fun, to them suddenly being, like, 'What you doing?'

MELISSA: Yeah, it was exactly like that. Everywhere you walked, you'd get stopped, and it's, like, why you stopping us for? I remember one time, I got a mate who's Albanian, and policeman come over and was like, 'You think you're black don't you mate?' And then we're like What?' And he's like, 'Remember you ain't even got a visa'. This is what he's saying to the boy, and I'm just like hold your tongue, he wants you to say something to him. Don't say nothing, just walk off and stuff. Like, that's how police was round there ... just, Smethwick police was racist, they actually was racist. That's all I'm saying, a lot of them was racist. After school, they'd just pick on the dark-skinned people, yeah.

It is interesting that Melissa uses 'dark-skinned people' as shorthand here, even as the story about her Albanian friend points to forms of racialisation which cannot be neatly reduced to phenotype.[14] Crucially, in Melissa's account, immigration control is invoked directly by police officers – 'Remember you ain't even got a visa' – which reminds us that immigration controls produce new narratives on and targets for popular and police racism (for example, when 'asylum seekers' are attacked in the streets while being hailed *as* 'asylum seekers').[15] Discourses on immigration at the national level permeate society and get mobilised in local interactions.

In this way, Melissa's anecdote reminds us that meanings about the nation's racialised outsiders are produced and negotiated at the border.[16] Therefore, immigration controls do not simply exclude racially undesirable migrants, they also define the very terms of racial differentiation and exclusion in the first instance.[17] For this reason, it is an oversimplification to say that Ricardo was first racialised as black, then subject to heavy policing, and subsequently deported. This account is too linear and, in an important sense, the expulsive logic of immigration control, the will to deport, preceded Ricardo's experiences of racist policing. Put differently, these two instantiations of state racism – racist policing and deportation – share certain logics and reinforce one another, and thus they are mutually constitutive rather than sequential. As James Ferguson argues:

> The policing of the border is intimately tied to the policing of Main Street in that they are both rituals that enact the encompassment of the territory of the nation by the state.... Both types of policing often demarcate the racial and cultural boundaries of belonging and are often inscribed by bodily violence on the same groups of people.[18]

And so, while it is true that black men are *discriminated* against and treated *disproportionately* within the criminal justice and immigration systems, the relationship between immigration control and racism is about more than discrimination and disproportionality. These concepts are too flat; they lack purchase on how racial distinctions and hierarchies are actively produced and reproduced, and the danger is that they lead us to assume that we know what 'race' is – i.e. skin colour difference – before proceeding to measure its impact statistically.[19] In fact, 'race' is not reducible to skin colour, and both criminal justice and immigration control are central to the very production of racial distinctions, hierarchies and dynamics.[20] In short, immigration controls do not simply discriminate on the basis of something stable called 'race', they are implicated in the very production of racialised meanings and social relations.[21]

Police racism in multi-status Britain

The racist actions of particular police officers are inseparable from the wider politics of immigration – most clearly demonstrated when one officer reminds an Albanian child that he does not have a visa. However, it is not only that police officers are influenced by anti-immigrant sentiments circulating in wider discourse. In fact, the police are now tasked with carrying out bordering tasks, and thus the relationship between immigration control and policing is made concrete.[22] Since 2012, the police have been working with the immigration authorities under a joint policy called Operation Nexus. The policy has several components, the most straightforward of which involves embedding immigration officers within police stations. As a result, when someone is arrested and taken to the station, Nexus custody officers can check their immigration status on Home Office databases.[23] This policy received bad press when it was discovered that victims of crime were also being referred to immigration enforcement, but it has become a fairly routine and unquestioned aspect of policing practice.[24] Indeed, in 2019 the police introduced on-the-spot fingerprint scanning ('stop and scan'), so they can check the fingerprints of people they stop in the street against criminal and immigration databases (using portable scanners).[25]

Operation Nexus also allows the Home Office to build deportation cases against individual non-citizens on the basis of 'non-convictions' – this is not my term but the official double-speak of policy.[26] As such, people can be deported as 'foreign criminals' because on the 'balance of probabilities' it is determined that they are likely to have committed criminal offences, even when this has not been decided by a criminal court. In these cases, police intelligence – in relation to 'criminal associations', arrests and charges short of convictions – feeds directly into the deportation process, sometimes without any judicial oversight. This raises obvious questions about institutionally racist policing.

Especially relevant here is the fact that many Operation Nexus cases are based on 'suspected gang membership', and 'the gang' is a highly racialised label attached primarily to groups of black men and boys. The processes by which the police identify 'suspected gang members' remain opaque, and it is not clear how an individual ends up on the gangs database (or how they get off it). The police claim that the function of gangs policing is to combat 'serious youth violence'; however, when Patrick Williams and Becky Clarke compared the ethnicity of those convicted of 'serious youth violence' offences against those on the gangs databases, the results were striking. In London, 72% of those on the gangs matrix were black while only 27% of 'serious youth violence' was committed by black people; in Greater Manchester, only 6% of 'serious youth violence' was committed by young black people, and yet 81% of those listed on the gangs matrix were black.[27] Amnesty International found that many of the young black men on the gangs databases had no criminal record at all.[28] In effect, young black men end up being identified as 'gang members' based on their encounters with the police and not their convictions, which is especially significant for heavily policed people like Ricardo and his friends. Under Operation Nexus, this now has deportation consequences.

At an institutional level, then, the policing of 'gangs' is now connected to controlling immigration. In many Operation Nexus cases, police officers provide written witness statements to the immigration courts, and even attend immigration hearings to provide oral evidence of 'bad character' and 'suspected gang affiliation'. In light of police involvement in deportation cases, we might question whether the police officers who harassed Ricardo and Delon were not in fact vindicated by their deportations. Ricardo and Delon were harassed, surveilled and excluded from public space, and they were denied basic rights of citizenship – to free association, the presumption of innocence and to childhood – but in fact they were not citizens and therefore they did not belong. In one sense, the actions of racist police officers merely hastened their rightful deportations.

More broadly, what does it mean to condemn racism within the police force while at the same time involving them in immigration control? Surely, the very logic of immigration control licenses racist policing? While discrimination between British citizens on racial grounds is unlawful, discrimination on national grounds is the essence of immigration control, and of course in practice these modes of discrimination are impossible to isolate: 'Both types of policing often demarcate the racial and cultural boundaries of belonging and are often inscribed by bodily violence on the same groups of people'.[29] In this light, immigration controls are motors of racist discrimination among police officers, who are increasingly tasked with 'finding foreigners'.[30] Thus, it is not only that racist policing has deportation consequences, but also that deportation policies shift the dynamics of racist policing in turn.

Delon's Bar and deportation as death sentence

This chapter is about the relationship between racist policing and immigration control, and the story of Ricardo's brother Delon is just as instructive here. I learnt more about Delon when I visited Ricardo's cousin, Louis, at his restaurant in Oldbury, a town not far from Smethwick. I travelled there one evening, and I was caught in the rain, which made Oldbury look even gloomier than usual. There were more closed shop fronts than open, and so I found the restaurant easily, spotting the faded Jamaican flag out front. I entered 'Delon's Bar' to Beyoncé blasting from the speakers, and the young woman working explained that Louis was out on a delivery. She told me I could I sit down and wait for him. The tables were slightly grubby, and there was a boxing arcade machine in the corner – the harder you punch the higher the score.

When Louis returned, he recognised me from Ricardo's WhatsApp pictures and smiled warmly. He was much shorter than Ricardo, and spoke more quickly and openly than his cousin. 'Give me two secs', he said, as he disappeared off into the back kitchen to prepare another order. I sat waiting, looking at my phone, straining my ears to listen to the conversation in the kitchen.

As I sat there, I realised that the restaurant was a kind of shrine to Delon. His image sits on top of the takeaway menus, his bulging muscles, arms crossed. The same picture is on the menu boards behind the counter, and on the big sign at the front of the shop. Delon looks eerily like Ricardo. Delon's Special recipe, marinade and mix are scattered around the menu, and behind the till there are more pictures of Delon, as well as some family collages. In the back yard, 'RIP Delon' was scrawled in white paint on the mouldy wooden fence, and Louis often wore a t-shirt with the same message: 'RIP Delon'. Louis had grown up with Delon; they were cousins by birth but Louis explained that they were 'more like brothers'. The restaurant, 'Delon's Bar', was his eulogy.

I had been sitting for half an hour, fidgeting at the table, looking at images of Delon everywhere, when Louis darted out of the kitchen and told me to grab a can of soft drink. He would give me a lift back to Smethwick via his last delivery and that way we could chat in his car. Louis drove fast and we arrived at the place I was staying within 20 minutes. Sitting in his car, smoking his post-work spliff, not far from where he grew up, Louis reflected on the deportation of his brothers. Louis had lost two brothers to deportation, one forever, and so when I asked him questions about Ricardo, it was inevitable that his responses became about Delon too: 'That's what's so fucked up about it all man, now I'll never see Delon again. Ricardo has gone, and Delon was killed because they sent him back.'

I cannot know what Delon was like, but Ricardo's friends described him as 'hard' – he had 'a reputation' and apparently he was 'like a king to people in the area'. However, they were evoking memories of Delon from when he was young, and it is important that we think critically about age in all these biographies. Delon's first period of incarceration was when he was under the age of 16. When he was around 17 or 18, he was threatened with deportation and told that if he reoffended he would be sent to Jamaica. Soon after, he was convicted of burglary, and then spent nearly a year in immigration detention before being deported, aged just 20. When Ricardo's friends described Delon as 'bad', 'hard' and 'into crime', I had to keep reminding myself that they were talking about someone they knew between the ages of 14 and 18. And so while Delon might have been 'like a king to people in the area', he was also a child. Ricardo's friend Marcus put it disturbingly well:

> MARCUS: We was all kids when you think about it. We didn't have our heads. Kids ain't got heads blud, it's true though innit! But they don't look at it like that, they just think yo, these lot are just criminals, full stop, innit. Let's delete 'em.

When I went back to Jamaica in 2016, I asked Ricardo some more questions about his brother. By this point, Ricardo and I knew each other well but we had hardly broached the subject of Delon. Ricardo is not the most expressive person and he tends not to elaborate much on his feelings without significant prompting. 'Sometimes it's hard to talk about him; it depends what mood you're in', he explained one evening. Over time, I came to realise how important Delon had been to Ricardo. Delon was 18 months his senior and they shared their childhood together. Ricardo remembered Delon from when they were small children in Jamaica, and in his earliest memories Delon was always there. He had memories of 'being in country' with his older brother and being happy. They were separate for two years when Delon first moved to England, but soon Ricardo had joined him and they both moved in with their 'auntie' and cousins. In this house, for many years, they shared a bedroom. When I asked Ricardo how he responded to Delon's death, which happened while Ricardo was in prison, he replied: 'I didn't really take it in. I guess I didn't really believe it like that, and that's what Tinesha's always saying, I need to grieve, I need to.'

Ricardo had pictures of Delon on his phone, and he would often select one for his WhatsApp profile picture. He also had a small picture of Delon stuck on his bathroom door, in a flat with otherwise bare walls and doors. Ricardo did not talk about his sadness, but I began to think about his body as a medium of expression. When Ricardo went to prison, and spent nearly three years inside, he committed much of his energy to working out.[31] Of course, this is about performing and enhancing masculinity, but his obsession with his body was, in part, an expression of brotherly love and familial attachment. The body can be 'a medium and a fleshy canvas through and on which belonging and structures of feeling are expressed'.[32]

As Les Back notes, the interview method 'privileges the idioms of elaborated communication, so often infused with class bias', and we need to find methods which recognise that 'people express themselves through a wider range of cultural modalities that operate beyond the word'.[33] For Ricardo, his body is one way in which he identified with Delon, using diet and intensive exercise to get bigger, and to approach likeness with the brother he lost. In early 2017, Ricardo posted a picture of himself on social media, arms crossed, beneath a tree on a shaded beach in Mobay. His caption read: 'I'm trying to Looking like Delon 💪 miss you bro R.i.p 💪.'

Conclusion

In 2017, when I returned to visit Ricardo in Mobay, he was living in his own place with Tinesha, and working full time as a security guard in a bank. They invited me around for Sunday dinner and I brought my camera to take some pictures. In the morning, Ricardo and I watched Manchester United on his cable TV, the team we both support, and Ricardo proudly described how they had both saved for the television, the furniture and the washing machine, which he had to carry up the hill on his back.

Tinesha laughed at me when I tried to hang up the clothes I had washed in their machine, before showing me how it was done. In the afternoon she cooked chicken with rice and peas, and a couple of their friends came over and joined us.

Ricardo's friend Everton was one of them. He had also grown up in the West Midlands. After dinner, we laughed about the kids' television shows we used to watch after school, spending a good 15 minutes listing off kids' programmes, reminiscing and laughing loudly. 'Man used to watch *Tracy Beaker*, I'm not even gonna lie', Everton said, and me and Ricardo burst into laughter, admitting that we had too. Tinesha and her friend were confused and continued their own conversation in patois. All of this was a reminder that Ricardo's childhood memories, like most of his cultural references, were located in Britain, even as his first experiences working, paying bills and living independently were in Mobay.

I asked Ricardo if he would like to go back to the UK at some point and he said 'Of course yeah, but I would stay away from the West Midlands. If that's how the police treated me before I even did anything, just imagine now.' As his friend Melissa put it:

> MELISSA: What's he done since he's been out there, got himself a job, d'you know what I mean? So it shows you. He hasn't had no one harassing him over there, and he's progressed. Sometimes I say to him, maybe getting deported was for the best, even though it's not the best, I say to him, like, you've learnt so much being out there now.

The fact that deportation might appear to have been 'for the best' is a reflection of how difficult Ricardo's life was made by policing and incarceration in the UK. The intensity of racist criminalisation meant that deportation presented new opportunities for different kinds of freedom, however limited, and this represents the starkest indictment of the UK's criminal justice system.

Undeniably, the experiences of Ricardo and his friends provide a damning account of racist policing in the UK. However, the

Pictures 3.2 and 3.3. *Ricardo watching Manchester United and experimenting with my camera, Mobay (2017)*

point of this chapter has been to complicate how we understand that police racism. Clearly, disproportionate and discriminatory policing propels certain people towards deportation, and this affects young working-class black men in particular, but processes of racialisation, criminalisation and expulsion are not linear. Instead, discourses and practices surrounding immigration control reconfigure how race and racism operate. In this way, reflecting on Ricardo's story helps us reach a more sophisticated account of racism in anti-immigrant times.[34] Importantly, it is not only that racism in wider society determines who gets deported, but that deportation determines how racism operates in wider society.

In the next chapter, I interrogate the relationship between racism, criminalisation and immigration control from a different angle, arguing that Chris was deported not because he failed to 'integrate', but because he was too well integrated into an unequal, racist and sexist society.

Coda

In February 2018, Ricardo sent me a message. It read: 'What's up Luke, just to let you know Tinesha is pregnant. I will be having a son or daughter soon.' He and Tinesha were excitedly making plans, while Louis was arranging to send clothes, toys and 'baby stuff' from the West Midlands.

Ricardo is actually doing well now. His life in Jamaica is full and hopeful and deportation was as much a beginning as an end. Of course, deportation can mean many things, and it does not have to be the end. However, as Delon's story reminds us, sometimes it is.

Chapter 4

Chris

CHRIS: It's like I've got a split personality. Sometimes I'm, like, when I'm around good, decent people, I'm good and decent and I'm charming, I'm loving and caring towards those that I care about. But when I'm around the bad people, *when I'm around society and all of that*, like I'm hard and tough, and I'm this bad boy that has to be, like, that has to survive, innit. You get me? Like, once I say I'm going downtown, I'm one of the baddest mandem downtown. Literally I put my mind frame as that. But when I'm at home, or around you or around guests, I'm just kind, charming, I'm just normal and just a human being. You get me? *I think I have to be what society is.*

Chris meditated on his 'split personality' in one of our many interviews under the gazebo where he sat on night shift. In 2015 and 2016, Chris worked as an overnight security guard at a small guesthouse in Liguanea Plain, Kingston, and we spent many long evenings there, talking about his life. I would prop my microphone up between us, and Chris would explain the key moments and relationships that shaped his biography. Chris is a deeply reflective and intelligent man, and his thoughtful and analytical way of 'telling his life' made him the ideal interlocutor. He likes to talk, and he is very consistent with the things he says about his past, even when they are defined by contradiction.

When I first visited Chris at the guesthouse, he met me at the gate wearing a Chelsea shirt, and immediately offered me a cup of tea – a familiar gesture in the wrong place. On that first evening, he spoke about his predicament in Kingston and described his former life in England – first in London, then in Leeds. He switched between Jamaican patois and London English in the middle of his responses to my questions, using patois when describing his life in Jamaica, and yet sounding like a Londoner when talking about England. This switching is central to how Chris navigates very different social contexts, and is part of his ability to, in his own words, 'adapt'.

We covered much of Chris' life in that first recorded conversation. He told me about his criminal offences – first street robbery, then possession with intent to supply – and explained that he had two children in Leeds, a boy and a girl, both aged six at the time of the interview. Chris often spoke about his children:

> CHRIS: Yeah bruv, I'm not even gonna lie, I think god blessed her because she was really advanced, within like, before she could walk she was saying 'daddy' all the time. As soon as she see me through the window comin', she used to be like, 'daddy, daddy, daddy, daddy' and her mum used get annoyed that her first word was 'daddy', you get me? So, she learnt fast. I think she got that from me really cos I'm a quick learner innit [laughs].... My son as well, every time I went over the house, he used to just hide round the corner, and just smile, giggle, wait for me to step inside the house and then he would just pounce on me and from then on it would be non-stop playing, non-stop playing until either he would fall asleep in my arms, every night. That was one of the greatest things I had with my son, like he used to just fall asleep in my arms. He had his bed and stuff, like, and he had his mum to put him to bed, but me not living with them, like, spending those times like, that was our thing.

Chris felt that he had let his children down: 'All I have left them with is my name', he said on several occasions. He tried to keep in touch with them, and spoke to his daughter roughly once a week, often in the middle of the night local time, before she went to school, but sustaining these relationships was not easy: 'If I don't contact them they don't contact me at all, completely', he explained. Aside from a handful of prison visits, Chris had had only a year or so with his children, and he continued to feel that the worst thing about deportation was separation from them. When Chris appealed against his deportation in 2011, he wrote to the judge: 'I now have two children and I have tried my best to be there for them as much as possible so that they will have a father who loves and cares for them as I didn't have that'.

I did not notice it straight away, but Chris has a tattoo on his arm that reads: 'A Gangster and a Gentleman' – a reference to one of his favourite albums, by Styles P. For the four years I have known Chris, I have been trying to understand the tensions between the gangster and the gentleman, his being both and neither. Indeed, I opened the chapter with this particular quote because it seems to reveal so much about Chris: *'I think I have to be what society is'*. Chris consistently explained his criminality in terms of 'adapting' to his surroundings – to being what society was – and so for Chris his criminality was not a mark of his foreignness, but quite the opposite. He put it in the most simple terms when he said 'England made me a criminal'.

Within the Immigration Rules, however, criminality is often seen to demonstrate 'a lack of social and cultural integration', and this lack of integration then justifies deportation.[1] Writing against this Home Office version, this chapter argues that, in practice, the UK deports people who are *too* well integrated, rather than not integrated enough.[2] The chapter therefore takes Chris seriously when he says that 'England made me a criminal', and this requires alternative theorisations of integration, culture and crime. In effect, criminalisation and deportation operate to individualise and externalise wider forms of inequality and violence, thereby obscuring broader causes of social harm.[3] Indeed, my argument is that Chris might have something important to teach us about the society into which 'migrants and minorities' are expected to integrate – a society which is violently unequal, racist and sexist.

Picture 4.1. *Chris under the gazebo in the guesthouse at Liguanea (2015)*

Defining 'integration'?

My argument in this chapter is that Chris did not fail to integrate, but was perhaps too well integrated into an unequal, racist and sexist society. But what do I mean by 'integration'? According to policy makers, integration is about the strengthening of social cohesion, democracy and citizenship in the context of 'ethnic diversity' and demographic change. In particular, 'migrants and minorities' are expected to integrate into host societies, by demonstrating their adherence to shared civic values of tolerance, democracy and the rule of law.[4] Thinking more critically, however, 'integration' functions primarily as a codeword for racial anxieties and resentments; integration is about 'what *we* do with *them*', central to the policy discourses through which 'migrants and minorities' are constructed as problems.[5] In contemporary Europe, debates on integration are focused primarily on Muslims, providing an apparently racially neutral, although in fact profoundly racialised, way of talking about difference and belonging in the context of widespread fears about 'internal enemies' and 'civilisational threat'.[6]

In the case of deportation, though, 'social and cultural integration' is operationalised in a slightly different way. To demonstrate their integration, 'migrants' appealing deportation must demonstrate that they are financially independent (not claiming benefits); that they have been in the UK lawfully (not as 'illegal immigrants'); and that they have abided by the law (not committed any criminal offences). To be integrated, then, is not merely to have lived in the UK for a long time, but to be able to demonstrate that one is a 'good citizen'.[7] In the Home Office's own words, 'mere presence in the UK is not an indication of integration',[8] and migrants should 'work hard, play by the rules, speak English and get on through merit'.[9] My intention here is certainly not to claim that Chris meets this definition, but rather to critique the very logic of 'good citizenship', and to offer instead some alternative ways of thinking about integration, culture and crime.

Chris, like many of the deported people I met in Jamaica, described himself as integrated into British culture and society. He did not claim to be a 'good citizen', but referred to the inevitable processes through which he had made friends and become part of the places where he lived. He described himself as a 'normal black guy in London', suggesting that his cultural identifications were profoundly local. He said that his decision to engage in street robberies as a teenager was a measure of his boyish camaraderie and 'neighbourhood nationalism' – not a reflection of his 'foreignness'.[10] Later, when he sold drugs in Leeds, he viewed it not as a mark of his individual moral failure or cultural alienness, but a response to material hardship in

Picture 4.2. *Chris in his Chelsea shirt, my flat, University of the West Indies campus (2015)*

the context of family responsibility. In other words, Chris felt integrated, and working with his own interpretations we can better describe what it was he was integrating into. This allows for a much deeper critique of inequality and 'integration' in contemporary Britain.

Street robberies in London

Chris's mother moved to London when he was 10 years old, but he stayed in Kingston for a few years with his father, before joining her in 2001, aged 14. He adapted quickly and made new friends in West London, but he started getting into trouble not long after finishing secondary school:

> CHRIS: My dad had died a couple of years before, so I was in that free mind to say I've got no one to tell me what to do, my mum has brought me up as good as possible. But it weren't enough no

more.... Then, I started to smoke weed with friends, in college, you get me, started to drink, have parties, stay up late, and then the influences started to happen, took a toll on us. We started to be on road, and be like 'Who are you?' I see my friend knock out this guy, and then I threw in a punch, and then another guy threw in a punch, so we end up rushin' one guy, and that adrenaline felt good. We're boys, we've got a crew! I'm thinking, I wasn't in no crew in Jamaica, you get me, but now I'm here this is what we're doing. We smoke weed every weekend, drink and we'd go out and fight, you get me?

When he was 17, Chris started committing occasional street robberies in West London, mostly on weekends:

LUKE: Did you make much money from robbing people?
CHRIS: Hundred quid a week. I didn't rob much people. I robbed like two people a week. And because there's a few of us doing robberies we just split the money, so we weren't making anything, we weren't robbing no banks or nothing, or post offices, we were just robbing random people. We're just having fun. By the time we finished getting pissed out of our heads, and we're going on the road, we'd be like 'Oi, you come here!' And then we just beat you up and rob you, just randomly.
LUKE: How do you feel about that now?
CHRIS: I feel like an idiot.
LUKE: Because I was just thinking, like, imagine it was me at the bus stop.
CHRIS: You woulda been robbed [*laughing*]! You woulda been robbed, honestly, back then you probably woulda been robbed.
LUKE: Was it fun though?
CHRIS: It was fun [*laughing*]. It was fun, it was adrenaline. We was young and we was teenagers. We didn't know right from wrong really, you get me, and it was fun. Like skinny me punching somebody, it was a lot of fun. Should have took up boxing really, would've been better, but....

When Chris was 18, his mother moved to Leeds but he decided to stay in West London with his auntie:

CHRIS: Like, my family was breaking apart so she moved, just to get away from the family bullshit and such, but I stayed because I was a Londoner innit. And I thought, 'Hey, my boys are here, I don't need you. You've helped me so far but I can take care of myself now.' I started doing robberies to support myself now. First it was for fun, now I took it up as a profession. One too many robberies went bad. I went on a robbery with my cousin, in Walthamstow, East London, Chingford area like, I didn't know the area. Robbed a group of people. As we're getting away we ran into a bag of police, got caught. I thought, fuck, I should've stayed in West London, where if I robbed a few people, I can get away because I know the area.

After Chris was arrested in East London, he was charged with street robbery and attempted street robbery, and later sentenced to 20 months in prison (to serve half). The Home Office tried to deport him during this sentence, but he successfully appealed on the basis of 'family life', his lack of previous offences and the fact that he had indefinite leave to remain (i.e. permanent residence). Chris would have found it much more difficult to win the same appeal 10 years later, given changes to immigration policy (see Introduction), but in 2007 he avoided deportation and retained his indefinite leave to remain.

Black culture, black crime

As a teenager, Chris found fighting and robbing people exhilarating: 'that adrenaline felt good'; 'skinny me punching somebody'. He described drinking, fighting and robbing people on the streets of London, at a specific time in his life, in ways which emphasised friendship, the peer group and experimentation. My intention is not to absolve Chris, but to recognise that turning these behaviours into 'crimes' worthy of custodial punishment takes ideological and legal work. Importantly, this ideological and legal work is connected to histories and processes of racialisation. Put simply, street crime is imagined as 'black crime', and this authorises heavier policing and tougher sentencing.[11]

Since the early 1970s, street robbery, or 'mugging', has been characterised in terms of lawless 'black youth' violently robbing innocents in deprived areas of urban Britain.[12] In this way, fears surrounding 'street crime' have consistently channelled wider concerns about immigration and multiculturalism. Racial anxieties and resentments – in relation to changing demographics, youth culture and the city – are powerfully mobilised and veiled within discussions about crime.[13] Through media reportage and political debate, specific 'criminal problems' (i.e. 'street crime') are associated with, or fixed onto, specific 'criminal populations' (i.e. 'black youth'), which are then made to symbolise moral and national decline.

In relation to 'black youth' and 'street crime', an array of explanations on 'absent fathers', 'cultural deprivation' and 'generational conflict' have been solicited to explain why young black men, in particular, 'turn to crime'.[14] There has been a broad consensus claiming that the apparently inordinate involvement of 'black youth' in violent street crime can be explained in reference to 'culture'. As Claire Alexander notes, in this context culture is understood both to mark ethnicity and difference, and to refer to deviant youth subcultures. In relation to 'black crime', these two formulations are used interchangeably, and criminality is blamed on the failures of family and community, and on depraved and nihilistic youth cultures.[15] As Paul Gilroy argued back in 1982:

> The emphasis on black culture legitimates the idea that any black, all blacks, are somehow contaminated by the alien predisposition to crime which is reproduced in their distinctive cultures, specifically their family relations…. The neat scenario which presents rising street crime as the cause and police militarization as the effect, places the blame for this state of affairs squarely on the shoulders of a minority of deviant blacks.[16]

Importantly, these racialised discourses on 'black culture' and 'street crime' have had significant consequences for policing, sentencing and legislation: street robbery is heavily penalised, and first-time offenders over the age of 18 almost invariably receive custodial sentences.[17] It is the racialised history of 'mugging' which underwrites the severity of criminal punishment, and thus racist ideas about 'culture' have real consequences in terms of who gets criminalised and how they are punished.[18] Returning to Chris's first conviction, the simple point is that not everyone who drinks, fights and steals ends up losing their liberty, and it is the histories of race and racism that underpin these processes of differential opprobrium and punishment.

It might be argued, however, that 'mugging' no longer preoccupies journalists and judges. This is largely true, but the same narratives on 'black culture' are now enlisted to explain 'knife crime' and 'gang violence'. In 2018, tabloid newspapers reported almost daily on the apparent epidemic of 'knife crime', linking it to 'gangs' and 'gang culture', both of which were constructed as a predominantly 'black problem'. Comment pieces predictably focused on the role of 'absent fathers',[19] while London's Metropolitan Police Service justified the disproportionate use of stop and search against black boys by arguing that young African Caribbean men were disproportionately affected by 'knife crime', both as victims and as perpetrators.[20]

The media focus on 'knife crime' and 'gang violence' between 2017 and 2019 was certainly relentless, but the narratives were well rehearsed. In 1998, the Metropolitan Police set up Operation Trident, the first dedicated unit tasked with policing 'gun violence' and 'the gang', with a particular focus on African-Caribbean 'gangs' from its inception. In 2007, Prime Minister Tony Blair stated that 'the black community ... need to be mobilised in denunciation of this gang culture that is killing innocent black kids. But we won't stop this by pretending it isn't young black kids doing it.'[21] In 2009, new police powers were introduced under the Policing and Crime Act, which introduced gang injunctions and limited the association of 'gang members' in public places. Two years later, in the wake of the 2011 disturbances, Prime Minister David Cameron announced a 'concerted all-out war on gangs and gang culture' and stated that 'stamping out these gangs is a new national priority'.[22] The Offensive Weapons Act 2019 introduced 'knife crime prevention orders', which can be issued by the police to anyone over the age of 12 who officers *believe* or *suspect* is a habitual knife carrier.[23] The orders can include curfews, geographical restrictions on where people can go and with whom, and limits on the use of social media (see previous chapter on Ricardo's ASBO). Breach of these orders can result in a prison sentence of up to two years.

These legal instruments and policing practices obviously have deportation consequences (as explored in the previous chapter). In Jamaica, I met several young men who had been criminalised, and subsequently deported, for carrying knives. Chris himself carried a knife, and like the other men I spoke to, he did so for protection, particularly against the threat of being 'rushed' or 'jumped'.[24] Chris spoke about his fears of violence as a teenager in London, especially when travelling to school or football practice: 'Sometimes I didn't even go to college, bruv. I stopped playing football because of that bullshit, bruv, and I was good too.' The fact that Chris stopped going to college and stopped playing football illustrates that fears of serious violence circumscribe young men's lives. While politicians, journalists and senior police officers repeatedly blame 'knife crime' on the 'black community', and by extension on 'black culture', Chris carried a knife in response to the very real threat of violence, which impacts young men living in particular parts of urban Britain. For Chris, carrying a knife had nothing to do with being black. In fact, Chris described himself as a 'Londoner', and he reminded me that his friends were multi-ethnic. In short, there was nothing 'black' about his criminality. In this light, to challenge the racist logics of 'black crime' and 'black culture' we need to think more critically about *lived culture*, pursuing an alternative definition of culture as radically open, something which cannot be reduced to or fixed onto 'race'.

Lived culture and conviviality

Chris and I spent most of our time together in Kingston, but we also went on trips out of the city. We climbed Jamaica's highest peak, Blue Mountain, and stayed in Portland for a weekend, the rainy parish in the north-east of the island. It was nice to be 'in country' with Chris, where everything moves slower, and this seemed to make him especially nostalgic. Indeed, it was in Portland that Chris spoke most extensively about his early years in the UK, describing how at home he felt in West London, in his neighbourhood and in his school in particular.

Much has been written about how young people in London tend to identify strongly with their local area: whether in terms of the city, their specific area defined by postcode or as locally as their housing estate. It is argued that divisions around ethnicity, nationality and religion tend to be less prevalent than these more local identifications. Les Back termed this 'neighbourhood nationalism', and as a teenager Chris clearly found his place in the world through identifying with 'his ends'.[25]

> CHRIS: It was our boys. If anybody try and mess with us, that was it ... we learnt to defend people as a group together. We had fun together. We was like NWA ['Niggaz Wit Attitudes'] really, you get me? [*laughs*]
> LUKE: All black guys then if you're saying NWA?
> CHRIS: Noooo! [*high pitched*] We was mixed. I think I was the blackest [*we both laugh*].... We had Sam. Sam was white. Yanick was mixed race, Antoine was mixed race, Charlie was white, I was black and Radelle was black.

Like Ricardo in the previous chapter, Chris was keen to emphasise that his friendship group was multi-ethnic. Arguably, this simple fact negates those racialising claims about 'black crime' and 'black culture' discussed above. However, recognising the multi-ethnic character of his peer group does not necessarily negate racism. Indeed, when historian David Starkey infamously claimed that 'the whites have become black', he was mobilising long-held ideas about 'black culture' as contagion.[26] The power and versatility of culturalist racism is that it can be detached from any particular racial group, and thereby freed from accusations of biological racism (after all, your culture is something you can change, unlike your skin colour). As Starkey put it: 'The whites have become black, a particular sort of violent, destructive, nihilistic, gangster culture has become the fashion, and black and white, boy and girl, operate in this language together'.[27]

Of course, when Chris and Ricardo emphasised that their friendship groups were multi-ethnic, they were not referring to those inter-racial cultures of criminality and gangsterism dreamed up by Starkey, but to the mundane fact that they shared their lives with friends of different ethnicities. Indeed, everyday interactions across lines of racial and ethnic difference are unremarkable in contemporary Britain, and scholars have described these forms of *everyday multiculture* with reference to Paul Gilroy's concept of 'conviviality'.[28]

Conviviality is a generative concept because it offers 'an alternative understanding of culture that focuses on what people do every day rather than always reducing them to their cultural origins'.[29] Focusing on what people do every day requires a definition of culture which cannot be fixed onto any single racial grouping. This refusal to let culture become a codeword for 'race' has been central to the firmly anti-racist strain of British cultural studies.[30] This tradition has tended to celebrate the radical openness of lived culture, viewing culture not as ethnic property but as the site of struggle over shared meaning.[31] For Gilroy, 'the convivial metropolitan cultures of the country's young people are still a bulwark against the machinations of racial politics'.[32] This everyday multiculture offers 'a ready-made counterpoint to nationalist capture', one that wages 'an everyday battle against the wider forces of nativist racism'.[33]

Chris's multi-ethnic affiliations were not confined to his early years in London, however. When he finished his first

10-month sentence, he moved in with his mother in Leeds (a city in the north of England) and spent much of his time in the neighbourhood by her house. The ward where she lived was low income and ethnically diverse, with around two-thirds of the local population defined as 'Black and Minority Ethnic'.

> CHRIS: There was Bangladeshis, Pakistanis, Africans, mostly Bangla-deshi and Pakistani Muslims really. Then, there was even this white Muslim guy, and Arabs, Kurdish, Afghans. It was mixed, the Muslims, you get me, it was mixed. The Kurds was there. I associated with the Kurdish Muslims as well, because there was a Kurdish shop next to me. They sell Caribbean foods, weirdly like, but they control that shop and whenever they cooked their Kurdish food they would invite me, because they lived on top of the shop, you get me, and I would go up there, and they showed me, we used to smoke shisha pipe, shisha innit, like fruity flavoured whatever like. We used to sit and smoke.

Chris spoke about how the Kurdish men 'shared everything' with one another, showing their generosity by offering food to him and his mother. He was impressed by their expressions of brotherhood and began taking an interest in Islam. Chris's oldest and best friend Jae was also a Muslim (Jae features in Chapter 6), and these positive encounters prefaced his conversion to Islam in prison during his second sentence. For the time I knew Chris, he was intermittently practising, and he said that his religion helped him when life was especially difficult (in 2017 and 2019 I took him prayer beads, thobes and skull caps). His conversion to Islam might be seen as evidence of the openness of culture, of dialogue and of the ways in which people live together and learn from one another in contemporary Britain – although in the current political climate it is likely to be made to symbolise something far more sinister.[34]

Conviviality is a useful concept, but it should not become 'a by-word for saccharine diversity fantasies'.[35] Simply recog-nising that people get along despite their differences is not enough. Conviviality helps us challenge and unmoor the logics of racism and nationalism, but this is only part of the political struggle. For Gilroy, ordinary multiculture is precious precisely because it exists in the context of deepening racism, nationalism and various forms of disentitlement under neoliberalism. Put another way, conviviality reminds us that we are not that different after all, and this allows us to focus on the vulnerabilities we share, which are particularly stark in the context of widening inequality, austerity and urban displacement. Thinking about lived culture differently allows us to overcome the traps of absolute difference, which can then bring our shared violation into view.

Indeed, this is precisely Gilroy's political project: if only we could see through the false promises of race and nation, by viewing cultural difference not as a site of danger but as one of dialogue and movement, then we might turn our attention to what really matters – the struggle against racism and the degradations of late capitalism. For my purposes, this means rejecting culturalist explanations for crime, recognising the importance of multi-ethnic affiliation and care, before then pursuing a material account of why people commit crime and are criminalised. Chris's experiences in Leeds are instructive here, reminding us that most people are criminalised in the context of poverty, social marginalisation and profoundly limited options.

Selling in Leeds – unemployment, benefit sanctions and rent arrears

I wanted to see where Chris had lived in Leeds, and so I arranged to stay in the city for a few nights in the summer of 2016. I messaged Chris and he told me to head to a particular KFC outlet in Leeds and then to call him on WhatsApp for a guided tour of the area. I wandered around his old neighbourhood with him in my earphones, speaking from Kingston. I walked down the road on which he was arrested in possession of heroin and crack cocaine, and he described that night to me again. He then directed me to his mother's old house, which was just around the corner (she now lives in London), and on the way there he told me to look out for the barbershop, a place in which he used to 'hang out and take calls'.

It was a warm day, with blue skies, and I told Chris that the area seemed nice. He laughed and replied, 'It's a shithole'. A few days later, when I met the mother of Chris's daughter, Tara, she gave her own description of the neighbourhood:

> TARA: Everyone's really nice here and just gets on with each other and stuff, but there's a lot of, erm, you see a lot of the young boys – you can tell they sell drugs. You see a lot of crack heads as well round here. You can always tell who they are.

Indeed, Chris referring to the area as 'a shithole' points to some of the struggles he had there. In his first year in Leeds, he was unemployed, he had no money and he was bored; he relied on his mother and was mostly eating at her house. Later, when he had his own council flat, he still spent much of his time at his mother's house, helping to look after his two younger brothers and often 'crashing on the couch'.

Unlike Jason and Ricardo, however, Chris had indefinite leave to remain, and so he was legally permitted to work and claim welfare support. He was in receipt of unemployment benefits for most of this time (Job Seeker's Allowance), and that gave him around £45 a week. A condition of Job Seeker's Allowance, however, is that the individual be actively looking for work, and Chris had to meet with his benefit caseworker every two weeks to provide evidence of the jobs he had applied for. He also had to attend work placements, and he was very sceptical about them. As he put it, 'Tesco were just using people as free labour innit; they never got no job at the end'. Chris worked at an Oxfam charity shop for one of his work placements, and when he missed a day they told him not to come back. When

Chris missed work placements like this, or skipped meetings with his caseworker, he was sanctioned, and his Job Seeker's Allowance was stopped, which led to the removal of his housing benefit. Indeed, he was sanctioned several times and fell into rent arrears on three occasions.[36]

At this point, Chris had had no meaningful experiences of paid employment, and he was aware that his criminal record put him at a profound disadvantage in the labour market. Unemployment among 16–24-year-old black men was over 40% in 2010–2012 (when Chris was in Leeds), and the proportion not in education or employment was over 20%.[37] In the words of Chris's mother: 'If you're black and you've got a record, no one's gonna trust you'. The recession of 2008 hit young black men particularly hard, and Chris had a criminal record, no qualifications and lived in a poor ward in a city in the north of England. His employment prospects were fairly bleak. Meanwhile, he was facing regular benefit sanctions and ultimately he lost his council flat when his rent arrears reached a certain point.

It was during this period that Chris discovered he would be a father, not once but twice, and this was when he decided to sell heroin and crack not far from his mother's house. With seemingly few alternatives, Chris found work in the flourishing economy in the neighbourhood he knew well.[38] However, his position in the drugs trade was high risk and low reward. As he put it: 'I was never sitting pretty ... I'm not no Scarface or no, like, Escobar or anyone. I'm just a nobody really.' However, when the Home Office sent Chris his deportation decision letter two years later, they had no interest in these qualifications. As the letter stated: 'You chose to deal class A drugs (rather than seeking legitimate paid employment, as your immigration status allowed you to)'. From Chris's perspective, he *chose* to sell drugs because he was unemployed and homeless, and because he had two children on the way, but the Home Office did not think these circumstances relevant. Chris reflected on this in the scrapbook I gave him, writing the following line in a reflective piece titled 'Decisions, Decisions, Decisions':

> I've seen white men get caught with a house full of drugs and walk away with a fine, but cos I'm Jamaican and I had a handful of drugs, I got to go back to where I came from.... Racist cunts.

In 2013, the year Chris was deported, over half of the 'foreign criminals' sent from the UK to Jamaica had been convicted of drugs offences.[39] Many of these individuals, like Chris, will have sold drugs in the context of poverty, unemployment and insecurity – and many, like Denico in the next chapter, because they were prohibited from working legally. Recognising that drug economies employ young men who are excluded from the formal labour market offers an important response to the Home Office's individualising and externalising narratives on 'lack of social and cultural integration', as well as those racist arguments on 'black crime' and 'gang culture' discussed earlier. Of course, racism within the criminal justice system is also central here, and the focus on poverty and unemployment in this chapter must be read alongside the account of racist policing documented in the previous chapter.

Unlike the other three men in this book, Chris had the right to work and to claim benefits, and this is significant. However, persistent unemployment and punitive benefit sanctions meant that he had no income and no means of supporting himself or his family. In this way, Chris's decision to sell drugs shares much with British citizens who make similar decisions in similar contexts, and who are also incarcerated for their crimes. Chris had not failed to integrate, then, but was in fact too well integrated into a violently unequal society. His criminality did not reflect a lack of 'shared values', but *the lack of things shared fairly*.

Ultimately, Chris's second offence of possession with intent to supply propelled him towards deportation, and in the next section I focus on his legal appeal against his deportation. I explore the ways in which his 'family life' was constructed within deportation proceedings – which prefaces a longer discussion of 'family life' in the next chapter – arguing that Chris was invested in the same gendered ideals as the Home Office, even if he failed to embody them successfully.

Deporting 'feckless baby daddies'

Chris was arrested in possession of a small amount of crack cocaine and heroin in January 2011. He was released on bail and not tried until May, when he was sentenced for two years, to serve half. After a few months in prison, Chris was served with a 'Notice of Intention to Deport' letter, explaining that the Home Office planned to deport him when his sentence was finished. Legal arguments were attached, and the letter said that if Chris wanted to appeal the decision, he had to reply with any reasons why the Home Office should not deport him within 28 days. Thus began the legal battle between Chris and the Home Office.

Chris replied to the letter with some information on why he should not be deported, but the Home Office briskly rejected his submissions. Chris therefore found a solicitor and appealed to the immigration tribunal. Chris's argument, broadly put, was that he should be allowed to remain in the UK to stay with his family. The Home Office, on the other hand, argued that his deportation was in the 'public interest'. Chris's deportation case therefore hinged on a proportionality assessment, in which criminality and the 'public interest' were weighed up against his right to 'private and family life'. As a result, Chris had to demonstrate the substance and the quality of his family connections, and when his appeal reached the First Tier Immigration Tribunal he made every effort to get his family together to attend the hearing. As he explains:

CHRIS: My kids couldn't come, because that would literally influence it. Because they're gonna see the bond I have with my kids, so they [the tribunal] said nah, they don't want no influences in the court room. My mum came up from London; my cousin, my best friend as well, he drove them up, and both my baby mothers came. So we was all in the court. The solicitor went up and said his piece. I stood up, said my piece. They asked loads of questions and I was, like, really, come on man, look, you can see how good we are – we've all come together because we care. We've put our differences aside. Yes, my relationship might not be a top grade-A relationship, but it is a relationship. Like, who has a perfect relationship? You can't just base it off the Beckhams, or the Kardashians, or some rich kids. You can't base it off that, like, some people have broken-down relationships, *but it works*. It's the kids; I've got a bond with the kids. You can't take me away from it. So I was, like, really, kind of shocked. I don't know, I got angry at certain stages because they was saying I was lying, and I'm, like, come on man, just give a brother another chance, I've literally changed my whole life.

Chris is astute here. He realised that the state's definition of 'family life' would likely exclude his relationships, rendering his intimate connections illegible. Of course, the fact that there is such a thing as the 'right to respect for family life' demonstrates that liberal states are concerned with protecting 'the family'.[40] However, only some kinds of families are recognised, and the value attached to different family forms is profoundly racialised.[41] When Chris asks 'who has a perfect relationship?', he is questioning what metric Home Office decision makers and immigration judges are using to reach their decisions. In fact, the Home Office had already made its position clear in its correspondence with Chris:

The birth dates of your two claimed children have been noted and it is apparent that both of the mothers of these children would have been pregnant at the same time....

It is apparent that neither of these women, nor their children can rely on you for stability in their lives, or rely on you to take responsibility for your actions. You have demonstrated that you are quite prepared to move on to new relationships, and father more children without considering the needs of the child you have already fathered, or behave as a responsible father which is paramount in these young children's lives. Your actions cannot be considered the actions of a responsible adult who claims to be devoted to them.

You cannot be considered a suitable role model for these children given the nature of your offences, your blatant disregard for the laws of the United Kingdom, and your failure to behave as a responsible father.

The Home Office censured Chris for having two children by two women within six months and emphasised his lack of personal responsibility. The language used to assert that Chris was not 'a suitable role model' is notable for its resonance with wider discourses on 'absent black fathers', who are routinely blamed for the 'pathologies' of black children (especially boys).[42] The Home Office view is that responsible fathers maintain monogamous relationships and support their families through legal employment. Indeed, the Immigration Rules recognise relationships between partners as 'genuine and subsisting' only if they involve either marriage or relationships 'akin to marriage' (i.e. involving co-habitation). For this reason, fathers are assumed to be peripheral if they do not live with their children.[43] This is not just a matter of immigration judges using their discretion to enforce norms of respectability, then: these standards are actually codified in immigration policy. According to the Immigration Rules, migrant fathers should be financially independent (i.e. not claiming benefits), they should live with their children and they should play an active role in their lives, making decisions about where they go to school, for example.[44]

These rules are likely to be interpreted in particular ways in relation to African-Caribbean appellants. Chris was constructed as irresponsible for having two children with two women within six months, and while this reflects the legal preference for nuclear and monogamous family forms, it is important to recognise that cultural ideas about the irresponsibility/absence of black men inevitably permeate the court room. In short,

Chris was not just deported as a 'foreign criminal', but as a 'feckless Jamaican baby daddy'. My argument here is that culturalist and racist tropes on black masculinities take on renewed significance in immigration cases – even if in ways which are difficult to measure. As Peter Wade puts it: 'People in schools and city administrations [for my purposes immigration judges and Home Office decision makers] pursue their goals with the resources (material and symbolic) at their disposal; they understand the problems confronting them in ways influenced by ideas of nation and race, but not necessarily with these ideas at the forefront of their minds'.[45] In this light, histories of racialisation which have produced tropes on 'criminal black youth' and 'absent fathers' inevitably shape decision-making processes within the immigration system, even if their impact is impossible to quantify. In this way, racist culture and structural racism are mutually constitutive.

By critiquing Home Office decision making, however, I am not arguing that Chris was in fact a responsible father and a 'good man'. Nor do I want to pretend that Chris always treated the women in his life well. In fact, I want to make almost the opposite point, recognising that Chris's gendered identifications are profoundly damaging, and yet they are deeply normative, significantly overlapping with the ideas about masculinity and family that are written into UK immigration policy.

Masculinity denied

I became frustrated with Chris's narratives on women when I returned to Jamaica in 2016. My field notes are interspersed with complaints about Chris calling women 'bitches'. It is important to note that in many of my relationships with deported men I felt uncomfortable with their perspectives on and behaviour towards women. I conducted interviews with one man who was a violent domestic abuser throughout his whole adult life, another who was convicted for statutory rape (who was murdered in Clarendon one year later), and another young man whose comments on women were so vile that I found it hard to be around him. In this context, then, Chris is not an extreme case, but perhaps that is why he is better to 'think with'.

In 2016, after a couple of weeks struggling with Chris's incessant misogyny, I broached the subject with him in a bar. He recognised that he harboured anger towards women, and he heard me out when I expressed my views, but he continued to emphasise that Jamaican women were, in fact, 'disloyal bitches'. He also felt that women from his life in the UK did not care about him any longer, and they blamed him for his deportation: 'I'm tired of being sorry for it. I didn't leave. I wished I could stay. I fought. I tried.' Separated from his children, and struggling to develop intimate relationships with women in Jamaica, it was clear that Chris felt that he was ageing without meaningful gendered relationships. Of course, Chris's misogyny did not magically appear with his deportation, but his anger and frustration surrounding the immense dislocation that deportation wrought were predictably channelled into anger towards women, who, he thought, probably fairly accurately, were not interested in a man with no money, house or job. While I found Chris's narratives frustrating, sometimes upsetting, even as my own maleness licensed his tirades, it is important to situate them within a wider critique of gender.

In Jamaica, Chris felt like a failure, and he described his destitution and deportation as forms of emasculation. Central to his feelings of emasculation was the inability to raise his own family. As he repeatedly said of his two children in the UK: 'All I left them with was a name' – that last vestige of connection, family continuity and patriarchal responsibility. Indeed, returning to Chris's second criminal offence, it is important to recognise that he sold drugs in Leeds because he felt compelled 'to provide for his children':

> CHRIS: I felt a bit of pressure. I could afford one, but not two, at the same time.... I thought, what the fuck? I ain't got shit. I need to buy shit. Reality hits me, I need to be a responsible dad. My dad didn't do shit for me.

Chris aspired to the ideals of hegemonic masculinity and responsible fatherhood, the very norms encoded in immigration policy.[46] He was deported because he failed to meet these ideals, rather than because he rejected them. This analysis is not meant to detract from the depressing reality that, after he had been deported, Chris's experiences of isolation, destitution and loneliness were worked through in hateful and angry monologues about women. But it does suggest that Chris was invested in the same gendered aspirations as those valued in UK immigration policy: biological reproduction, co-habitation and 'breadwinning'. The observation here is a simple one: both Chris and the Home Office shared a concern with the performance of 'proper masculinity'. While I often felt that Chris should have reworked the gendered scripts available to him, and that he might have made different decisions if he had, the same is true for the Home Office.[47]

Relatedly, the (over)valuing of nuclear family forms in immigration law also renders wider networks of family support invisible. In Chris's case, his relationships with his mother and his siblings were deemed wholly irrelevant. Chris was very close to his mother, and still is, but relationships between adult children and their parents are deemed wholly irrelevant in immigration policy (in all but exceptional circumstances).[48] Chris was also very close with his two younger brothers:

> CHRIS: Yeah, I basically raised my two brothers, as if they was my own. Seen from they was born, up to this day. I raised them, changed their nappies, everything, took them to school. Really played a father role in their life as well as a brother.

Despite his closeness to his brothers, Chris was not their primary carer and so their connections were deemed irrelevant.

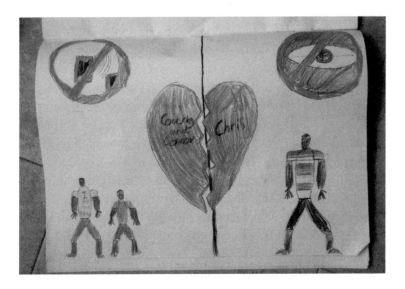

Picture 4.3. *Chris's younger brother represents deportation*

When Chris's brothers visited him in Jamaica, he asked them to draw whatever they wanted to capture what his deportation had meant for them. Chris's 10-year-old brother here offers his own portrait of the damage inflicted by deportation, which tells its own story about the violence of deportation and restrictive definitions of 'family life'.

Conclusion

Where the previous two chapters explain criminalisation and deportation primarily in terms of exclusion – Jason was excluded legally and therefore his very survival was criminalised, while Ricardo was excluded on racial terms, and his deportation was therefore hastened by racist policing – this chapter recognises that criminality often stems from processes of *inclusion*. It is important to recognise that non-citizens become part of the places where they live, and these processes of inclusion preface 'crime'.

In short, 'migrants' who end up with criminal records are not outsiders, but often quite the opposite, and viewing criminality as a mark of integration helps us to see certain things.

Chris experimented with drinking, fighting and robbery as a teenager, but his behaviours were hardly deviant or counter-normative. Then, as an unemployed adult, subject to benefit sanctions and with two children on the way, he sold drugs in his local neighbourhood. None of this points to a lack of 'social and cultural integration', and my argument is that Chris was well integrated into a deeply unequal, racist and sexist society. In this context, criminalisation and deportation work to individualise and externalise wider causes of inequality, violence and social harm. Prisons lock away social problems, individualising and invisibilising them,[49] while deportation seeks to expel them, as if their source were foreign, as if migration were to blame for people like Chris selling drugs.

Still, Chris is unlikely to be seen as deserving. He committed two criminal offences, his second after being threatened with deportation once before. He sold class A drugs, even when he had the right to work and claim benefits. He had two children with two women within six months. He carried a knife and often blamed women for his situation. Undeniably, he made bad decisions. However, by recognising Chris's flaws and complexities, I have tried to offer a fuller critique of deportation, one which does not rely on people being 'good citizens' or 'helpless victims'. Chris was not without personal agency, but he did have limited options. He made his way in profoundly unequal, racist and sexist social settings, and he reflected them back to us. This offers a rejoinder to racialising ideas about 'black crime' and 'gang culture', suggesting alternative ways of thinking about integration, culture and crime.

Chris was deported despite his family connections: to his children, his mother and his siblings. He was defined as an irresponsible father figure, and his 'family life' was deemed less important than the 'public interest' in his deportation. This is how deportation and immigration controls actively enforce and reproduce particular ideals surrounding gender, sexuality and the family. This argument is further developed in the next chapter, in the discussion of Denico's story.

Coda

Towards the end of my final fieldwork trip, in 2017, I visited Chris where he lived in Rockfort. He was staying in a house on Wareika Road, not far from where he grew up, sleeping on the floor of his friend's room. The taxi refused to drive up the lane and the driver seemed worried for me as he dropped me off, but Chris assured me that it was 'calm up there'. Once at his place, we played a few games of Pro Evolution Soccer on his Xbox, before walking down to his local bar on Windward Road.

Picture 4.4. *Chris and me playing Pro Evolution Soccer in the room he was sharing, Rockfort, East Kingston (2017)*

As we walked in, an older woman chided me for bringing food in without enough for everyone, while Chris took his seat at the bar and began talking with two older men, in patois, about the day's news. Everyone in the bar knew Chris, and most remembered him from when he was a boy. They all knew that he was 'a deportee', but that was unremarkable in Rockfort. I bought us a drink and Chris continued to make boisterous conversation at the bar. The men laughed loudly, but I was unable to keep up. Chris noticed and turned to me to explain, in his London register, what they were talking about. Chris seemed happy to show me his 'humble little area', to explain and translate the place for me. I was struck by how, despite everything, Chris seemed at home, 'centred in place'.[50] His ability to read his surroundings, to adapt and to develop friendships had followed him throughout his life, and it seemed that, in the context of even greater hardship, Chris was making his home again.

Chapter 5

Denico

On Boxing Day of 2015, I visited Denico where he lived for the first time. He was staying in Rockfort, East Kingston, with his two cousins, in a small two-room tenement paid for by their mother, who was working as a domestic worker in the Cayman Islands. They shared their kitchen and bathroom with four other families. Denico shared a bed with his cousin, Omar, and slept on the floor when Omar's partner and young child stayed over. When I arrived, Denico was sat on the bed, and I perched at its foot, given there was space for little else in the room. I asked how his first Christmas in Jamaica had been, and he replied: 'Shit … really shit'. We sat in silence for a moment. Denico then showed me a video of Tamara and Maisy, aged six and three, opening presents back in the UK. The girls were excitedly showing him their presents, sending a Christmas message to their 'second dad'. I said they were very sweet, and he didn't respond. I wasn't sure whether he wanted to show me the video, or whether he just wanted to watch it again.

Denico always made clear that the most painful thing about deportation was the separation from his partner, Kendal, and her two daughters, Tamara and Maisy. In all our conversations, we never drifted far from Kendal and the girls. I might ask him to focus on his early years in Jamaica, and somehow we would end up talking about Kendal again. During interviews, when we

Picture 5.1. *Denico on his phone, Treasure Beach (2016)*

would break to smoke a cigarette, he would look at his phone, often taking time out to call Kendal, and usually returning looking deflated, reminded again of everything. Kendal, Tamara and Maisy were always what was at stake, and both he and Kendal found it impossible to deal with their separation.

To understand how and why Denico was deported, I will quote from immigration policy and lift excerpts from Home Office correspondence with Denico, juxtaposing official narratives with Denico and Kendal's account. As in Chris's case, Denico appealed against his deportation on the basis of 'family life', and thus the Home Office decision to deport him reveals the ways in which family norms are defined and enforced at the border. Indeed, deportation is a key site at which we can observe the state's regulation of gender, sexuality and family.[1] To extend my critique of these processes, I introduce two other deported people, Darel and Michelle, who were also exiled from their families. Their stories reveal the damage inflicted by restrictive and heteronormative definitions of 'family life', as well as some of the gendered impacts of deportation. I go on to argue that immigration controls actively shape how people make decisions about their intimate and family lives, which presents another example of how borders are productive of certain relations, identities and exclusions.[2] Before engaging in this critique, however, it is important to describe how Denico was criminalised and deported, and to hear him describe his family relationships in his own words.

'You think if I had my stay I would sell drugs'?

When I first met Denico in September 2015, he had been back in Jamaica only a few weeks. He was very cautious about travelling alone, after being robbed at gunpoint in downtown Kingston just a few days after returning, and so he spent most of his time in Omar's room, mostly on his phone, occasionally venturing out into Rockfort to buy cigarettes, phone credit, or to collect money from Western Union, usually sent from Kendal. When I returned in 2016, Denico had moved out of Kingston and was living in St Elizabeth – the dry, hot parish in the south-west of the island – with a family friend. He moved partly to give his cousin Omar some space, and partly because he preferred the slower and calmer tempo of things 'in country'.

However, things had not improved much for Denico in St Elizabeth. In 2016, he seemed even more exhausted and flat than during my first trip. He was not working and had no money, and so his sadness was inflected with boredom and inertia. In an attempt to cheer him up, I invited him to spend a week with me in Treasure Beach, a sleepy tourist village 35 miles south of where he lived. It was a holiday for both of us, and while Denico was often sad, I always enjoyed spending time with him. He is one of the most gentle and considerate people I have known.

In 2017, we made similar plans and stayed in Treasure Beach again for a few nights. At this point, Denico was working full time in the butchery of a supermarket, and while he was happy to be busy he found it hard to save any money from his meagre wage (he earnt around £35 a week working over 40 hours). Still, we enjoyed a few days together, catching up, recording conversations on my phone and being tourists in Treasure Beach again, before Denico had to return to work. On that second trip, Denico opened up more about his father. For all the time I had known him, he had remained fairly quiet about both his parents, but for some reason in 2017 he was much more forthcoming.

Denico moved to the UK aged 13, and his father was his primary carer. They lived in London until he was 16, when they moved to Birmingham with his father's new partner and children. However, when Denico's father applied for indefinite leave to remain, he did not include Denico in the application:

> DENICO: Yeah. And to be honest, like all of them got their stay apart from me in the house, and that kind of hurts me even more.
> LUKE: How did he get his stay then?
> DENICO: They all filed, they all put their thing in together as a family.
> LUKE: And why didn't you get included – because you're not her kid?
> DENICO: I don't know why. He claimed that his name wasn't on my birth certificate. That's what he says. But that could've easily been done or whatever. I don't really wanna get into it, because it hurts me, because he feels himself that I got myself into this situation, because I couldn't be a bit more patient. But I've tried.

As with Jason, Denico's difficult relationship with his father was fundamentally entangled with immigration control. His feelings of exclusion, resentment and the sense that his father did not really care about him were intimately bound up with his experiences of illegalisation. Denico's relationship with his father remained tense, and when he was 18 he was kicked out of the house following a fight. He spent the next few nights in a homeless shelter in Birmingham, before being taken in by a friend. Over the next few years, Denico lived with friends, his girlfriend and at one point with an elderly woman from the church he was attending. During this time, Denico sought employment despite his status as an 'illegal immigrant'.

He worked for a while as a car mechanic and then in a Caribbean restaurant, but his labour went mostly unpaid. He managed to get some occasional cash-in-hand work as a painter-decorator but nothing consistent. As he explained: 'None of that really worked, without a National Insurance number, you can't really do much'. Denico also worked two seasons picking strawberries. He was paid £1.50 to fill a tray of 12 punnets, and at his speed he made around £18 for a seven-hour day. Petrol costs were deducted from this, and so he came home with around £13.[3] He explained that many of those working alongside him were Polish migrants:

> DENICO: Polish yeah. I gotta take off my hat to them. Dem work. Wen mi say dem work mi mean dem work! They go in. No time to jibby jabby, jibby jabby. When I'm sitting down some-times taking breaks, they just work, because it's like, a long, long stretch, and it's like you're under a tent, yeah. Strawberry picking made me think different about everything. The hard work that people have to do to just get things on the shelves.

Denico had tried to earn money in different ways over several years, but it was only in selling drugs that he found some consistent income. He first started selling to save for his immigration application, and once he had paid solicitors and applied for his leave to remain, he stopped. His application was rejected a few months later, however, and he could not hide his distress from Kendal. Indeed, this was the first she heard of his immigration status. Following the rejected application, Denico decided to appeal, and a few months later he started selling drugs again to save for legal fees and for the wedding he and Kendal were planning. It was during this second period that he was arrested in possession of heroin.

In January 2014, Denico was charged and held in prison on remand for five months. In June, he went to trial pleading not guilty, but he was convicted and sentenced to four years and six months (to serve half). After trial, his case was reported in the local press, and some of the articles included his mugshot. Kendal told me that people were sharing the articles on Facebook: 'It was awful', she recalled. In one of the articles, the detective involved said: 'These men were street dealers and their activities had a big impact on the community. There was a lot of concern, not least because this was going on near a school.'

Denico often spoke about how out of character he felt selling heroin: 'I used to sometimes think, what am I doing? How did this happen?' Denico always saw selling drugs as short term, and his decision was largely an effect of his inability to secure income by any other means. My intention here is not to recast Denico as a 'good migrant' who had no choice but to sell drugs – we should not lose sight of the arguments around poverty and racism presented in previous chapters – but there is an obvious and important truth to his claim that he sold drugs because of his immigration status.

> DENICO: You think if I had my stay I would sell drugs? I would not even look at it, I would not even know what drugs look like. And that's me being honest.

'This is my home now, this is my life now'

Denico had spoken about Kendal from the first day I had met him, but when I turned on the microphone and began recording our first interview, he started from the beginning. Kendal was a friend of a friend, and Denico had known her for a few years before they started dating in the summer of 2012. Denico narrates the events of that summer in the way one does a well rehearsed family story. Usain Bolt had just broken the 100-metre world record at the London Olympics, and Kendal and Denico had been watching the gold medal race in different houses. After the race, Denico was driving with his friend when he saw Kendal walking on the street. He jumped out of the moving vehicle to stop and speak with her: 'See, I nearly killed myself for you' was his line. Denico told me this story more than once, and when I met Kendal she told the same story and laughed at his 'cheesy chat-up line'. They arranged a date, and spoke on the phone and on Facebook over the next few evenings, often until the early hours. 'She is a friend more than anything else, that's what is so hard', Denico told me several times. Denico met Kendal's young daughters very early on and they all 'hit it off straight away'.

> DENICO: Meeting Kendal give me so much hope and belief. I finally find somebody that genuinely loved me, you know what I mean? The two girls that she had as well, they kind of, like, helped me together. And when I look at it, I look at my home and I'm thinking, yeah, this is my home now, this is my life now. And then I was fixing up the house and everything was going into plan. That's how we planned it. We was going to get married. And then bam!

I wanted to hear from Kendal too, and so I went to meet her in her home town of Bromsgrove, just south of Birmingham in the West Midlands. I got the train from Manchester, and as I stood waiting for her to pick me up it started snowing, which was bizarre in late April. I was reminded that Denico missed the cold, and often complained about the heat in Jamaica – which was perhaps the reason he walked so slowly. After a few minutes, Kendal arrived in a small Ford Ka, having just passed her driving test, and drove us to a large family pub a couple of miles from the station, not far from where Denico was first incarcerated. She appeared slightly nervous and later told me she was apprehensive about whether she would be able 'to talk about it all'. But once we found a seat in the pub, and I began recording on my phone, Kendal offered a lucid account of her relationship with Denico:

Picture 5.2. *Denico at Treasure Beach (2016)*

KENDAL: When I got with him, I made sure I told him, listen, you know I've got two children. I'm not being with … if I get in with somebody, I want you to be there. I don't want him to just be there when I'm on my own or. I'm not asking for a father figure, because they've got their own dad, but, you know, we come as a pack, do you know what I mean? But he was, he didn't care. He didn't care.

A few months later I went to meet and interview Kendal's mother, Tracy, also in Bromsgrove. Her semi-detached house was filled with trinkets, with photos of her children and grandchildren on the walls. About an hour into our conversation, Tracy offered me another cup of tea, but I worried I might be holding her up: 'No no, this is important', she replied, 'I'd stop anything for this'. In the end, our interview lasted over two and a half hours, and it was clear that Tracy cared deeply about Denico and felt angered by his deportation.[4] I asked her to describe his relationship with the children:

TRACY: When I first met him he was very quiet, erm, but he was so good for them girls. He'd read with them. We took pictures of them out in the snow playing. I said, 'Kendal, look at this, look at this. Their own father doesn't do this'. And he'd also, like, they'd come home from play school or school, and of course he knew

Maisy from five months. He just knew what to do. And they really respected him. And if he said something, he was listened to.

LUKE: What, like, kind of quiet discipline, sort of thing?

TRACY: Yeah. Yeah. He wasn't a shouter, no he's not a shouter. And he got Kendal motivated.

LUKE: In what way?

TRACY: You know, just around the house, and feeling like she's worth something. Even though Kendal's stubborn, so I think with her seeing how I was with her father, how he was very, erm, dominating and tried to take over everything, she'd never allow that. And I said, 'He's trying to help you. He's not trying to take over you or control you. It's a different kind of help this man is.' Yeah, really good for her, really good for her. But no, Christmases, he just loved the fact that, he loved seeing us as a family. Which apparently he never had.

After they had been together for just over a year, Denico proposed, Kendal said yes, and they began planning a wedding.

TRACY: Oh my goodness me. It was just, she'd met a man that she [*laughing*], that they actually bounced off each other. Just to know that you've got the right person must be a bloody amazing feeling. It must be. Just, *gunf*, when it hits you like that. She goes, 'Mum … you just know'. I was, like, that, 'Wow, I've never got it right' [*laughing*]. This woman, looking at dresses, she goes, 'I can't show my arms'. She's obsessed about her arms. Oh, it was just lovely. Of course the children were involved.

LUKE: Oh, so the kids were excited about the wedding?

TRACY: Yeahhh. And then it just all *wadooshed*. It's just gone, it's gone. It's all the highs and then the lows, innit.

Tracy went on to describe Denico as 'old-fashioned', and I recognised her description. He desperately wanted to work hard and to 'provide', to marry Kendal and for their wedding to be 'special', and to be a responsible father figure for the girls. In Jamaica, Denico wore the loss of that possibility.

***

One afternoon in December 2016, just before his second Christmas in Jamaica, Denico came to visit me on campus. It was a sunny day and we walked down to the Mona Bowl where the athletes train. We walked over to the running track, where Usain Bolt and Yohan Blake, the two fastest men in the world, were training, right in front of us. Denico was fairly calm about the whole thing, a reminder that he had always found Kendal more interesting than Usain Bolt. After being politely asked to leave the track, we walked aimlessly toward August Town at a pace somewhere between mine and Denico's preferred speed. I asked him how everything was going with Kendal. He sounded tired: 'Everything is stressful, it's all just stressful. Sometimes I feel like I should just give up and tell her to get on with her life. She needs to focus on herself.' He sighed and we slowed a little more: 'We both need to be patient, but it's just so hard'.

That same afternoon, I bought us a couple of bananas. Denico smiled and said: '"Narna" – that's what Maisy used to call it'. It was clear that he missed the girls deeply, and he also worried about Kendal and her mental health. Both Denico and Tracy told me that Kendal had been struggling with depression since Denico's deportation. He was her best friend and she was unable to entertain 'moving on', in no small part because her children spoke about Denico so often. She first felt the pain of separation when Denico was in prison:

KENDAL: It's hard. What makes it harder is the fact that the girls were so attached to him. I think if the girls weren't so attached to him, or we didn't really have that relationship, it would still be hard but it wouldn't be as hard. And I think the fact of seeing your children react in a certain way, or act out, do you know what I mean, like Maisy. He was really close to Maisy, so, as a baby, if she'd wake up in the middle of the night, he'd see to her, obviously because after I had her, after about six months, she became like really a bad sleeper, so I was getting really stressed about it. I hardly got any sleep at all, so he'd kind of take that role in the night-time. And she just, like, literally would go to sleep straight away. So, her not having that, when he left, she cried. I remember her even crying out Nico, Nico, Nico for weeks. And just laying in bed listening to it, obviously her being in her cot next to my bed, it was just hard, really hard.

Luke: And how old was she then? When he first went inside?
Kendal: She was two, yeah.
Luke: So he'd been there since she was six months.
Kendal: Yeah, yeah, five months. Seeing him from five months.

Maisy was separated from Denico first by prison, then by deportation, and as Kendal's mother Tracy explained to me when we met in 2016, he was still 'constantly on her mind':

> Tracy: Even this morning, I slept in the spare room, and they had my bed, and little Maisy, she's a funny little thing, she come into my bedroom, and she said, 'Alright nan', and she gets in and I said, 'Are you alright?' and she said, 'Yeah', and I said, 'Did you have any good dreams?' And she said, 'I had a good dream nan', and I said, 'What was that then?' and she goes, 'There was me, there was Nico, there was mum'. It's constantly on their mind. And she's four.

Denico's absence clearly had profound emotional and material consequences for Kendal and her two girls, but this was not enough to prevent his deportation. In legal terms, the rights of Denico, Kendal, Tamara and Maisy to have their 'private and family life' protected were ultimately outweighed by the 'public interest' in Denico's deportation. In this context, we need to interrogate the legal and bureaucratic processes through which these decisions are made, and through which lived family connections are effectively rubbished. In the next section, I question how Denico's deportation was justified by the Home Office, *in spite of* his intimate relationships.

Article 8, the Immigration Rules and the denigration of family life

While Denico had been subject to removal for many years, it was following his criminal conviction that his deportation became inevitable. Since the 'foreign national prisoner crisis' of 2006 (discussed in Chapter 1), it has become increasingly difficult for non-citizens with criminal records to make the case that their connections to the UK outweigh the 'public interest' in their deportation.[5] Changes to law and policy have been complemented by widespread cuts to legal aid and the removal of appeal rights. The only option for Denico, like most of the deported people I met in Jamaica, was to appeal his deportation on the basis of 'private and family life' under Article 8 of European Convention on Human Rights.

Article 8 states: 'Everyone has the right to respect for his private and family life, his home and his correspondence'. This mirrors Article 16(3) of the Universal Declaration of Human Rights, which states: 'The family is the natural and fundamental group unit of society and is entitled to protection by society and the State'. But what does 'the family' look like? If there are many different kinds of family, then what is so natural about it? Indeed, feminists and gay liberationists have long 'drawn attention to the violence and degradation hidden within the walls of the nuclear household, and to the broader social and economic inequalities connected with it', arguing that 'the family' is a site of social discipline and control, with often devastating and violent implications for women, children and queers in particular.[6] This has led some to call for the *abolition of the family*.[7] This critical body of political and intellectual work teaches us that states do not merely 'respect' family life, but actively produce, demarcate and enforce it.[8]

Scholars such as Eithne Luibhéid have shown that, historically, immigration controls have been key sites for the regulation of gender and sexuality; liberal states define and enforce norms surrounding gender, sexuality and 'the family' at the border. We can apply these insights to UK deportation policy. When people like Denico and Chris appeal their deportations, they are required to prove they have a 'family life' and to frame it within the terms of the Immigration Rules. This is far from straightforward. Within immigration law, ties of blood, marriage and monogamy are favoured, and it precisely these processes of legal definition which imbue the norm with its power and solidity. Of course, from the perspective of liberal states more broadly, not everyone is fit to parent, and not every relationship is genuine, but within the politics of immigration these questions take on added significance, determining who can stay within the national territory and on what terms.

For Denico to prove he had a 'family life', he had to demonstrate that he was in a 'genuine and subsisting' relationship with Kendal, and in a 'genuine and subsisting' *parental* relationship with the girls. He then had to argue that it would be 'unduly harsh' for the children to move to Jamaica, or to remain in the UK without him around. This wording comes directly from the Immigration Rules.[9] However, it was difficult to make the case that separation would be 'unduly harsh', because Denico had been in their lives for only 18 months before going to prison. While Denico was very close with Tamara and Maisy, he was not their biological father and their primary carer had been Kendal, who had raised them, largely independently, from birth.

The Home Office went on to question not only the quantity of time spent together but also the *quality*, constructing Denico's involvement in the girls' care as limited and unimportant: 'You did not live as a family unit prior to imprisonment … you [only] stayed over'. Indeed, the Immigration Rules state that for unmarried couples to meet the definition of 'family life', they have to be 'living together in a relationship akin to marriage', which at the very least implies co-habitation. This ignores the many complex reasons, often practical and economic, why people might not co-habit, or be able to prove that they do.[10] In fact, Denico did stay at Kendal's house for most of the week, but he was not on the tenancy agreement – after all, he was an 'illegal immigrant' with no 'right to rent'.

Things were then made immeasurably more difficult by Denico's incarceration. If it was hard to prove 'genuine and subsisting' relationships before Denico went to prison, it was almost impossible afterwards. As the Home Office put it in their letter rejecting Denico's appeal:

> You have not provided any evidence which would suggest that your relationship with any of Ms Walker's children has been maintained during your imprisonment.

The Home Office suggested, as is very common in these kinds of cases, that prison already constituted separation. Kendal, Tamara and Maisy might not want Denico to be deported, but they had already effectively been separated from him by prison. In practice, though, people maintain their connections despite incarceration, and Kendal visited Denico in prison every few days. Her youngest, Maisy, got used to getting patted down by the prison security guards: 'Literally she'd run up and she'd be all excited putting her hands out, to get patted down', Kendal recounted. Kendal also described Denico's attempts to maintain connection with the children through something called 'story-book dads':

> KENDAL: Yeah, basically it was where he could read a story book, and in front of the camera. He had this annoying monkey next to him, that kind of moves, so this guy behind the bit of fake tree was there doing this, and Nico was reading the story, and talking to them at the same time. So obviously when I used to watch it, I used to laugh, erm, and even Nico, like, obviously he speaks English but he's still got that kind of twang of, like, patois, and he can't really pronounce certain words, so I was laughing at the fact that he was, like, quite awkward reading the book as well. And Tamara was like that, 'Why is he doing that expression? Why is he reading like that?' So she was kind of laughing with me, at him, and then Maisy was just there, listening to him. He'd probably do one every three months, and they'd send them to the house. So that was kind of a nice thing as well. The girls kind of looked forward to getting the CD, the DVD through the door, and they'd constantly watch it, like every night.

Despite Denico and Kendal's best efforts, the Home Office stated that prison amounted to separation, which thereby made deportation less disruptive. They argued that the prison log book did not prove ongoing contact, and thus the pained and yet resilient way in which Denico and Kendal dealt with his imprisonment was rendered obsolete. This is a finding which came up repeatedly in my conversations with deported men in Jamaica: families made as many prison visits as possible, over long distances and with limited funds, and yet still this was deemed insufficient to prove 'ongoing contact'. In Denico's case, the Home Office argued that because he had already been separated from Kendal's children by prison, his deportation could not be seen as 'unduly harsh' (to appeal successfully against deportation under the Immigration Rules, an appellant must prove that deportation would be likely to have 'unduly harsh' consequences for the children who remain):

> There is no evidence before us to conclude that your presence is needed to prevent any of those children claimed from being ill treated, their health or development being impaired, or their care being other than safe and effective.

This formulation offers a negative construction of 'family life'. As British citizens, Kendal and her children had the right to protection from being 'ill treated' in the event of Denico's deportation, nominally at least, but their love for him alone was not enough to outweigh the 'public interest' in his deportation.[11]

Ultimately, Denico was unable to convince the Home Office that his relationships with Tamara and Maisy were 'genuine and subsisting', and it was not any easier in relation to Kendal. In fact, it was near impossible because the Immigration Rules state that a relationship with a qualifying partner must be 'formed at a time when the person was in the UK lawfully and their immigration status not precarious'. By definition, then, Denico and Kendal's relationship could not be relied upon because Denico was an 'illegal immigrant' for its duration. According to policy, if a British citizen enters a relationship with an 'illegal immigrant' – even if they are not aware of their migration status, as in Kendal's case – then their relationship is effectively illegible and void. This policy is in no small part a response to long-standing concerns around 'sham marriages', in which immigrants like Denico are constructed as 'using' marriage as a means of securing residence rights.[12] For 'illegal immigrants', relationships with British citizens are defined as inherently instrumental, love merely a ploy motivated by cold calculation. For this reason, relationships between citizens and 'illegal immigrants' cannot be trusted, and by definition they cannot be 'genuine'.

While 'the right to respect for private and family life' is a human right – applicable to both citizens and non-citizens – it is not an absolute one. UK immigration policy works to restrict the protections this right affords. For people like Denico and Kendal, this means that their lived forms of connection, care and mutual support are actively denigrated and deemed illegitimate through the Home Office's bureaucratic and legal manoeuvring. The experiences of Kendal, Tamara and Maisy demonstrate the immense suffering caused by these processes, and unfortunately their stories are far from unique. In the next section, I turn to Darel's story for another account of how deportation impacts partners and children.

Darel: deportation and the (British) women and children who remain

While this book focuses on four deported men, the consequences of deportation were also borne by women. This was true for Kendal, who became a 'single mother' again when Denico was deported. She stopped working and had to rely on welfare benefits and support from her mother, while she took on the full-time care of her children. It was not that Denico had been 'the bread-winner', but rather that he had helped with child care, collected the children from nursery and helped with housework in ways which granted Kendal more time. Kendal had plans to train as a midwife, but when Denico was imprisoned and deported her plans were forestalled. Clearly, women and children suffer immensely as a result of deportation policies which primarily affect men, and I want to explore this point further by reflecting on Darel's experiences.

When I returned to Jamaica in September 2016, I landed just a few days after a mass deportation charter flight that had taken 38 men and four women from the UK.[13] I contacted some of those on the flight and Darel was keen to share his story over the phone. Darel was 32 when we spoke, and he had lived in the UK since he was seven years old. He had six British children, four of them with his partner Shanice:

> DAREL: I was the one what took them to school, picked them up from school, made lunch, cook them dinner, made sure dinner was ready for when she [Shanice] got home. She was out in the morning at 5 a.m. for work. Before, I would be supporting her to go to work by looking after the kids, but now I'm here, she's lost her job. She is worried that without work they're [the council] gonna move her to some place far like Birmingham or Milton Keynes.

As in Denico's case, Darel was not the 'breadwinner'. He was the primary carer for four of his children, in no small part because his immigration status prevented him from working. The fact that he was deported in spite of this care work demonstrates the invisibility of, and low value accorded to, reproductive labour. Feminists have long made this argument in relation to women's unpaid labour, and here we see the undervaluing of care work when performed by poor black men.[14] Gendered narratives on men's patriarchal responsibility to 'provide' – and the related assumption that care work performed by men is always secondary to that of the mother – have profound implications in deportation cases. In the last chapter, we saw that Chris was deported because he failed to provide for his children economically, while with Darel and Denico we see that reproductive labour is disregarded as an alternative form of 'providing'.

Remarkably, Darel's only criminal offences were for possession of marijuana. But he was deported under Operation Nexus on the basis of police intelligence alleging gang involvement (see Chapter 3).[15] As he explained: 'It wasn't a gang, we all just grew up together, on the same estate, you get me? They can't prove I'm in a gang, it's just because of my pictures [on Facebook], with people from the area'. Darel had not spent any time in prison, and had only been cautioned for possession of cannabis, but he found himself propelled towards deportation on the basis of police intelligence (in relation to suspected gang involvement and previous arrests, which are referred to as 'non-convictions' under Operation Nexus policy), and because he was an overstayer. On this basis, he was constructed as a 'foreign criminal' and thereby exiled from his British partner and six British children.

As Darel's case reminds us, racism determines not only who gets criminalised (see Chapters 3 and 4), but also whose 'family life' is recognised. As Eithne Luibhéid notes: 'although patriarchal heterosexuality has been elevated as a national imperative, race and class dimensions further determine whose heterosexualities are valued and whose are subject to surveillance and punishment'.[16] Ultimately, Darel's deportation resulted from the convergence of several processes: the devaluing of social reproductive labour; the aggressive criminalisation of black men who are associated with 'the gang'; and the political imperative to deport any and all 'migrants' associated with criminality.

After being deported, Darel lived with family members he did not remember, scared to go outside and constantly on the phone back home:

> DAREL: Every night I talk to my kids. They're crying every minute. My missus is stressed, and I'm stressed. The other day I was so depressed I couldn't get up. I had aches and pains all over.

> Sometimes I just feel like I wanna kill myself right now. Being away from my family, everything. I'm sleeping on the floor. When I had my nice house, and my kids, and my routine.

Darel's partner Shanice, meanwhile, was trying to navigate work, benefits and the threat of eviction. She had to quit her full-time job so that she could take the children to school, and this meant she could no longer afford the rent. Shanice knew that if she was evicted it would be very unlikely that she would be given accommodation in West London, where the children went to school, and she had heard about people being moved as far as the West Midlands.[17] The material consequences of Darel's deportation, then, were not borne by him alone, and the restrictive definitions of 'family life' within immigration policy justified the destruction of his functioning family unit.

Michelle – the heteronormative compulsions of immigration control

As I have shown, deportation disproportionately affects men and yet has specific gendered consequences for partners who remain in the UK. That said, this should not imply that women only experience deportation vicariously. In fact, 15% of those deported to Jamaica in 2013 were women.[18] Most of the deported women I met in Jamaica were middle-aged and had moved to the UK as adults to work and remit money to children and family back in Jamaica, often paying for school fees and housing costs. Many of these women had been 'working illegally' in the UK, often in the hospitality and care sectors, before being removed as overstayers. In other words, their migration histories and the structure of their transnational family lives differed markedly from those of the younger men who feature in this book. However, not all deported women fit this description. Michelle, a 27-year-old woman who was deported on the same charter flight as Darel in 2016, had a similar profile to the men in this book.[19]

Michelle moved to the UK aged 12, to join her mother. Like Denico, she lived in London when she first arrived, and then moved to Birmingham after school. When she was 19, she received a two-year sentence for intent to supply class A drugs, after helping to transport drugs with her friend who was in rent arrears and facing eviction. After spending one year in prison, she was held in Yarl's Wood Immigration Removal Centre for over 11 months while the Home Office pursued her deportation. During her detention, she claimed asylum on the basis of her bisexuality. However, her claim was refused because she could not prove it:

> MICHELLE: I had a female relationship before, and *that's the only route you have*, but I had no proof. I couldn't find the woman I was with or any women that I had any intercourse, or like, relationship with.

Michelle's suggestion that claiming asylum on the basis of sexuality is 'the only route you have' points to something crucial about the ways in which immigration controls delimit how people are able to define themselves. As Sarah Keenan shows, refugee law 'demands a unitary, discrete subject', and this affects 'the way individual queer women asylum seekers present and perform their identity'.[20] Michelle would likely have stood a better chance of securing asylum if she had frequented 'gay bars' or was in a long-term relationship with a woman (and could document both), but these markers obscure how financial resources, racism and proximity to the city affect how people express (or consume) their sexual identities, while also prejudicing bisexual, 'closeted' and non-monogamous people.[21] What does it mean, as Michelle puts it, to have proof of one's sexuality?[22]

After nearly one year inside detention, Michelle was released while her asylum appeal was being processed. She was then signing on at a reporting centre for a couple of years, but when she received a letter threatening her with deportation she decided to stop signing on and go 'under the radar'. During this time, she attempted to have children with her partner, a British citizen:

> MICHELLE: I thought my best option was not to sign on, stay out of trouble and have a child. Three years passed, we were trying, and it wasn't happening. In 2015 I decided to submit another application, given it had been three years, and I'd been out of trouble. I thought that would prove to them I had reformed, but that was basically a foolish mistake. I thought they would look into the fact that I'm looking after two step-kids who've got no mum, and my partner is working, and I'm trying to help him out with the kids as well. They became my family. But they refused it.

Like Denico, Michelle felt that her role as a step-parent was undervalued. In this light, I asked her if having her own children would have made a difference to her appeal:

> MICHELLE: Once I had a young baby, it would've been harder for them to remove me from the UK. Yeah, if I had a child, 100%, that would never happen. That's what happened to my co-d [co-defendant], and that's what stopped her getting deported. Basically, 99% of the time, having a child by a British citizen does remove deportation from the picture.

Michelle knew that if she had a child with a British man, that child would be a British citizen. However, her claim that this would prevent her deportation is questionable. Women with British-citizen children can be deported, and their children taken into care or encouraged to leave with them.[23] That said, Michelle does capture an important reality here: mothers of British citizens are harder to deport than fathers, largely because they are defined as primary carers. A 2015 study of mothers with 'no recourse to public funds' found that Jamaican women were the single largest national group.[24] These Jamaican nationals were 'illegal immigrants', usually overstayers with similar migration histories to the men in this book, and yet their British children made them eligible them for some forms of child support and afforded them some protection from deportation. This should not be overstated; in many cases, these women are totally excluded from welfare benefits, and suspended in legal limbo. However, Michelle's point remains true: if she had had a British child, she would have been less likely to be deported. By and large, this does not apply to fathers like Darel and Chris, and certainly not to step-fathers like Denico.

The fact that Michelle was unable to have children when she tried to raises broader questions about sexuality and immigration control.[25] In the context of widespread concerns about the 'fecundity' of immigrant women, there is a particular irony in Michelle being deported after trying and failing to become pregnant. Consider these headlines in major British newspapers: 'Up to three in four babies born last year in parts of the UK had foreign mothers, official figures have disclosed';[26] 'Migrant baby boom: Third of babies born in England and Wales in 2015 have at least one foreign parent'.[27] Widespread anxieties about the fertility of migrant (and minority) women are central to broader concerns about immigration and demographic change. In this context, if Michelle had become pregnant she would have been another 'illegal immigrant' relying on her children to evade deportation.[28] As it stood, she was unable to have her own children, and was therefore more easily deportable as an 'illegal immigrant', whose role as a step-mother was deemed completely irrelevant.

The crucial point, though, is that Michelle made her decisions about family, children and relationships in light of her illegality and deportability. She tried to get pregnant partly in an attempt to prevent her forced exile from her friends, her mother, her partner and her step-children. Her motivation to have children was shaped by immigration control, even as immigration controls stipulate that such decisions should be solely about 'love' or 'choice' – as if decisions about marriage, parenting and family life could ever be isolated from economic and material considerations.[29] As such, immigration controls not only differentiate between non-citizens along lines of sexuality, marital status and family life, they also influence the decisions people make in this regard. As argued in previous chapters, immigration controls are productive of certain types of relations, and Michelle reminds us that borders encourage particular ways of thinking about and acting within intimate relationships.

This applied to Denico too. When Denico first proposed to Kendal, he was very clear that he was not marrying her 'to get his stay'. However, immigration controls privilege marriage in ways which imbue it with real material benefits. Immigration law encourages people to make decisions in relation to marriage, parenting, co-habitation and even sexual preference in ways which enforce heteronormative and nuclear family scripts. However pitiful and uncertain, there remain dividends in following these scripts, in the vague hope that the British state might recognise co-habitation, marriage and biological parenting as badges of 'family life' which qualify individuals for protection from deportation. Most of these attempts might prove unsuccessful, but they remind us that it is the legislation of the norm which enshrines it.

Against family

Today, immigration law still promotes sex and childbearing within marriage, endlessly reproducing both heteropatriarchy and classes of immigrants who face exclusion for nonreproductive sexuality or childbearing outside marriage, or childbearing within marriage that costs the state money. – Eithne Luibhéid[30]

The fact that people must appeal their deportation on the basis of connections with children, in which biological connections are afforded greater significance than step-parenting, is profoundly limiting. The idea that couples should co-habit and live in a relationship 'akin to marriage' is restrictive. When family life is defined as nuclear, relationships between extended family members are rendered invisible (such as between siblings who do not live together). These questions arise before we even ask how non-monogamous, non-sexual and queer forms of intimacy and care might be recognised in law. What about friendship, for example?[31] As Bridget Anderson notes:

> The logic of job, family, and citizenship, assumes a certain community of value. Moving beyond the choice between exclusion or exploitation through beginning, not with a job, but with the need for subsistence, *not with a spouse, but with the need for mutual care and support,* and not with the right to exclude, but with the assumption of people's full inclusion, has the potential to open up politics and analysis.[32]

Beginning not with a spouse, or children, but with the need for mutual care and support can open up politics, allowing for different relationships to become legible and valued. Indeed, it was the terms of immigration law that forced Michelle, Darel and Denico to define their right to remain in the UK exclusively in terms of their relations to partners and children. This does not mean they were lying or exaggerating when they described their relationships, but they might have liked to express their belonging in Britain in other ways. They might have mentioned their extended families, their friends or their relationships to places and memories.

My point here is that we need to resist the argument that 'deportation is bad because it destroys families'. As Sophie Lewis notes, 'the family is not an innocent organism upon which traumatic events descend from the outside'.[33] In fact, norms surrounding 'the family' are produced and enforced at the border, and therefore the critique of immigration controls is greatly enriched by the refusal to defer to the family as 'the natural and fundamental group unit of society'.[34]

Conclusion

DENICO: What's the reason for someone to gaze a lot? Out into space? I've been doing that a lot since I've been back.

LUKE: Maybe because your head is somewhere else?
DENICO: Yeah, yeah.

On 23 June 2016, while the British public voted on whether to leave the European Union, I was going through Denico's legal files. In his legal bundle were photographs submitted as evidence of his relationships with Kendal, Tamara and Maisy. In my print-out, the images were hard to make out, overly saturated with black ink, but I could recognise photos of Denico and Kendal together, dressed up, kissing, arm in arm, as well as photos of Denico with the girls, a few years younger then. Denico and Kendal had gathered up these images, imbued with such sentiment and memory, and submitted them for Home Office scrutiny. The Home Office response was brisk and dismissive:

> You have provided photographs which you claim depict you, Ms Walker and her children, however these photographs are undated and there is no way of ascertaining who each person is, in particular the children. Photographs such as those provided are evidence of instances of contact, rather than a consistent and ongoing pattern of contact.

When Denico returned to Jamaica he burnt the legal documents he had carried with him and it is not hard to see why. There was no way for him to articulate what his relationships meant to him – the love he felt for Kendal, Tamara and Maisy – and his submissions were treated with scepticism and derision. Indeed, there is something profoundly violent about the destruction of people's lives and relationships via this kind of legal and bureaucratic process, in which lived forms of mutual support, care and connection are subject to administrative scrutiny, and summarily disbelieved and disregarded. And yet, this was the kind of story I heard most frequently across all my conversations and interviews with deported persons in Jamaica.

Deportation proceeds not only through assertions of criminality and illegality, then, but also in relation to 'family life'. People are deported *in spite of* family connections, and through the denigration and devaluing of lived family relationships. To justify deportation, normative ideas about gender, sexuality and 'the family' are mobilised and enforced in profoundly restrictive ways. As such, any radical critique of immigration controls demands a refusal to defer to 'the family' as 'the natural and fundamental group unit of society', even if the people impacted by immigration controls narrate their own experiences through the prism of family.

Taking these arguments in a different direction, the next chapter engages with the accounts of the family and friends who remain in the UK, questioning what their experiences of witnessing deportation reveal about citizenship, racism and inequality in multi-status Britain.

Coda

In 2017, Denico and I took a route taxi from Treasure Beach to a place called Lovers' Leap. I had been before, but I wanted to show Denico the incredible blue of the sea from up there.

Picture 5.3. *Denico and me at Lovers' Leap, St Elizabeth (2017)*

Pictures 5.4 and 5.5. *Denico at Lovers' Leap, St Elizabeth (2017)*

Lovers' Leap is a 1,700-foot cliff overhanging the sea, and the legend associated with it is one that most Jamaicans know well. Once I returned to the UK, and was drafting this chapter, I asked Denico to describe the legend to me, and he replied, somewhat poetically, in a voice note he sent me via WhatsApp:

> DENICO: The story of two persons, from Lovers' Leap, that was run under one master. They didn't know where life was going to take them, but they ended up seeing each other and fell in love, fell in love so deep that they would be willing to do anything to not be apart. To love someone so much, and then being told that you have to be torn apart, that's heart breaking. Words can't really describe the feeling it gives, to know that someone you love so much is going to be taken away from you. But love is a funny thing. Love makes you do things you would never imagine yourself doing. For them two, to love each other so much, and being told that they had to be apart, well, they were willing to sacrifice their own lives, just to be together. And so they jumped.

Denico sent me this voice message late one night, and I could hear that he was outside, somewhere quiet, feeling reflective. He took long pauses, the sound of crickets offering him some accompaniment.

When we visited Lovers' Leap, Denico suggested we walk down the trail to the sea. The sun was at its highest point, the trail overgrown and rocky, and I was in flip-flops, and so we made it only halfway down, much to Denico's disappointment. For whatever reason, he really wanted to get down to the shoreline.

Denico and Kendal have been separated, but not totally. Perhaps, then, there is something fitting about Denico going to Lovers' Leap, getting halfway down the hillside, that bit closer to the sea, before turning around, walking back up, buying a bottle of water and a cigarette, and borrowing some mobile data from me to check back in with Kendal.

Chapter 6

Family and friends: witnessing deportation and hierarchies of (non-)citizenship

The previous four chapters examined how and why Jason, Ricardo, Chris and Denico were deported. By describing processes of criminalisation, illegalisation and expulsion, I developed a critical account of immigration controls in contemporary Britain. In Jason's chapter, I argued that deportation begins long before anyone gets on a plane, which means that immigration controls both produce and shape various forms of inequality *within* Britain. When discussing Ricardo's experiences of racist policing, I suggested that immigration controls not only reflect racism in wider society, but actively shift how racism gets articulated thereafter. In the next chapter, I argued that Chris had not failed to 'integrate', but was in fact too well integrated into a racist, sexist and unequal society. Finally, in Denico's chapter, I demonstrated that heteronormative and restrictive definitions of 'family life' are defined and enforced at the border.

Structuring the chapters as individual portraits allowed me to draw out and elaborate on these distinct themes and issues. The four men were very different to one another, and it made sense to focus on homelessness and illegality with Jason; racist policing with Ricardo; integration, culture and sexism with Chris; and 'family life' with Denico. However, it is important to recognise that their experiences overlap extensively. Both Chris and Denico fell into homelessness, just as Jason had; of course, Ricardo was not the only one who faced racist policing, even if his experiences were the most extreme; like Chris, all four men found ethnic and racial difference ordinary, and all felt that they were integrated and at home in the UK; and all of the men went through a profoundly violent legal process, in which their connections to family and friends were denigrated, even if I chose to explore this issue substantively with Denico and Chris. In short, the four chapters should be *read together*, in their connections as well as their specificities. Read together, the chapters highlight broader patterns, processes and themes which are of wider significance to the study of deportation, racism and immigration control. With this in mind, the book now moves away from individual portraits, and this chapter turns to family and friends.

Across the previous chapters, I described my encounters with the family and friends of Jason, Ricardo, Chris and Denico, who I met in different parts of the UK between 2016 and 2018. However, in this chapter I want to put their experiences and perspectives at the centre of my analysis. In particular, I am interested in how they made sense of deportation, in how it affected them, and in what their accounts might reveal about immigration control, racism and citizenship in contemporary Britain.[1]

The family and friends I met in the UK were situated very differently, in terms of their citizenship and immigration statuses (their vulnerability to illegality and deportation); their migration histories (whether they were born in the UK, or whether there were naturalised citizens); and their 'race'/ethnicity (whether they were racialised as 'properly British') – as well as in terms of their age, gender, class and where they lived in the UK. Given these differences, clearly there is no neat distinction between citizens (who are fully included) and migrants (who are fully excluded), and I have found it useful to think about these dynamics in terms of hierarchies of citizenship and non-citizenship. The accounts of family and friends in this chapter reveal some of these hierarchies of (non-)citizenship, which were in many cases shaped by the experience of witnessing deportation. This chapter therefore suggests new ways of thinking about racism, immigration control and citizenship in Britain, from the perspective of the family and friends of deported people.

Citizenship and racism in multi-status Britain

In ideal terms, citizenship is defined as a form of *full* political membership and belonging. Citizens are the state's insiders, and they are equal under the law. Despite their many differences, citizens share the same rights and responsibilities in the public realm.[2] This ideal of full, abstract and equal citizenship is connected to ideologies of nationalism, which construct the nation as a horizontal community of compatriots.[3] But, of course, some citizens belong more than others, and some citizens' rights are more well protected than others. In the UK, prisoners cannot vote; 'dual nationals' can have their citizenship stripped; and many poor citizens encounter the state as both abandoning and punitive (in relation to welfare, education, housing and social services).[4] In other words, there are hierarchies of citizenship, shades of citizenship and deep divisions within the citizenry.[5] This much should be obvious, but it is the necessary starting point for any critical theorisation of citizenship.

In this light, racism within any given nation-state produces *hierarchies of citizenship*. Citizens who are negatively racialised – defined as minorities, outsiders and foreigners despite their legal membership – do not enjoy full membership or homey belonging. They tend to be discriminated against by different institutions of the state, have unequal access to employment, housing and healthcare, and to be vulnerable to racist violence in public space.[6] Their equality under law is therefore nominal, and quite demonstrably illusory in most instances. Of course, 'race' is not the only way in which a given citizenry is divided, and critical work on gender, class, sexual orientation, age and disability all refer to hierarchies of citizenship – in terms of who is ignored, punished and unprotected by the institutions of the state.[7] However, in this chapter I focus specifically on the relationship between racism and hierarchies of citizenship.

Undeniably, evidence of these hierarchies of citizenship is invaluable for people seeking policy change. In relation to British racism in particular, demonstrating the 'ethnic penalty' in the labour market, the attainment gap in higher education and disproportionality within the criminal justice system all provide concrete evidence of structural racism and inspire calls to action. But what about the vexed question of who counts as a citizen in the first place? Most sociological accounts of racism assume the national scale of analysis, so that racism concerns unjust and unequal relations *between citizens*. As Linda Bosniak puts it: 'ample attention is paid to "second-class citizenship" in various guises ... [but] the issue of formal noncitizenship simply does not arise'.[8] When accounting for racism in Britain, then, where do non-citizens fit?

Non-citizens who live in the UK are subject to British law, but they do not belong to the state and can therefore be deported. Given that many of these deportable non-citizens are racialised as black and brown, and often hail from the same countries as the UK's largest 'ethnic minorities', we might question what their legal exclusion has to do with racism affecting minoritised British citizens (those aptly named 'alien citizens' by Mae Ngai).[9] What is the relationship between racism affecting black and brown British citizens and the system of illegalisation, detention and deportation affecting 'migrants' who are racialised in similar ways, and who might be part of the same communities and families? Discrimination against 'immigrants' is legal and necessary – how else could immigration controls be enforced? – while discrimination against minoritised citizens is not, which is why we have equality law and the Race Relations Act, and yet, clearly, we miss the point if we view these two sets of processes as distinct.

The friends and family members I met around the UK made it clear that these forms of discrimination were not distinct and could not be neatly separated. Despite their different circumstances, they were all deeply affected by deportation, and they often related deportation to other experiences of racist exclusion, thereby connecting the legal force of immigration control to the racist spaces, cultures and institutions they navigated in their everyday lives. This provides another reminder, if it is needed, that borders are not neutral instruments that distinguish political members from non-members, but technologies of differentiation which take force and become meaningful in spaces structured by racism. To describe Britain as multi-status, then, is not merely to state that 'legal status matters', but to recognise that *how* legal status comes to matter is intimately connected to racism. This much should be clear from the previous chapters, but I want to develop the argument from the varied perspectives of family and friends who remain in Britain.

Overall, this chapter is intended to complicate and challenge the idea that immigration controls are neutral and fair mechanisms for ordering and filtering 'migrants', and the related argument that borders protect citizens. In reality, immigration controls are enforced unevenly, in the context of structural and institutional racism, and they often have adverse impacts on citizens. To work through this argument, this chapter begins with the friends and family who were most vulnerable to deportation, and moves gradually through to those who were least. The next section therefore focuses on Ricardo's friend Marcus and cousin Louis, who both remained vulnerable to deportation. The chapter then moves to 'migrants' with indefinite leave to remain, then naturalised citizens, then black

British citizens born in the UK, and finally to Chris's friend Emma, a white British citizen. Focusing on these friends and family members – who were positioned in very different ways – allows me to examine shades of deportability and hierarchies of citizenship in multi-status Britain, as well as the ways in which witnessing deportation affects how people understand racism and belonging. These varied accounts remind us that there is no neat binary between inside and outside, included and excluded, and citizen and migrant.

Importantly, this chapter is not solely about the impacts of deportation on citizen partners and children (see previous chapter), but instead focuses on wider networks of multi-ethnic and multi-status friends and family.[10] In fact, the largest part of the chapter focuses on the friends of Ricardo and Chris. Unfortunately, this extends the male-heavy focus of the book, but the arguments can be transposed to other kinds of stories, groups and dynamics in multi-status Britain. In the next section, I turn to Ricardo's friend Marcus and his cousin Louis, who reached for different explanations when articulating the relationship between immigration control and racism.

Black and alien

I went to meet Marcus, one of Ricardo's oldest friends, in Derby, where he was living with his heavily pregnant girlfriend at her mother's house. He came to pick me up at the train station on foot, because his girlfriend was using the bus pass they shared. Our walk from the station took us over a series of large dual carriageways, and then into the quiet low-income housing estates of Chaddesden where they lived. On our walk, Marcus explained that he had not been in trouble for nearly three years, since he was 18:

> MARCUS: This is the longest I've been out. As a child I was always inside, man. I was the mad one. I've never been on road longer

than a year. I was just getting done for dumb, stupid street robberies, no force or nothing ... this was my way of retaliating against the system, when you think about it.

Marcus was born in the Democratic Republic of Congo (DRC) and although he had moved to the UK as a four-year-old, he had not been able to secure British citizenship. As a result, when he was 18, after being released from prison, the Home Office tried to deport him. Unusually, Marcus won his deportation appeal, primarily because social services decided it was their responsibility to fund his legal fees. This is by no means the norm for care-leavers, and I met several people in Jamaica who would have benefited enormously from such support. Even though Marcus had won his appeal, however, the Home Office had not sent his Biometric Residence Permit, which would allow him to work. He was convinced that the Home Office was testing him, encouraging him to 'fuck up' and 'commit more crime', so that he could be deported back to the DRC.[11]

Marcus is two years younger than Ricardo, and they met when he was around 10. They lived a few roads down from one another in Smethwick, and Ricardo remembered seeing Marcus on the road, looking distressed. 'Marcus couldn't handle things in the house any more', Ricardo told me, there were 'fucked up things happening', and so Ricardo took him into his house, where they phoned Childline, the confidential counselling service. Not long after, Marcus entered the care system, and was 'looked after' by the state from the age of 11. He was excluded from school before he reached 13, by which point he was regularly interacting with the police. He spent most of the next few years in secure units – children's homes where the doors are locked at night – and although he was moved around the country, he would often escape and return to his friends in Smethwick.

At first I found Marcus slightly unnerving. He wore his anger outwardly, and laughed manically when describing traumatic experiences from his childhood. His posture was tense, and he spoke loudly and urgently, swearing almost automatically when talking about the police, immigration authorities, lawyers and youth offending teams. But we soon grew into one another's company, and by the time we reached the house my only concern was that I would forget all the important things he had already shared with me. On our walk, he spoke about staff within the youth criminal justice system with disdain, and explained that he had to learn how to fight in juvenile prison to protect himself from white boys: 'Them lot were racist, man; I had so many scraps it got boring, like boring bro.'

Like Ricardo, Marcus had many stories about the police. They had verbally abused him, and once taken him to the station and strip-searched him when he was 16, without an 'appropriate adult' present. He described another occasion when he was alone, walking on the street, when a police officer said: 'You fucking little nigger'. Marcus tried to stay calm, but was arrested all the same. As he explained: 'All of this shit is because man are black bro. I'm telling you.' Marcus's experiences with the police, with social workers, prison guards, lawyers and immigration authorities led him to the conclusion that they wanted to see him and Ricardo deported, right from the beginning:

> MARCUS: What I think is it's harassment, straight. It's no excuse to be kicking down people's doors bro. They was up our arse, yeah, they was up our arse. This is what I'm tryna say: they've had us from the start. *They must've been planning this shit from the start.*

By 'this shit', Marcus is referring to Ricardo's deportation and perhaps to his own. Marcus even thought that 'they' would deport his British friends if they could: 'I know they hate that they can't do it to Josh and them lot. They must hate that.' It is unclear who 'they' are in Marcus's account. Clearly, he views the police and immigration authorities as co-conspirators. He does not separate out deportation from policing practices, and sees deportation as another tool that 'they' can use to punish and control people like him. At other times, Marcus seems to include social workers, care workers, teachers, lawyers and prison staff into this 'they'.

I had at first thought about Marcus's 'they' as conspiratorial. I thought that he had a naïve understanding of how things *really work*, and that he was too reliant on a conception of knowing conspirators. But as I try to conceptualise the relationship between racism and immigration control, I keep returning to Marcus's 'they'. He is telling us that he lived these forms of state power in a *continuous* way. One thing followed on from the next. The institutionally racist criminal justice system inordinately punishes black young men, especially care leavers, and immigration controls and citizenship laws are designed to identify and exclude 'criminals'.[12] In this way, Marcus was right: deportation might not have been actively planned from the start, but it did follow an all too familiar pattern. Importantly, the glue that bound Marcus's 'they' together was racism. He called his care workers racist, he said the police were racist, and he thought the Home Office was racist too.

More specifically, Marcus said that 'All of this shit is because man are black', and so he was specifically naming anti-black racism. Chris's mother made a similar point when she said: 'If you're black and you've got a record, no one's gonna trust you'; 'Legal aid doesn't help when you're black'; and 'They complain about black fathers but it's them that are making single parents'. Chris's mother viewed her son's deportation as consistent with the wider oppression of black people, and many of the people I met in Jamaica evoked similar sentiments, saying things like 'The British just hate black people'. In this account, deportation was not necessarily a rupture from what preceded it, but rather an extension of various expressions of anti-black racism, whether in relation to Britain's racist criminal justice system or in light of longer histories of slavery and empire.[13]

When Marcus says that 'All of this shit is because man are black', he suggests that immigration controls extend and enforce the forms of anti-black racism which he experienced in school, children's homes, youth prisons and at the hands of the police. When he says that 'They must've been planning this shit from the start', he connects deportation to those other forms of racist state violence that also produced non-belonging. He points to the ways in which he was, like Ricardo, already denied rights of citizenship, way before his deportation order was signed: the right to innocence, to free association, to liberty and to childhood. Interestingly, Marcus did not draw attention to the distinction between his experiences and those of his British-citizen friends, but instead suggested that 'they' 'must hate' the fact 'they can't do it [deportation] to Josh and them lot' too. In sharp contrast, Ricardo's cousin Louis was very eager to emphasise the divergence between his experiences and those of his black British friends, pointing to the difference that legal status makes.

* * *

I introduced Louis briefly in Chapter 3, when I described visiting his restaurant, 'Delon's Bar', in Oldbury. Louis is Ricardo's older cousin – although in his own words 'they grew up in the same house as brothers' – and like Ricardo, he grew up as an un-documented 'overstayer' (at the time of our interview he had secured only temporary leave to remain). Twice when visiting Louis, I helped out in the restaurant (Louis relied on the labour of his friends but was unable to pay them because he was barely making ends meet). During these visits, Louis drove me around when he was making deliveries, and I recorded our conversations on my phone, placed precariously on his dashboard. I asked Louis about the kinds of problems he and his brothers faced when growing up, and he said it was hard being 'illegal', immediately underlining his legal status in a way that Marcus had not. 'You're an alien, you haven't got equal opportunities', he explained, emphasising how difficult it was to get a driving licence and to earn money. Indeed, Louis said that immigration status was the main thing that divided him and his 'brothers' from everyone else, even when I encouraged him to talk about racism:

> LUKE: Like, what is the effect of racism, in the context of trying to understand Ricardo's life? What role do you think racism has?
>
> LOUIS: I wouldn't even put it down to racism, because, erm, like I says, the reason what separates us is that we're not British, and that's just it, so it's not just that we're black, it's that we're not British. So when you say race, it's a bit more ... what term, what word would you use for that? I don't know what term you would use for that.

Louis is trying to work through a difficult question here, on the relationship between racism and legal status. He suggests that his experiences of state power are fundamentally different to those of a black British person, because he is subject to exclusions from work, education and welfare benefits, and, most importantly, because he is deportable: 'If we got stopped and we both go to jail, I know where I'm ending up', he reflected. However, as our conversation continued, Louis did qualify this position somewhat, especially when discussing Delon's deportation – his cousin who was deported following criminal conviction and later killed in Jamaica (see Chapter 3):

> LOUIS: The only time I would say race comes into it, is the fact of Delon's situation where, don't get me wrong, obviously Delon was just Delon innit. It's fucked up yeah, because obviously he done what he done, but at the same time the police made sure that that happened if that makes sense? They made sure they got rid of him, if you get what I'm tryna say? So, if you're on about racist in that sense, yeah, *racist in the sense of how much force the police used against us*, how much they pressured us. If you wanna look at that as being racist, then fair enough.

Louis's point here is that police racism hastened the deportation of his two cousins. We continued driving around Walsall, and on our way back towards the restaurant Louis interrupted me to say, 'That's police'. I looked behind at a BMW that had just pulled in. To me, the car looked unremarkable, so I asked how he knew, but he interrupted again to say 'That's police in front as well'. Again, the car appeared like any other. He looked slightly concerned and was seeing something I was not. We drove a little further before the car ahead pulled in quickly to the roadside to block in an SUV, which was then quickly flanked at every angle by three unmarked police cars, and then a riot van. Louis slowed right down so that we could watch, and we saw a female police officer walk around the riot van with an automatic rifle in hand. There were two white men being arrested on the pavement, and Louis wound his window down to film the drama on his phone, pointing out the helicopter above. It was all strangely calm after the urgency of the ambush. 'I don't know who that is you know; maybe a big dealer or some shit', Louis remarked.

We left the police cars, rifles and helicopter behind and drove back to the restaurant, feeling animated by the scene. I was still dumbfounded that Louis had seen it all coming. He laughed and said, 'You're more or less a posh, yute, innit!', explaining that he 'just knows' the police – he grew up with them. He used to be able to recognise their number plates in their unmarked cars and he learnt to recognise 'how they do things'. In short, Louis was highly literate in something I knew nothing about. That incident reminded me that while Louis distinguished the racism facing black British citizens from his experiences as a non-citizen, in practice he encountered the border *via* the police and criminal justice. Put simply, the police were the institution Louis encountered most often, not border guards.

This is not true for all deportable non-citizens: asylum applicants who sign in at immigration reporting centres fear being detained when doing so; undocumented migrants working in car washes or takeaways fear immigration raids at work; other illegalised non-citizens fear dawn raids on their homes.[14] Louis, however, had temporary legal status and so he did not fear these forms of border enforcement. His problem was and always had been the police. While his encounters with the police were very similar to those of his black British friends, the consequences of those interactions were decidedly different. Indeed, Louis had already indicated as much when he said, 'If we got stopped and we both go to jail, I know where I'm ending up'. The example he enlisted to explain his deportability referred directly to the police and to arrest, a reminder that his vulnerabilities to state racism were both different from and similar to those of his heavily policed, although non-deportable, black British friends.

* * *

An important difference between Marcus's and Louis's accounts was the relative emphasis they placed on immigration and citizenship status. Marcus described his violation at the hands of the police as something he shared with his British-citizen friends, most of whom were racialised as black, and he thought that 'they' would deport his British friends too if they could. Louis, on the other hand, drew a clear line between his experiences as a deportable non-citizen and those of his black British friends. Whether 'they' would like to deport his black British friends is not the point; the point is that they could not.

In fact, given Louis's emphasis on legal status, alienage and deportation, we might ask how this connects his experiences to other non-citizens who are made illegal and deportable, but who are not racialised as black or criminalised in the same ways. In other words, Louis's difference from his black British friends might also denote his similarity to other deportable migrants. These connections and disconnections point to some of the complexities of racism in multi-status Britain. Chris's friend Kyle, who is also black and from Jamaica, seemed to make similar points to Louis when I asked him about the relationship between racism and immigration control:

KYLE: I wouldn't say so much that racism is related to it [immigration control]. Because even if you're black or you're white and you're not from here, they'll still send you away. They don't really bother about the colour of your skin if they wanna send you away. Basically, what I think it is, once you're not born British, that's where the problem is. Once you're not born here, it doesn't matter what colour your skin is, you'll always have problems.

Kyle identifies the shared vulnerability to deportation among different national groups, but clearly his suggestion that 'it doesn't matter what colour your skin is' is unsatisfactory. Kyle himself described the innumerable ways in which he had been attacked, abused, made to feel unsafe and made to fight because he was black, and his own account, like Marcus's, therefore testified to the role of anti-black racism in processes of criminalisation, illegalisation and deportation. However, what Kyle does point to is the complexity of racism in multi-status Britain.

In the end, though, it is important not to make too much of these quotes taken out of context, or to imagine that different points of emphasis amount to substantive disagreement. I am convinced that if Kyle, Marcus and Louis were to talk it through, it would not take them very long to agree on the same points I want to make here: racism makes some people more vulnerable to deportation power than others, and the heavy and disproportionate policing of young black men is central to the deportation of Jamaican nationals. However, and as importantly, immigration controls make the experiences of black non-citizens distinct from those of their black British friends, and in some ways this makes them similar to other groups of illegalised migrants who are not racialised as black. And so, returning to Marcus's claim that 'All of this shit is because man are black', the point is that deportation both is and is not about being black – not reducible to anti-black racism but neither explicable without it.

Indeed, my own analysis of these narratives is not meant to identify substantive disagreements but rather to draw out nuance and complexity. Louis highlighted the significance of being foreign, legally, and the difference that legal status makes between black British citizens and deportable black non-citizens, while Marcus described the significance of always having been rendered foreign through violent forms of popular and state racism. Ultimately, both of these points of emphasis are indispensable in any account of racism in multi-status Britain.

Significantly, both Marcus and Louis were deportable when we spoke. They both had only 'temporary leave to remain', and witnessing Ricardo's deportation made them feel more vulnerable to deportation. Both were trying to stay out of trouble, avoid the police and to earn money through legal employment, because they knew that the Home Office was capable of deporting them if they made the smallest slip-up. This points to the fact that witnessing deportation affects how people navigate their own lives in the UK, and witnessing deportation often makes non-citizens more mindful of their own deportability. However, as I would soon find out, this also applies to people whose immigration status is settled (i.e. they have permanent residence), and even to those who have naturalised as British. In the next section I turn to Jae, Kyle and David to further examine how witnessing deportation reminds some people of their own non-belonging, provisional inclusion and the revocability of their settled status.

Witnessing deportation and feelings of deportability (even with a red book)

Jae is Chris's best friend, a Ghanaian national who moved to the UK when he was 10 years old. He grew up in West London and attended the same secondary school as Chris, but he moved to Northampton for university and stayed on. I went to visit him there in May 2016, taking the train from London. Jae collected me from the station, and when he arrived he laughed at my large rucksack: 'Are you going camping mate?' he joked as I got into his car. He drove us back to his slightly cramped three-bed flat where he lived with three other men. They had turned the lounge into a fourth bedroom, and so we recorded our interview in Jae's room. Once we were settled, I asked him to reflect on how Chris's deportation had affected him:

> LUKE: Did that shock make you reassess your situation more then? That shock of being like, 'Oh shit, they still deported him even though he had all his ties'.
>
> JAE: Yeah, it did. It did. I had to sit back, and make sure I don't get myself in any trouble. To be honest I think that's probably one of the reasons why I decided to stay here rather than go back to London.
>
> LUKE: Really?
>
> JAE: Yeah, I would say. Like, as I said, down here is a bit quieter. I don't really associate myself with anybody as much. I know people down here, but they're not my friends, they're just associates, where if they say 'You comin' out today?', I can be like 'You know what, I don't really want to come out'. Like, there's no obligation for me, to help them out if I don't want to. I'm quite happy just to sit down here and just ride my time and let time fly, until the next day, and the next day, and the next day. You know, just seclude myself away from all of the problems that I have, you know, and the people that will get me into more trouble. Like I say, I learnt, I watched Chris's case behaviour, movements, and just learnt from it. Like, don't associate yourself with everybody, because certain people are just not there to help you. That's probably one of the main reasons why I stayed down here [in Northampton] to be honest.

Jae talks here about secluding himself away in Northampton, even as his extended family and oldest friends live in West London. He was working in retail in Northampton, struggling to make ends meet on zero-hours contracts, and he knew that he would have more options for work in London, but somehow he felt that he was more likely to get into trouble there. This is not because Jae was tempted by 'criminality', but because in London, if he was out with his old friends, he would be obliged to them in different ways, and thus might be more likely to get 'caught up in some situation'. Jae needed to reduce any risk because he had been unable to naturalise as British, mainly because he had received a two-month sentence for carrying a knife when he was a teenager. Indeed, Jae's decision to stay in Northampton was also shaped by his memories of heavy policing growing up in West London:

> LUKE: When you say the police would always be around, how often did you get stopped and searched then?
>
> JAE: Aight, growing up, Brentside, when I was there, pff, like weekly, about three times a week. Depending on the time of day. But, monthly, you're looking at the same, about 12 times in a month. It depends how often I go out.

Here, Jae reminds us that heavy policing determines which non-citizens become especially vulnerable to deportation power, and witnessing Chris's deportation affected how he understood and navigated these risks. He knew that heavy policing in West London made him more likely to end up facing deportation, and Chris's removal reminded him of just how careful he needed to be. As a result, he decided to remain in Northampton, despite his precarious employment and the distance from his family. Of course, not all deportable 'migrants' have to navigate the same risks in the same ways.

For example, white Australian overstayers working in bars simply do not experience the institutions of policing and immigration enforcement in the same way as racialised non-citizens like Jae, Marcus and Louis, even though, in law, the Australian overstayer is the 'illegal immigrant' among them. Immigration controls are implemented unevenly, and some people are more vulnerable to enforcement action than others; racism determines how people become vulnerable to expulsion power. This means that immigration status alone does not predict who will be deported, and by extension people with the same immigration status understand their own belonging and deportability in very different ways. Indeed, even some British citizens who are not subject to deportation power are made to feel vulnerable to it.

***

In July 2016 I travelled to Leeds where Chris had lived, and interviewed his friend Kyle at his council flat near the hospital. Kyle spoke with a broad Yorkshire accent, although, like Chris, he could switch to patois when necessary. He had moved to the UK with his mother and brothers when he was 10 years old and had naturalised as a British citizen when he was 13. While I learnt some new things about Chris from our conversation, it was more interesting to hear Kyle talk about his own experiences of racism, his thoughts on the recent Brexit referendum and his perspectives on (his own) British citizenship. Importantly, despite possessing a British passport, Kyle still felt that the British government could deport him: 'Even with the British passport, you're still liable for deportation, they've told us that', he explained. I asked him who 'they' were and he said 'I've just heard that's the law, someone told me that':

> LUKE: Have you worried about this before, or is it just something that you're thinking about now we're talking?
> KYLE: Nah, I've thought about it quite a lot, which is why I learn from certain people's mistakes and just try my best not to let certain things behold me. Because you never know, to be honest with you. Every day you hear of a new law, or a new this and a new that, so you can never be sure; you feel like anything can happen.

Witnessing Chris get deported made Kyle feel less secure in his own status as a naturalised citizen. 'Every day you hear of a new law', Kyle said, and he was aware of the direction of travel in immigration policy more broadly. Kyle had thought extensively about how he might lose his British citizenship, even though he had never been convicted of a criminal offence and nor did he intend to commit one. This was an issue I encountered again with Denico's friend David, another naturalised British citizen:

> DAVID: Maybe if I got done for manslaughter, I dunno, like in the nursing home where I work, if someone's death was caused by

an accident that I made, then I'm liable. I'm thinking, could that then be the reason that I get sent home? I dunno. Like you said, it's unlikely but at the time it was on my mind, like that could happen. Could be a reason why I get sent back to Jamaica.

It has been argued that citizenship can be defined as the right not to be deported: 'Every act of deportation might be seen as re-affirming the significance of the unconditional right of residence that citizenship provides'.[15] However, Kyle and David invert this claim: deportation might reaffirm the value of citizenship *for some*, but it also sharpens hierarchies between citizens. In this case, witnessing deportation sharpened how Kyle and David understood divisions between naturalised citizens and those who were 'born British' – a distinction with inevitably racialised contours.

To be a naturalised citizen or a 'dual national' is not supposed to be a form of second-class citizenship, however, and liberal states want to maintain the view that all citizens are equal under the law. As Mae Ngai notes, naturalisation 'is important because it recognizes the moral and political imperative of equality that is central to liberal democracy'.[16] Further, given that the UK's naturalisation policies require a clean immigration history, long residence and 'good character' – although the whole process can be rapidly expedited if you have enough money[17] – those who do manage to naturalise are supposed to be welcomed into the horizontal community of citizens. And yet, Kyle and David's fears of deportability are not unsubstantiated; they do in fact remain deportable, in the sense that their citizenship can be stripped.

The UK has long had the power to deprive people of their citizenship, but before 2002 the power was used very rarely (only once between 1960 and 2002).[18] Since 2002, however, increasing numbers of British citizens have been denationalised, with a sharp spike in 2010 (in early 2019 Home Secretary Sajid Javid admitted that around 150 people had been stripped of their citizenship since 2010).[19] The power has been reserved for 'national security' cases in relation to the 'War on Terror', and those stripped of their citizenship have been defined as terrorist threats (read 'Muslim terrorists').[20] The one notable exception was in relation to the Rochdale 'grooming gang', in which three of the men who were convicted of sexual offences against tens of girls in the north of England were stripped of their citizenship so that they could be deported to Pakistan at the end of their sentences.[21] This was the first use of denationalisation powers in the absence of accusations of terrorism – although evidently it relied on similar ideas about Muslims as the 'enemy within'.[22]

The crucial point for Kyle and David, though, is that laws around citizenship are not fixed but constantly shifting. For dual nationals, British nationality remains revocable; dual nationals are thus less secure in their Britishness than those citizens who have no other nationality.[23] Importantly, it is cultural meanings about an individual's *foreignness* that licence these forms of expulsive state power. As Bobbie Mills argues: 'If citizenship deprivation is considered a necessary step to enable deporta-tion – a measure reserved exclusively for foreign nationals – then the individual in question must *already* appear as foreign for the very notion of these measures to occur to the public imaginary'.[24] For Kyle and David, both racialised as black and having migrated from Jamaica, powers of citizenship deprivation appear to be creeping towards them, and while the targets today might be 'terror suspects' and 'grooming gangs', it is not clear where the line will be drawn tomorrow. In the context of this uncertainty, and following the deportation of their close friends, people like Kyle and David begin to feel deportable, despite their British citizenship.

In this section, I have described the ways in which witnessing deportation made Jae, Kyle and David feel deportable, despite the fact that they either had indefinite leave to remain or had naturalised as British. However, not everyone who witnesses deportation feels more deportable as a result. As described in the last chapter, deportation has profound effects on partners, parents and children, who might not be liable for deportation themselves but whose lives remain structured by it. In this way, deportation produces and deepens various hierarchies of citizenship for the mothers, partners and children who remain – especially along lines of race, gender and class – and these processes should be central to any account of racism and immigration control in multi-status Britain.[25]

Mothers, partners and children: the left behind

Chris's mother, Angelique, was a naturalised British citizen like Kyle and David, but she did not feel deportable. Given her age and her British children, she was not worried about being criminalised, losing her nationality and then being sent to Jamaica. That said, her eldest son Chris had been taken from her and there was very little she could do about it, except incur debt and bear the stress. This is an experience that the majority of British citizens do not have to worry about, especially white Britons, and yet there are thousands of mothers like Angelique living in the UK, many of them naturalised British citizens, who have watched their children being deported. In my experience, their stories tend to involve migrating from places of insecurity and limited opportunities, navigating restrictive immigration policies in the UK, working and bringing up their children, only to then observe one of them, usually a son, being criminalised and later banished 'back to where they came from'. These stories are both tragic and increasingly common in multi-status Britain, and yet there is hardly any academic analysis or social commentary on what these stories reveal about racism, migration and citizenship.

Ricardo's auntie also experienced the deportation of her (adopted) sons. She was a black British citizen, born in the UK, who raised Ricardo, Delon, Louis and his brother, all Jamaican nationals who had overstayed the visitor visas they had obtained when children. In the end, she saw two of them incarcerated as adolescents and then deported to Jamaica, where Delon, who she had legally adopted as her child, was murdered in Montego Bay aged 22. How should we conceive of her citizenship rights in this context, particularly in terms of the 'right to respect for family life'? Ultimately, Ricardo's auntie was punished because the children she raised were 'foreign', and she had very little power to prevent their being exiled.

Another group who might not fear deportation themselves, but who are profoundly affected by immigration controls are the British-citizen partners of 'deportees'.[26] In the last chapter, I described how Kendal and her children suffered due to Denico's deportation. Kendal had to stop working to take care of her children, and was effectively prevented from training as a midwife because of the emotional and material impact of Denico's enforced removal. I also described how Shanice, a black British woman, was threatened with eviction from her council house after Darel was deported. Deportation affected these women in the most profound ways, and tended to deepen and extend existing social inequalities surrounding race, class and gender.

Importantly, 'ethnic minority' British citizens are more likely to be in relationships with non-citizens. Kendal is mixed race, and the two mothers of Chris's children are non-white (Tara is black British and Hayley is mixed race). It is hardly surprising that the deportation of Jamaican men disproportionately impacts black and mixed-race citizens, but the more general point is that immigration controls reproduce and reaffirm racial hierarchies *within* the citizenry. We can observe similar patterns in relation to 'British Asians' who engage in transnational marriages, and who therefore encounter restrictions on their family life through controls on marriage migration.[27] More generally, British citizens who want to sponsor a 'foreign spouse' must now earn at least

£18,600 a year, and this inordinately affects working-class and 'ethnic minority' women.[28] Clearly, immigration controls have adverse consequences for citizens, and the impact is most keenly felt by ethnic minority citizens.[29] This reflects the fact that immigration controls are expressly designed to prevent people moving from where ethnic minority citizens are thought to have 'really come from'. As Sivamohan Valluvan puts it:

> Racialised nationalism anxiously scans the border and the exterior only because it already takes issue with the interior and the many problematic minorities that are in some form already deemed excessive – excessive in the sense that they are simply too many, have been given too much allowance, wield too much power, or threaten to wield too much power if not preemptively stymied.... The exterior is therefore rendered a threat partly because it is seen as replenishing, enhancing or emboldening the already problematic interior.[30]

The effects of deportation are also borne by British children. Kendal's children were profoundly distressed by Denico's absence; two of Darel and Shanice's children started 'playing up' at school; and I heard many accounts of young children who started bed-wetting following their fathers' detention and removal. These consequences of deportation are now routine. Indeed, even when children are not affected in these more immediate ways – as with Chris's children – they are still effectively barred from seeing their fathers indefinitely. In fact, some British citizen children are actually compelled to leave when their parents are deported, and they are thereby separated not from their parents but from the country of their citizenship – from their friends, schools and homes.[31] When British children are effectively deported with their parents, we are provided with the starkest reminder that not all citizens are equal.

Overall, then, deportation causes profound emotional and material hardships for the British-citizen parents, partners and children who remain, or who are compelled to leave with loved ones facing deportation. These impacts tend to deepen existing inequalities along lines of race, class and gender. What was most interesting in my admittedly limited research with friends and family, however, was that it was Chris's friend and former 'fling', Emma, who had encountered immigration controls most often, and she was 'white British'. Indeed, while immigration controls disproportionately impact 'ethnic minority' citizens, white British citizens also share their lives with deportable non-citizens. I conclude the chapter with Emma's perspective, and that of her son Callum, because they remind us that the social implications of immigration control are far-reaching, and not necessarily restricted to 'migrants and minorities'.

White Britons in multi-status Britain

I met Emma in Leeds, in a McDonald's, with her 11-year-old son Callum, who needed to eat after football practice. Emma had just finished a long shift at a care home for the elderly, where she worked as a manager, and had collected Callum from football practice before coming to meet me. While Callum ordered his food, she explained that she and Chris had become friends and were 'seeing' one another around the time he was arrested for selling drugs. Emma said she still spoke to Chris on WhatsApp, and when I asked her to describe him she paused and said, 'Well,' he's a mummy's boy!' When Callum returned with his food, he smiled when I mentioned Chris – two days earlier Chris had sent Callum a recipe for brown-stew chicken over WhatsApp because Callum loved cooking Caribbean food.

As our conversation progressed, it became clear that Chris was not the only person Emma knew who had been deported. She knew several men who had been sent to Jamaica and Nigeria, including her sister's ex-boyfriend, her friend's partner and Callum's friend's dad. In fact, Emma's current boyfriend was appealing his own deportation to Jamaica at the time, and had spent some months in prison and immigration detention over the last two years. Emma had also encountered women at work who had overstayed their visas, were working illegally, and were later detained and removed. In short, even though Emma is 'white British' she has had several encounters with the border. In this context, it was partly through witnessing deportation that Emma and Callum made sense of race and racism in the UK, and our conversation moved naturally from deportation to discussions of racism more broadly.

Callum found racism particularly upsetting, and he described a recent football match in which some of the black boys on his side had experienced racist abuse from the opposing team and their fathers. It was interesting that a conversation about deportation so easily became a conversation about racism among British children. For Callum, an 11-year-old white British boy from Leeds, who loved Jamaican food and music, 'race' became most significant when white boys abused his black friends during a football game, but also when his friend's dad was deported to Nigeria. In his words, both were 'unfair'. Callum's reflections remind us that encounters with immigration controls shape how 'race' becomes meaningful for many people living in multi-status Britain, including for white Britons.

While our conversation was brief, it stuck with me because it captured the ways that citizens and non-citizens of different ethnicities share lives in the UK, despite difference, division and exclusion, even as borders carve through their neighbourhoods, classrooms and intimate lives.[32] Immigration controls violently enforce racial and national distinctions, but often in the lives of people who demonstrate the inevitability of their banal transgression. Emma and Callum, in quite unremarkable ways, embraced urban multiculture and were against racism. They present a very different image of the 'white working class' to that invoked by both left-wing and right-wing communitarians in debates about migration and borders.[33] Ultimately, Emma and Callum remind us that Britain's multi-status character is

socially significant not only for 'migrants and minorities': immigration controls structure racial meanings and hierarchies for
everyone living in the UK.

Conclusion

According to the states who implement them, immigration
controls protect citizens. But which citizens are really protected by the exclusion of 'migrants'? As Bridget Anderson and
Vanessa Hughes argue, 'emphasising the inclusions/exclusions
of citizenship encourages an assumption not only that immigration controls have no direct adverse consequences for citizens
but also that all formal citizens are fully and equally included'.
In so doing, immigration controls turn 'attention away from
the gendered, classed and racialised borders within formal
citizenship'.[34] As I have shown, immigration controls often
have severely adverse consequences for citizens, and deportation
therefore actively produces and entrenches 'gendered, classed
and racialised borders within formal citizenship'.[35] In short,
immigration controls do not protect citizens but differentiate
among them, especially along lines of race, class and gender.[36]

Also, according to the states that implement them, immigration controls are filters that sort migrants into different
categories. These processes of sorting and filtering are imagined
to be neutral and fair. However, even migrants with the same
legal statuses are differentially vulnerable to deportation, and the
enforcement of immigration controls is highly uneven. Rather
than neutral sorting mechanisms, borders produce complex
lines of difference, division and hierarchy. Therefore, the legal
and bureaucratic filtering of 'migrants' cannot be separated
from the ongoing cultural and structural force of racism. This
book is concerned precisely with these connections between the
'filtering' of migrants and the production of racialised distinctions and hierarchies. The experiences and narratives of the

family and friends featured in this chapter – who are legally and culturally positioned in very different ways – help us better appreciate how these complex connections are understood and lived by people living in the UK.

The overall argument in this chapter is that racism in multi-status Britain is precisely about the production of hierarchies of (non-)citizenship. This offers a method for analysing what immigration controls do and how they are lived in societies structured by racism. Importantly, immigration controls do not only confirm pre-existing racist exclusions – for example further excluding 'blacks' and 'Asians' – they also create new dynamics and complexities, thereby reconfiguring racial distinctions and hierarchies.[37] In my view, we can better understand both citizenship and racism if we trace how immigration controls produce hierarchies of (non-)citizenship, and this can generate a rich and textured picture of multi-racist, multi-status Britain.

Of course, this demands a more critical account of citizenship – not as equal, inclusive and abstract – but as highly differentiated and differentiating. In the next chapter, I further develop this critical account of citizenship, but this time by thinking globally about what citizenship does in the world. Indeed, the final two chapters of the book move away from multi-status Britain to examine racism, borders and citizenship in and from Jamaica.

Chapter 7

Post-deportation: citizenship and the racist world order

The chapters so far have focused mostly on racism, criminalisation and immigration control in Britain, even if narrated from Jamaica. In this chapter, however, I want to think from and about Jamaica, questioning what deported people encounter when they return, and what their experiences reveal about citizenship in global perspective. Where the previous chapter offered some tools for theorising hierarchies of (non-)citizenship in contemporary Britain, this chapter explores *hierarchies of citizenships*, globally. It questions what citizenship does in the world, from the vantage point of the Jamaican 'deportee' (as noted in the Introduction, I use scare quotes around 'deportee' throughout because the term has some pejorative connotations in the Jamaican context).[1] Ultimately, I argue that citizenship functions globally to manage and fix highly unequal populations, in space and in law. As such, citizenship is central to the reproduction and reconfiguration of colonially forged global disparities, through the ordering of space, mobility and population.[2]

This chapter also provides some space to describe the hardships deported people face in Jamaica, which were only hinted at in previous chapters. While *Deporting Black Britons* is not a study of post-deportation, I want to include a fuller account of how people struggle to survive and rebuild their lives once they are deported. I do not, however, want to isolate the experiences of 'deportees' from those of other Jamaicans struggling with poverty and insecurity on the island. Of course, deported people experience their hardships specifically in relation to their exclusion from the UK, but they are not the only Jamaican nationals who are immobilised and fixed in place, fenced out of countries where there are greater opportunities, higher wages and better living conditions. Neither are deported people the only Jamaicans who have transnational family connections, or who dream of escape and flight.[3] Frustrated and restricted mobilities are the stuff of Jamaican citizenship.[4] This observation brings a much wider group of people into the frame, and the discussion therefore becomes less about individual 'deportees' and more about the broader role of citizenship, which functions to immobilise the majority of Jamaican nationals on the island.

That said, the position of deported people does lend particular clarity to my reflections on the global function of citizenship. Their out-of-placeness 'at home' reveals the violence of citizenship as the global regime which assigns individuals to states.[5] In this way, the experiences of deported people in Jamaica are useful to think with, and in this chapter I develop a wider set of arguments about what citizenship does in the world from the perspective of the 'deportee'.

The chapter proceeds with a description of what people face after deportation – focusing on poverty, violence, insecurity, ill-health and unemployment – before situating these hardships in historical and global context. I trace contemporary economic and social relations in Jamaica through slavery and colonialism, before offering a broad theorisation of citizenship in global perspective. Ultimately, my argument is that citizenship is fundamental to the racial ordering of the world and the (re)production of a racist world order. These arguments are profoundly broad in their scope, but they emerge from close attention to the experiences of deported people. In the next section of this chapter, therefore, I turn to Chris, who offered an unsettling account of his return to Jamaica.

Returning to 'the ghetto'

CHRIS: This man on the road, like all he does is just drink alcohol, and chats a bag of shit. But majority of the times what he's sayin' makes sense. Because he's drunk he don't care if it hurts your feelings or not, and so he said openly one time: *'When deportees can't get money, dem mad'*. I'm thinking, when you look at a lot of these deportees out here, that are homeless, that are beggin' on the roadsides because they can't take care of themselves, because they're having financial problems and difficulties.[6] It's a good statement he made, and it's a fact, *it will drive any person insane*. You know, you live a certain lifestyle, and then you get degraded so far below people, you get me? I used to be in a nice house, three-bedroom house with my mum and that, heated, big 40-inch TV, and 30-inch TV in the bedroom or whatever. We used to live comfortably. And for me to leave that, and then to come to Jamaica to live in a board house, with no TV, and not even a little piece of bed. Like when there's lizards and roaches and everything, just crawling in and out of the place. So from a good lifestyle, well, a below-average lifestyle, below yours, but then to go to worser than that, to homelessness, it will drive a person insane, you get me, it will.

When Chris moved back to Jamaica, he first lived with his cousin in a 'ghetto area' called Harbour View, East Kingston. He was smoking weed all day, calling friends and family in England, and surviving on the small amounts of money and essentials his mother sent from London: 'When I first came my mum sent me a barrel yeah, with like tinned stuff like baked beans, corned beef, tuna, pasta, rice, bulk rice, you get me, like peanut butter, sugar, so, it's a big shop and it will last like two, three months', Chris recalled.

In Jamaica, children whose mothers have emigrated are sometimes described as 'barrel children', because their mothers send back necessities, and perhaps affection, from the UK and North America, in large blue barrels. Chris became a grown-up 'barrel child' again following his deportation, and the fact that he received sugar from the UK, of all things, tells its own story.[7] But Chris's mother could not keep sending barrels. She was no

Pictures 7.1 and 7.2. *Photos taken by Chris – East Kingston (2016)*

longer working as a hairdresser due to ill-health, and she had to support her other four children in London. Soon Chris had to find ways to survive without regular remittances, and when the food and money ran out, so did the hospitality of his hosts. After an argument with his cousin, Chris was told to leave the place in Harbour View, and so he turned to his mother's brother for some support:

> CHRIS: I'm sleeping on the floor, and my uncle is, like, 'Bwoy, if police or gunman come look for you, I don't want them to come in my house'. And I'm like, 'But nobody's gonna come look for me. I just ain't got nowhere to go because I fell out with my cousin out there, and I'm lost right now. I just need a little bit of understanding, a little bit of support.' He didn't give me nothing.

After being kicked out of his uncle's house, Chris had nowhere to go and no one to call on. He walked aimlessly up Windward Road towards 'town', and by chance stumbled upon Open Arms Drop in Centre – the homeless shelter with bed spaces for 'deportees'. After speaking with the management he was able to secure a bed space in the large dormitory. This would be his home for the next seven months.

Chris's experiences are not uncommon. Deported people often leave their immediate family in the UK and so depend on estranged family members when they return. In Jamaica, almost everyone would 'go foreign' if they could, but it is the (predominantly black) urban poor who are most likely to migrate through irregular routes (e.g. overstaying visitor visas). The middle classes tend to utilise visas, green cards and transnational connections, while migrants from the 'ghetto' are more likely to be illegalised and criminalised in the UK and North America.[8] Deportation, then, reflects the transnational circuits of disadvantage which determine who is mobile and in what ways, and this explains why 'deportees' most often return to live with family members in the low-income urban areas still marred by the structural violence which precipitated their emigration in the first place.[9]

Once they return, 'deportees' are often stereotyped as 'criminals', described as individuals who had a 'golden opportunity' and wasted it. That said, attitudes towards 'deportees' are by no means uniform. While academic research has emphasised the stigma confronting 'deportees' in Jamaica, it is important not to flatten out or oversimplify how deported people are received.[10] Firstly, we should recognise that we are talking about a significant number of people here. Tens of thousands of Jamaican nationals have been forcibly returned in the last two decades. Indeed, around 2–3% of the Jamaican population living on the island are people who have been deported since 1996 – mostly from the US, Canada and the UK.[11] The majority of these are men (85% of 'deportees' in 2013 were men, for example) and most are between the ages of 20 and 60.[12] Further, because the overwhelming majority of the deported population are poor, they most often live in low-income urban neighbourhoods. This means that in any given 'ghetto' – what Jamaicans call 'the garrison'[13] – there are likely to be several people, especially men, who are 'deportees' from North America and the UK. Many will be easily distinguishable by their accent and mannerisms, but others might not be identifiable as 'deportees' at all. This means that the social significance of have being deported varies in intensity with context and over time.

None of this is to suggest that having been deported is insignificant. It might be the reason someone does not get a job or is kicked out of their house. Many Jamaicans describe deported people as undeserving failures who squander opportunities 'in foreign', before then becoming dependent on estranged family members they had scarcely remembered to contact when they were abroad.[14] That said, these narratives are complicated by the widely held conviction that people who left Jamaica as infants should not be deported. Many of the Jamaicans I spoke with thought that 'deportees' who were raised in North America or the UK suffered an injustice when they were sent back. Further, Jamaicans often recognise that 'foreign nuh easy' – that life in the UK and North America can he hard – but this does not necessarily negate their conviction that particular 'deportees' are to blame for their own predicament.[15]

In this context, whether an individual deported person is received with hospitality or hostility very much depends on a number of contingencies within individual and family biographies. Because of this, it is important to recognise the generosity and care as well as the stigma and isolation. For example, Chris's friend shared his small room in Rockfort with him rent free, as did Denico's estranged cousin when he first arrived back. Meanwhile, Ricardo's uncle provided him with shelter for a few months, even as he found more substantive support from his partner, Tinesha, and his friend, Everton.

That said, deported people do face specific obstacles in the immediate context of their return.[16] Most arrive without any money and with very few prospects for employment, especially in the first few months. In these circumstances they tend to rely on remittances from their friends and family in the UK, and this makes them vulnerable to robbery and extortion. For example, Denico was robbed just a few weeks after arriving in Kingston, after he had collected money from the Western Union downtown – clearly because he was visible as someone who had come back 'from foreign' (his assailants referred to him as 'yankee', mistaking him for a deported person from the USA).

Denico soon learnt how to act more discreetly in Kingston, and most deported people find ways to mitigate these kinds of risks. However, low-level extortion is both every day and unavoidable in low-income Jamaica. In the context of poverty and 'turf war', people in the inner-city communities are compelled to pay for their security. As Chris explained, 'It's just extortion, innit; everybody pays'.[17] Chris would pay 'rastaman' 100 Jamaican dollars a couple of times a week, depending on how he was doing for money. Denico gave money to men a few streets down, and Jason spoke about being extorted by men across the road from Open Arms, although this had very little to do with payment in return for protection:

> JASON: They are by the shop, yeah, near the bus stand, and I see them when I walk downtown. They say 'beg you a change, nuh?' but I haven't got nothing Luke! I'm just trying to buy one cigarette, and they think I'm working. One of them said, 'What, you don't think I'll shoot you?' People are trying to kill me down there, Luke. I need to get back to England!

Perhaps the most regular complaint I heard from deported persons concerned these kinds of threats of violence: fears of being robbed, attacked and shot. Chris spoke about hearing gunshots most nights in Rockfort, while Denico, who lived a few streets down, also described the unsettling sound of gunfire. Other deported people told me they had seen people killed 'in front of their eyes', in areas like Rockfort, Denham Town, Maxfield Road and Waterhouse. One young man, Omar, described vivid and repeated nightmares of being shot in the head by gunmen, just like his father had been when he was a child. Omar, at age 13, had fled Maxfield Road with his mother and moved to London. On his return, over 15 years later, it was the only neighbourhood he could return to. This kind of story is not unusual, and not only in downtown Kingston. Ricardo lived with his uncle in an area of Montego Bay called Norwood, and there were regular shootings in his neighbourhood. Montego Bay entered a 'state of emergency' several times between 2016 and 2018, in which military checkpoints and curfews were instituted, and Norwood was one of the areas worst affected.

Importantly, however, the threat of violence comes not only from local 'badmen' but also from the police. When Chris was living in Harbour View with his cousin, he started hanging out with some young men on his street. At one point, they had an altercation with another local group, and 'the beef' culminated in a fist fight and further threats of violence. The next day, a police SUV pulled in abruptly to where Chris was stood, and several officers emerged with guns raised, telling them to get to the ground. One of Chris's friends was hit over the eye with the butt of an officer's gun, while another officer held a gun to Chris's head:

> CHRIS: I literally begged and pleaded on my knees. The policeman had the gun to my head. He had his nine-millimetre Glock. I was in shock at the time, like, I forgot the procedure to take down his badge number and file a report, it just happened so fast, in a matter of seconds. He had his gun to my head, he looked at it, I seen him look at the gun, he put it on safety, you get me, but I didn't know if it was on safety or off safety, but he done something to it, held it my head, and squeezed the trigger and I heard 'click'. I thought, what the fuck.

Chris was accused by the other group of men of being a 'deportee' who had 'come back from foreign' and bought firearms for his friends. The police were acting on that information. In fact, police corruption and extrajudicial killings are endemic in neighbourhoods like Harbour View; Amnesty International reported that between 2000 and 2016, an estimated 3,000 people were killed by the police (over 200 people each year, or around 8% of the total homicides in Jamaica).[18]

> CHRIS: Out of everybody, I don't like the police, because they kill innocent people, you get me, innocent people. I don't like them.

Pictures 7.3 and 7.4. *Photos taken by Chris – East Kingston (2016)*

Many other deported persons spoke to me about their experiences of serious violence. I met one man who no longer had function in his left hand after being attacked with a machete in Montego Bay. Another man called Dwight was shot three times a few months after arriving back in Jamaica. He survived the attack, but I was reminded that when I met him just days after he had landed, he repeatedly told me that deportation was 'a death sentence'. I also heard of at least six deported men who had been killed, one of whom I had met, and one of whom was Ricardo's brother Delon. *The Guardian* revealed in May 2019 that five men deported from the UK to Jamaica were known to have been killed in the previous year – and these were just the cases the paper knew about.[19] Despite these risks, Jamaican nationals still find it very difficult to secure asylum in the UK, and these cases of murder on return demonstrate that the 'culture of disbelief' in the Home Office leads the UK to deport people to their deaths.[20]

The sickness of non-belonging

In the context of poverty, violence and isolation, many deported people I met said they felt paranoid and depressed, and some felt that they could not trust anyone in Jamaica. Jason often said 'I just need to get out of Jamaica, Luke', and Denico moved to

Pictures 7.5 and 7.6. *Photos taken by Chris – East Kingston (2016)*

St Elizabeth to get away from East Kingston. As Chris explained in 2015:

CHRIS: I don't trust not one person out here.
LUKE: Not one?
CHRIS: Not one person. Even my close friends out here, I don't trust them. I trust them to be them. But I know they're only out to get what they can get, for the time being, because that's how most Jamaicans are right now.

As was common with several men I met, Chris self-medicated by smoking weed, which he said made him feel less tense and made the days go quicker. He described his 'suicidal thoughts', and I heard similar accounts from many of the other deported people I met. Many complained about how much weight they had lost, and several people spoke about 'going mad'. In general, deported people were scared, they missed their friends and family in the UK and they were often just incredibly bored. One man I became very close with, Kemoy, experienced a mental breakdown in this context, and it is worth describing the episode in some detail.

I first met Kemoy on a visit to Dungavel Immigration Removal Centre in Scotland in 2015, while he was still fighting his deportation. Kemoy moved to the UK when he was 10 years old, and he lived first in London, some of that time in care, before moving to Scotland with his mother. When he was 18 he was convicted of drugs and robbery offences, and after pleading not guilty he was sentenced to six and a half years. Kemoy was then incarcerated from the age of 18 to 24, spending nearly five years in prison, and then one year in Dungavel Immigration Removal Centre, before being deported to Jamaica in 2016.

I met him in Jamaica just a few weeks after he had been returned, bumping into him by chance outside Open Arms where he was then living. We started hanging out, and met regularly up at the University campus. Initially, Kemoy seemed to be doing well, much better than when I had met him in detention. He was positive and proactive about rebuilding his life in Jamaica and he was making friends and spending time with family. Two years later, however, Jamaica had worn him down and he ended up hospitalised in Bellevue Mental Hospital for over four weeks after a serious mental breakdown. I met him again in 2019, after he had recovered, and he described his breakdown to me – what he called his 'sickness'.

While living in Open Arms, Kemoy began hearing voices and started over-analysing everything. His thoughts were running too quickly and he felt that people were talking about him. He began leaving Open Arms for days at a time, trusting no one, and walking for hours. He would walk for miles, aimlessly (at one point he was badly beaten up by police officers when walking in a wealthy neighbourhood). At some point, he stopped showering because he thought that when he showered people would get beaten up. He smashed his phone after reading too much into people's profile pictures on WhatsApp, and he was experiencing severe headaches. During this time, he was smoking weed almost compulsively, and not eating, sleeping or washing regularly.

Kemoy explained that when he was trying to sleep in Open Arms, the voices became too loud, almost deafening, and he had to leave. He was not sure if the voices were in his head or not, but he also believed he could hear other people's thoughts. They were saying: 'Why are you staying here? This is not your bed. You don't belong here. Go and find where you live!' As

Kemoy explained to me, 'I felt like, I don't know where I live. If I knew where my place was I would go there'. When those voices became too loud, he would walk. He still heard voices, but they were not as loud when he was out on the street, and even if he was not sure where he was going, he was in motion, following the signs he identified in the traffic lights, wind direction and car number plates. On several occasions he walked down to the sea, sometimes immersing himself in the water.

On these walks, Kemoy was not sure where he was supposed to be, and this question haunted him – where did he belong? One evening, he decided he needed to get out of Jamaica. This was not the first time he had wanted to leave the island, but it was the first time he actively made plans. Remembering a shipyard he had seen on the bus, he decided to walk there, a distance of over five miles. He arrived, feet badly swollen, and was unable to climb the fence or find a way onto a docked boat. Clearly, he had not thought the plan through, but he felt compelled, somehow, anyhow, to leave Jamaica.

As Kemoy described his 'sickness' to me, it felt like an allegory for the experiences of many deported people I knew. Kemoy felt he did not belong in Jamaica and yet he did not know where his home was, or how to get there. He felt trapped on the island, alone in the country of his birth and citizenship. As Kemoy was concluding this account of his 'sickness', he reflected: 'People might tell you what it will be like when you come back to Jamaica – obviously, there's the sun and sea version – but no one tells you about the loneliness. No one tells you about how lonely you are going to be.'

Finding work and securing the means of life

Along with mental ill-health, poverty, family alienation and fears of violence, deported people in Jamaica also find it very difficult to secure employment. They usually lack contacts and networks to help in finding work, and it takes months to acquire necessary documentation – a tax registration number (TRN), a national identification card, a passport. Further, most employers request a police check, and whether the check comes back clean is something of a lottery. For example, Denico's drugs offence had travelled with him from the UK, and so he could not get a clean police check certificate. He was therefore ineligible for most jobs. Ricardo's record, on the other hand, was clear, despite the fact that he had received a longer sentence than Denico. Even when people find work, however, clean police record or not, it is usually poorly paid.

Ricardo had a series of jobs in Montego Bay between 2015 and 2019. He first worked on a hotdog stand in the town centre, where he regularly did double shifts, mostly unpaid, and came home with just over £35 a week. Later, he found work as a security guard, which was one of the better options for deported people with clean police certificates – after all, private security is big business in Jamaica. Still, on his wages Ricardo was unable to live independently, and he relied on his uncle before moving in with Tinesha. This was also the case for Denico, who found work in the butchery of a supermarket in St Elizabeth. Working around 40 hours a week, he still earned only £35 to £40 a week, and he spent up to half of his wages travelling to work and buying food while on shift. Denico said he was 'basically earning to pay to go to work'; without the ability to save and progress, he was effectively treading water.[21] In this context, both Denico and Ricardo still relied on remittances from the UK, especially if they wanted to save some of their wages, or to buy something substantial like a TV, washing machine or pair of trainers. This dependence on remittances, even while working, is a reality for many of Jamaica's working poor (indeed, remittances account for 16–17% of Jamaica's total GDP and it has been estimated that up to a third of the Jamaican population depend on regular remittances for their survival).[22]

Jason found securing employment even more difficult. In 2017, he was packing recycled paper into containers for a while, making around £5 a day, but he was being bullied by men he was working with and could not secure consistent hours. At one point in 2016, he worked as a kind of bailiff, but he was mostly not being paid (he implied that payment was on commission). He ended up in some dangerous situations, like when he was dropped in Trench Town, tasked with collecting court debts from an individual, and ended up being threatened with a machete and chased out of the neighbourhood. Two years later, after Jason had been kicked out of Open Arms, he spent his days at the market downtown, offering to help people carry their goods for small change, and then sleeping underneath the market stalls by night.

In many ways, the employment experiences of deported people are characteristic of work for poor Jamaicans more broadly. The minimum wage for a 40-hour week is set at around £40, which is way below a living wage. Unemployment stood at around 10.4% in 2019, with youth unemployment at around 25% (although this does not capture the kinds of work people are doing and whether it pays).[23] The financial crisis of 2008 hit Jamaica especially hard, with poverty levels increasing from 14% to 21% between 2007 and 2015, and a marked increase in the number of people employed in the informal economy (informal work accounted for around 40% of the total employed population in 2016).[24]

In a context in which so much of the workforce is employed informally, the statistics on unemployment do not capture the realities of widespread underemployment and poverty. Informal work often translates as small-scale entrepreneurial activities, like selling drinks, sweets and cigarettes from small carts, or running unlicensed fruit-and-vegetable stalls at the market ('higgling').[25] Notably, informal work is often intensely social, organised within networks and through social connections, and therefore deported people are likely to be profoundly disadvantaged in this regard.

The more general point here is that for most poor people in Jamaica, it makes very little sense to talk about unemployment, as though formal employment were the norm. In reality, for people living in the 'ghetto' there is no hope of their full inclusion, no role for them in the labour market and no possibility that they will successfully vie for jobs in the formalised service sector.[26] For people like Chris, Ricardo and Denico, there might be the option of working in a gas station, at a supermarket or as a security guard, but within such jobs there are very few opportunities for progression or job security, and wages are often far below what is required to pay for rent and essentials.

In fact, the broader point is that for most of the world's population the prospects of securing formal employment are remote. In the global South, informal employment is the regular mode of employment, and the normative waged/legally insured formal sector job was a feature of a very short historical period in the global North, now in decline.[27] In Jamaica, the lack of decent jobs means that it is increasingly difficult for people to secure the means of life (i.e. to survive and to socially reproduce),[28] which produces immense social and economic pressures that get only partly relieved through emigration and crime – particularly via extortion, 'lotto scamming' and the trade in drugs and weapons.[29]

The most important point to draw from this is that the employment experiences of deported persons, as well as their vulnerability to crime and violence, are symptomatic of the wider immiseration of the global majority. In effect, capitalist development has produced surplus populations in countries like Jamaica, and most people are not and nor will they be meaningfully incorporated into global markets.[30] Their labour is not exploited, and even when it is there are always many more people than jobs in the major extractive industries (including tourism). People in this situation must survive with a meagre income – acquired through formal work in badly paid, insecure, retail and service jobs, or through small-scale business activities in the informal economy, or through low-level criminality. Indeed, this explains why so many Jamaicans are forced to depend on remittances.[31]

The point I am emphasising here is that the hardships faced by deported people in Jamaica are as much about adjusting to these new realities and challenges as they are dealing with family separation and cultural alienation. Indeed, the quote from Chris early in this chapter captures exactly this, as he describes moving from the safety and security of his mother's warm three-bedroom house to 'a board house, with no TV, and not even a little piece of bed'. Put another way, the experiences of 'deportees' are not only or even primarily about out-of-placeness, but concern the most material questions in relation to securing the means of life. The bleak circumstances that await 'deportees' reveal the broader violence that defines Jamaica's economy and society. Of course, the prevalence of poverty, violence and insecurity in Jamaica is not incidental, and nor is it internal to the Jamaican polity. Jamaica's economic and social conditions have been constituted historically and globally, and in the next section I situate the experiences of 'deportees' in historical and global context.

The colonial pre-history of Jamaican citizenship

For here is the truth: each day contains much more than its own hours, or minutes, or seconds. In fact, it would be no exaggeration to say that every day contains all of history. – Kei Miller[32]

The historical facts of colonialism and slavery come to be dominating, recurring issues: not simply as events which occurred in the distant past, but as histories which eat into the present and whose afterlives still organize our contemporary post-colonial world. –
Stuart Hall[33]

In Jamaica, 'ordinary people' will invoke slavery when discussing the state of the roads, the price of goods and the lack of jobs. People in Jamaica know that today's insecurities can be explained only via slavery and colonialism. People in Jamaica also have some sense, however patchy, that their country is in debt because of loans made by the International Monetary Fund (IMF), reliance on imports and a lack of political and economic clout globally. They recognise that tourism primarily benefits foreign-owned hotel chains and cruise ship companies, and they certainly know that there are more opportunities in North America and Europe – which is why nearly everyone 'wants to go foreign'. Whether on radio talk shows or in everyday conversations in route taxis, there is an understanding that slavery, poverty, debt, crime, tourism, violence and emigration are intimately connected, and that these connections explain the 'sufferation' of Jamaican citizens today. In this section, I pick up the threads of this Jamaican 'common sense'.

As Jovan Scott Lewis explains: 'sufferation is a descriptive public discourse used in Jamaican society to denote a condition of being existentially and economically stuck'.[34] 'Sufferation' is 'not understood as discrete occurrences of financial insufficiency ... [but] as a *state*, a *condition*, and a *position* in which one economically struggles' – one of 'comprehensive and inescapable precariousness'.[35] Importantly, the concept of 'sufferation' is central to how many Jamaicans understand the continuities between their present condition and histories of slavery and colonialism. The discourse of 'sufferation' implies a particular kind of historical imagination, in which colonialism and slavery come to dominate the imaginaries of ordinary Jamaicans.[36]

It is hardly surprising that Jamaicans retain this historical imagination in relation to slavery. Jamaica was the largest British colony in the West Indies, with a disproportionate share of sugar plantations, and its economy was the most productive, diverse and complex in the British Caribbean (more than half of the estimated two million enslaved Africans brought to the British West Indies by 1807 were taken to, or through, Jamaica).[37] Indeed, Jamaica's physical and social geography – its ecology, its population and its infrastructure – have been formed by and through slavery. The island's only ruins, and indeed some of its main tourist attractions, are old plantation houses. The University of West Indies Mona campus, where I lived when I was in Kingston, was once the site of two large sugar estates, and most mornings I would walk past the ruins of the eighteenth-century aqueduct that carried water from the Hope River to those sugar estates. These ruins provide a reminder that Jamaica, like other colonial economies, was structured to produce mainly agricultural products for export to the metropole – specifically sugar, although later bananas and bauxite.[38]

Writing in the 1970s, George Beckford suggested that Jamaica could still then be described as a plantation economy because economic conditions and constraints remained structured by the plantation. Beckford noted that countries like Jamaica had been participating in world commerce for over 400 years and yet still they were characterised by profound underdevelopment.[39] Even with formal independence, the Jamaican economy has been heavily dependent on exporting a narrow range of commodities – and tourism is a kind of export here too – while the country imports manufactured goods, machinery, food and oil. Derek Walcott observes that 'absentee "power structures" [still] control the archipelago's economy',[40] and as former Jamaican Prime Minister Michael Manley put it: 'Today's world is the direct consequence and logical outcome of the economic arrangements and structures created by colonialism and imperialism'.[41] Of course, with emancipation (1834) and much later with independence (1962), the conditions of rule and of the conditions of possibility changed dramatically for Jamaicans. However, Jamaica's structural location, its place in the global economy, largely did not.[42]

Since the early 1970s, Jamaica has had a very low rate of economic growth. The response from multilateral organisations like the IMF, whose policies are determined in the interests of powerful states and corporations, has been to impose liberalisation policies that open up the economy to foreign exchange, and to privatise public assets, while also enforcing aggressive austerity policies (as in most postcolonies, the openness of the economy can be contrasted with the 'closed-ness' of borders). Unsurprisingly, these measures have increased economic and social inequality, leading to the decimation of small-scale agriculture, thus precluding Jamaica's ability to grow food for the island's population.[43] This has increased the dependence on imports, especially of food, which is prohibitively expensive in Jamaica.

Moreover, austerity measures have impacted the weakest sections of the population most severely, as the government has cut investment in education, healthcare and social programmes in the last four decades, with specifically gendered impacts.[44] As elsewhere, years of economic liberalisation and austerity have made the Jamaican economy particularly vulnerable to global economic shocks. The 2008 crash resulted in the final collapse of the major export industry in bauxite, a decline in inflows from remittances and a stagnation in earnings from tourism. Compounded by austerity and debt, these conditions have intensified the pressures on poor Jamaicans.[45]

In this light, Jamaica's *lack of sovereignty* is painfully obvious. Public debt stood at 116% of GDP in 2017. In 2014, Jamaica paid $138 million more to the IMF than it received in loans. Interest payments on these debts continue to soar, and in its 2012–2013 budget, Jamaica allocated 55% of its total expenditure to pay foreign and domestic debts. The government currently spends more than twice as much on debt repayments as on education and health combined. In 2015, Jamaica was running the most austere budget in the world, with a primary surplus of 7.5% (around double that of Greece in the same year). This programme of austerity has seen the maternal mortality rate double between 1990 and 2010, and the percentage of children finishing primary school fall from 97% to 73% over the same period. The price of basic goods, as well as electricity, has skyrocketed since the early 2000s, and youth unemployment hovers at around 25%.[46] Jamaica's economy is now therefore completely dependent on remittances and tourism.[47]

The economic violence of undemocratic IMF policies is implicated in the production of more generalised and inter-personal violence in Jamaica. In fact, to understand violence and crime in Jamaica, we need to trace the links between economic relations, party politics and local 'turf wars'.[48] Crime and violence in Jamaica have been deeply connected to party politics since the 1940s, when the two major political parties, the Jamaican Labour Party (JLP) and the People's National Party (PNP), first emerged. In exchange for voter loyalty, the two rival parties would provide work contracts or housing schemes to particular inner-city communities. 'Area leaders', or 'dons', acted as intermediaries between politicians and local constituents, deriving their power from the ability to determine who would benefit from the distribution of scarce resources (Carl Stone described these political rationalities as clientelism).[49] Crucially, though, resources and jobs were scarce precisely because Jamaica remained a 'plantation economy and society', still geared towards the export of single commodities, and still ruled by absentee power structures. In other words, government contracts were precious in the absence of other means of income and survival for Jamaica's growing urban poor.[50] In this way, the power and violence of 'dons' and 'gangs' has always been inseparable from party politics, which in turn have been structured by the deter-mining force of (neo)imperialism.

In the context of enforced austerity from 1980 onwards, the ability of the state to dispense resources to 'area leaders'

Picture 7.7. *Photo taken by Chris – East Kingston (2016)*

decreased significantly, and 'dons began to develop new sources of economic enrichment, turning away from declining government contracts and towards the transhipment of illicit drugs, primarily crack cocaine to North American markets and later the extortion of money from local commercial businesses'.[51] Unsurprisingly, these illegal and informal economies have been policed with violence, made more extreme by the ubiquity of firearms. These conditions explain Jamaica's staggering homicide rate, which is consistently one of the highest in the world. In 2017, there were 1,647 homicides in Jamaica, with a total population of just 2.9 million (compare that to England and Wales, in which there were 719 murders in the year to June 2018, with a population of 56 million).[52] The crucial point is that the hardships facing deported people are a symptom of structural and historical forces, and they are inexplicable without an examination of the devastating impact of externally imposed neoliberal economic and social policies implemented in a plantation economy and society.

This historicisation of Jamaica's contemporary economy and society is only a sketch, but it has important implications for the analysis of deportation. Crucially, it reminds us that the circumstances of deported people are not incidental, but reflect ongoing histories of colonial domination and dispossession.[53] Clearly, the inequalities between the UK and Jamaica are historical and relational – both in terms of the role of sugar and slavery in enriching the UK historically and in terms of contemporary relations of economic and political domination – and yet deportation relies on the myth that states are equal, sovereign and independent. Indeed, deportation would be much harder to justify if, rather than being labelled an administrative process through which foreigners are 'sent home', it was recast as a form of expulsion from the overdeveloped metropole to the underdeveloped former slave colony. In the next section, I develop this argument, offering a critical account of citizenship, sovereignty and the racist world order.

Citizenship, sovereignty and the racist world order

So far in this chapter, I have described the hardships faced by deported people when they return to Jamaica. I have situated their experiences of poverty and insecurity in relation to structural adjustment, enforced austerity and debt, which are explicable only with reference to histories of slavery and colonialism. Put most simply, when people are deported from the UK to Jamaica they are expelled from the (over)developed former metropole to the underdeveloped former slave colony, and yet these historical entanglements and relations are obscured through liberal claims surrounding citizenship, sovereignty and the rule of law. For this reason, it is necessary not only to recognise that slavery and colonialism eat into the present, but to use this as the starting point for thinking about citizenship and sovereignty differently.

As should now be self-evident, deported people live their Jamaican citizenship in relation to their British alienage.[54] For Jason, Ricardo, Chris and Denico, Jamaican citizenship was inseparable from their non-citizenship in the UK, but also their exclusion from other countries in the 'global North'. For example, when Denico was deported to Jamaica, his police record travelled with him. This meant that not only was he prevented from returning to the UK, he was also unable to migrate to North America, because his criminal record blocked him from securing a visa in the US or Canada. Denico was prevented from fleeing his predicament in Jamaica – one of isolation, underpaid work and profoundly limited opportunities – and in this way his citizenship status immobilised him. Denico was contained by his Jamaican nationality and by his criminal record, which were determined by the modern technologies that identify and fix individuals (passports, finger prints, electronic databases).[55] In this way, citizenship works as an international 'geography of containment'.[56]

For the late Barry Hindess, whose writing on citizenship has profoundly shaped my own thinking, it is useful to view citizenship not only in terms of internalist relations between a given state and its citizens, but also as 'a marker of identification, advising state and nonstate agencies of the particular state to which an individual belongs'.[57] Hindess notes that citizenship operates at the international level by allocating each individual to a state. The individual is then the responsibility of that state, and not the responsibility of other states. In this light, deportation is simply the realisation of citizenship: when individuals are deported they are 'returned home', legally and spatially reassigned to the state that they belong to. Deportation might be an extraordinarily violent and naked form of state power, but, as William Walters notes, 'it is actually quite fundamental and immanent to the modern regime of citizenship'.[58]

This way of describing citizenship is especially relevant for Jamaican nationals, who lack many of the rights ordinarily seen as fundamental to liberal citizenship, and yet whose Jamaican-ness is experienced precisely as 'a marker of identification' at the international level, a legal-political status which symbolises global marginality and restricted mobility.[59] Especially for 'deportees', Jamaican citizenship is not primarily about rights and responsibilities in relation to the Jamaican state, but represents a way of being positioned, managed and fixed globally. Indeed, citizenship as a legal regime is necessarily international: the men in this book were not only defined as aliens and non-citizens in the UK, they also had to be verified and produced as citizens of Jamaica (see Chapter 8). Both alienage in the UK *and* formal legal belonging in Jamaica were necessary to realise deportation, and thus citizenship is a 'supranational regime of government', an *international regime*, and a legal status which operates at the *global scale*.[60]

These observations are important when citizenship is so often celebrated as an ideal of political engagement and subjectivity.[61] Celebratory accounts of citizenship obscure its global function as a 'supranational regime of government', one which determines who belongs where, and in effect immobilising the global poor in conditions of scarcity (while also mobilising them in particular ways, as illegalised or temporary labour).[62] The experiences of 'deportees' highlight that citizenship is not some guarantee of homey belonging and political membership, but rather a global regime for the fixing of unequal populations.

If citizenship is in fact the global regime for the management of unequal populations, then it works to reproduce and perpetuate racialised global disparities forged through slavery and colonialism.[63] As I have already noted, the inequalities between nation-states and their populations are not incidental: they reflect histories of colonialism and its constitutive processes of domination, dispossession and uneven development. What is specifically postcolonial about today's global racial order, however, is that the racialised global poor are governed not as colonial subjects but as citizens of independent nation-states. They are governed through citizenship and incorporated into the global as citizens.[64] In this context, discourses on *sovereignty* prove ideologically pivotal, obscuring historical continuities through references to the apparent independence of formerly colonised nation-states.

Sovereignty refers to the idea that each state has ultimate authority over a particular territory and population, and that this authority is recognised by other states in the international system. However, in practice, assertions of sovereignty are highly abstract, and the formal sovereignty of nation-states tells us little about the historical, political and economic relations that organise international relations.[65] Indeed, it is precisely by acknowledging Jamaica's sovereignty, even while economically dominating the country, that countries like the UK and the USA have managed to claim that violence and poverty in Jamaica are somehow effects of Jamaican 'national policy' and the 'national economy'.[66] This nationalisation of Jamaica's problems also constructs the Jamaican citizenry as the sole responsibility of the Jamaican state, which then makes deportation not only possible but wholly legitimate.[67] But what does sovereignty actually mean in a country weighed down by the unrepaired histories of slavery and empire, and destabilised by the ongoing economic violence of structural adjustment, enforced austerity and debt?

In fact, Jamaican sovereignty is a *void sovereignty* – a term I borrow from Merav Amir in her discussion of Israeli statecraft in the West Bank. Amir argues that it is through the fabrication of a Palestinian sovereignty (via the Palestinian Authority) that the Israeli government is able to deny its responsibility for the welfare of the Palestinian population under occupation. The Israeli state is therefore able to double down on security-oriented forms of domination, because the responsibility to care for the occupied Palestinian population has been outsourced to the nominally sovereign Palestinian Authority. This fabrication of a void sovereignty – i.e. attributing to the Palestinian Authority wholly illusory forms of political authority and defining the Palestinian population as 'its responsibility' – is central to the justification for military occupation.[68]

While Jamaica is not Palestine (although Palestine often functions as a laboratory for emergent forms of coercive state power),[69] this fabrication of sovereignty, a void sovereignty, does seem to capture the meanings of sovereignty in many formerly colonised states – whether in Africa, Asia or the Americas.[70] Countries like Jamaica are unable to provide their citizens with the basic means of life, and this is largely an effect of their subjection to political and economic domination from without, and yet because these states are *independent*, they are blamed for any shortfall. As with the Palestinian Authority, the Jamaican state is afforded only illusory forms of political and economic power, and yet through the ideology of *sovereignty* the 'sufferation' of the Jamaican population is described as an effect of Jamaica's 'national economy' and 'national policies'.[71] In this light, sovereignty is not only void, it is also a kind of ruse, an ideological trick through which powerlessness and subjection are recast in terms democracy, citizenship and freedom.

As I have argued, liberal claims surrounding citizenship and sovereignty work to obscure the ongoing relevance of racism and colonialism in structuring global disparities. One way to rethink these relationships would be to demonstrate that citizenship, in a postcolonial world, does remarkably similar kinds of work to that performed by race under empire: producing fixed legal and social distinctions between cultural/ethnic/national groups; defining who can move and how; and justifying uneven development, differentiated incorporation into markets and stark inequalities between populations. Race and citizenship are both systems of population management – both work to define where people belong, and both underwrite legal and coercive forms of state power which fix people in social and literal space. Recognising the connection between racial and citizenship regimes helps us develop a more satisfactory account of what has changed and what has remained the same after the end of formal colonial rule, and by thinking about citizenship in this way we might be able to improve our understanding of what race and racism are and how they function.[72]

In this regard, we should note that racial differences and hierarchies have always been centrally constituted by relations of mobility (see Chapter 8), and both colonial states and contemporary liberal states have been centrally concerned with the ordering of mobility.[73] As Robert Young argues, 'colonialism operated through a forced symbiosis between territorialization as, quite literally, plantation, and the demands for labour which involved the commodification of bodies and their exchange through international trade'.[74] As Ann Stoler argues, the colony was '*a principle of managed mobilities*, mobilizing and immobilizing populations according to a set of changing rules and hierarchies that orders social kinds: those eligible for recruitment, for resettlement, for disposal, for aid, or for coerced labor and those who are forcibly confined'.[75] Today, liberal states describe their immigration policies in terms of 'managed migration', as they seek to fill gaps in labour markets while excluding and illegalising the vast majority of the global poor.[76] Indeed, the combined logics of territorialisation and selective mobilisation characterise contemporary immigration regimes, and the ordering of mobility remains constitutive of racial difference.[77]

This way of conceptualising race and racism – historically, spatially and globally – requires moving beyond definitions of racism as intolerance, discrimination and prejudice. To understand the contemporary racial ordering of the world, it is important to view racism in terms of the reproduction of structural and material colonial-racial inequalities in the present.[78] This is where critical theorisations of citizenship and sovereignty become especially urgent, because nationality is the key legal mechanism through which racialised global disparities are obscured and legitimated.[79] Immigration controls might rely on the disavowal of 'race', but they inevitably organise the world in its image.[80] To bring continuities between then and now into view, we need to think about racism not only in terms of ideologies of biological and cultural superiority, but to recognise that race and racism are fundamentally constituted by the spatial and legal ordering of global populations, markets and mobilities.[81]

Conclusion

This chapter has moved from the specific experiences of 'deportees' to a broad set of arguments about what citizenship does in the world. The discussion opened with a description of the hardships faced by deported people in Jamaica, focusing on poverty, violence, unemployment, social isolation and mental ill-health. I related these experiences to the plight of other Jamaicans struggling to survive on the island, and argued that the struggles of deported people are not only, or even primarily, about family separation and cultural alienation, but relate to the basic need for shelter, income and security. After describing how difficult deported people find it to secure the means of life, I sought to situate these experiences in global and historical context, explaining Jamaica's contemporary economic and social relations in terms of the structuring force of slavery and colonialism. I argued that structural adjustment, debt and enforced austerity have been implemented in an economy and society still structured by the plantation.

Indeed, once we recognise the colonial formation of the nation-state system, the claim that citizenship has nothing to do with race and racism becomes increasingly untenable.[82] If history does not pass but accumulates, then citizenship bears the imprint and the weight of race, and no amount of liberal pretension should obscure the colonial pre-history of contemporary citizenship.[83] Of course, the poor in formerly colonised countries are no longer governed as imperial subjects, and racial hierarchies are no longer formalised in law, but the global poor are governed *through citizenship*, which fixes them in space and in law. This fixing in space and law reaffirms global inequalities formed through colonialism, and in this way citizenship reproduces colonial-racial hierarchies in the present. Put another way, citizenship might appear to be a neutral and eminently sensible system for dividing up the global population, but it does so along grooves and map lines formed through colonialism. As a result, citizenship works as a system of colonial forgetting and racial disavowal.

However, stating that citizenship racialises the world by fixing unequal populations in space and law is only the first step. The next set of questions concern how citizenship distinctions are actually produced and enforced. What are the specific policy arrangements and political relationships through which immigration controls are enforced and mobilities governed? What do these historically specific arrangements reveal about international relations and global order? And for my purposes, what do the specific deportation arrangements between the UK and Jamaica reveal about racism, citizenship and the ordering of mobility? It is to these complex questions that I turn in the next chapter.

Chapter 8

Deportation as foreign policy: meanings of development and the ordering of (im)mobility

In the last chapter, I developed a critical account of citizenship from the perspective of the 'deportee'. I described people's struggles post-deportation, with a particular focus on Chris's experiences in East Kingston, and argued that poverty, insecurity and frustrated mobilities characterise citizenship for Jamaica's poor more generally. In this sense, the effective immobilisation of 'deportees' is symptomatic of the wider function of citizenship as a global regime which fixes people in space and in law. In this chapter, however, I want to think more carefully about how citizenship status is actually determined, by states and between governments, within deportation proceedings. Examining the inter-state relations that shape deportation practices allows me to extend and develop the arguments on race, citizenship and mobility introduced in the last chapter.

In a book about deportation stories, it is easy to overlook inter-state relations. As I worked on *Deporting Black Britons*, I found myself thinking about deportation primarily in terms of the before and after: the 'before' referring to people's lives in Britain – and their experiences of racism, criminalisation and illegalisation – while the 'after' refers to post-deportation in Jamaica, and people's experiences of poverty, social isolation and insecurity on their return. In this framing, the moment of deportation itself becomes the central turning point in each biography, the fulcrum around which each story pivots. The problem with this before and after frame, however, is that it misses what happens in between, and between states in particular.[1]

By the 'in between' I do not simply mean the flight. In fact, academic and journalistic accounts often focus on the flight itself as a space of violence.[2] Instead, I mean the ways in which deportations are arranged between deporting and receiving states. My point is that we miss something if we describe deportation too briskly in terms of a familiar chronology: illegalisation and detention; the brutality of forced expulsion; followed, finally, by abandonment and isolation in unfamiliar 'homelands'. What is missed is the necessary involvement of the receiving state in deportation, the ways in which the Jamaican government in this instance is absolutely fundamental to the deportation process. Once we recognise that deportation relies on working relationships between states, and often also NGOs, we must then situate deportation within the wider field of bilateral, foreign policy relations of which it forms a part.[3]

For me, Open Arms Drop in Centre was the best place from which to appreciate these inter-state relations. The homeless shelter in East Kingston has allocated beds for destitute 'deportees' funded directly by the British government through the aid budget – as part of the Reintegration and Rehabilitation Programme (RRP) in particular.[4] Consider, for example, the fact that Jason had his own room in Open Arms. While it was more of box, with thin partition walls and bed bugs in the mattress, Jason was provided with a room, with a door and a key, rather than a bed in the shared dormitory, because he was a 'deportee' from the UK. Indeed, it was in Kingston that Jason was first provided with consistent shelter paid for by the 'British taxpayer'.

As noted in Chapter 1, however, the UK does not fund Open Arms out of goodwill, but primarily to facilitate deportation. Open Arms is regularly cited by the Home Office to justify sending people back to Jamaica when they have no family

connections or means of social support on the island, suppos-
edly because the centre prevents destitution and helps deported
people to 'reintegrate'. In this way, Open Arms is not only a
'zone of social abandonment'[5] – a place where the unwanted and
sick are warehoused in a country with no functioning welfare
state – it is also a site of 'humanitarian bordering', and one
which actively facilitates UK deportations.[6] Importantly, Open
Arms has been funded through the UK's aid budget, as Official
Development Assistance, and this reminds us that immigration
controls are increasingly implemented through development and
aid policy.[7]

This means that to situate deportation in wider political
context, we need to think about contemporary meanings of
development. As I demonstrate in what follows, contemporary
UK development policy is preoccupied with security, bordering
and trade, all of which concern the management of mobilities.
We should therefore analyse immigration controls in relation
to the wider government of mobility, which can advance our
understanding of the connection between race and citizenship
discussed in the previous chapter.

Arranging deportation and 'coordinating the reintegration process'

In a world fully territorialised into nation-states, there is no
banishment, only return. As a result, every non-citizen that the
British government wants to deport must also be (made to be)
a citizen of somewhere else, and they must be verified as such
by both deporting and receiving states.[8] In short, deportation
is a form of expulsion that relies on inter-state cooperation and
this means that deportation is embedded within a wider field of
bilateral politics. To explore this point, let me first describe how
deportations are actually arranged, once the UK decides it wants
to send an individual to Jamaica.

Before anyone is deported, they must first be verified as a Jamaican national. Once verified, they can then be provided with travel documents by the Jamaican government (the Jamaican authorities usually have to provide individuals with emergency travel documents because most do not have valid Jamaican passports). To better understand how individuals are actually verified as Jamaican, I interviewed the Policy Director at the Border Security and Control Unit within the Ministry of National Security in Kingston.

When the UK authorities want to deport someone to Jamaica, they contact the Jamaican authorities. The Jamaican authorities, in particular the Passport Agency, will then attempt to find records on the individual, and in most instances will be able to provide emergency travel documents based on available records. However, if documentation is not easy to locate – for example, if the person has not had a Jamaican passport for decades and Jamaican agencies cannot locate a birth certificate – the prospective 'deportee' may be interviewed by staff from the Jamaican High Commission in the UK. These interviews usually take place in British detention centres, as Jamaican state officials posted in London interview prospective Jamaican nationals to acquire details of their personal history.[9]

In some cases, officials back in Jamaica then attempt to verify the information gleaned from these interviews. They might for instance question neighbours, family members and school teachers in Jamaica to confirm details of personal histories, which can thereby prove that the individual currently detained in Britain did grow up in Jamaica and is indeed a Jamaican national. This process makes deportation possible where the official records fall short. The Policy Director explained that, in most cases, the Jamaican authorities are able to identify Jamaican nationals through these methods of multi-agency cooperation (although this does not mean that people are not wrongfully deported).[10]

Casting a critical eye on these arrangements, we might ask why the Jamaican authorities prove so compliant. Why do they facilitate, indeed expedite, deportation in cases where the individuals concerned have been away for Jamaica for so long, and therefore have no documents? When I asked the Policy Director how he felt about accepting 'deportees' who had few memories of the island, he replied:

> POLICY DIRECTOR: There's not much we can do. We are obliged to accept people who have not been here, but who are Jamaicans, perhaps who left here as children. That presents a challenge. The most we can do is to coordinate the reintegration process, in terms of partnering with NGOs.

In some ways, the Policy Director is right here: the Jamaican government is obliged to accept its own nationals, just as the UK government is British nationals. This is an *effect of citizenship* as the international regime which allocates individuals to states. However, the bilateral working relationship between the UK and Jamaica constitutes more than mere obligation. The Jamaican government is proactive in the re-documentation process, thereby expediting UK immigration controls, whereas countries like China, Iran and Zimbabwe have at different times made it difficult for the UK to deport their nationals (there are many ways to be obstructive when it comes to verifying and documenting people).[11] Clearly, then, the Policy Director's claim that the Jamaican government has no choice but to comply obscures the Jamaican government's wider political relationships with deporting states, like the US, Canada and the UK. These relationships could be otherwise.

Further, when the Policy Director states that the most the Jamaican authorities can do is ease the reintegration process by 'partnering with NGOs', he is in fact referring to NGOs whose work is directly funded, and therefore made possible, by the British government. Indeed, both the Open Arms Drop in Centre and the National Organization of Deported Migrants

(NODM) have been funded by the British government through the aid budget, and therefore reflecting on these local NGOs allows for a deeper appreciation of the wider bilateral arrangements that frame deportation practices.

Open Arms Drop in Centre – a prison and a shelter

Open Arms Drop in Centre is just off the main road that runs east from downtown Kingston towards Rockfort, Harbour View and the airport, and it is situated between two notoriously dangerous 'garrison towns', Raetown and Dunkirk.[12] The Centre was established in 2006, operating as both a walk-in day centre for Kingston's homeless and as a night shelter, with two large dormitories that could accommodate around 60 men. In 2011, the British government began funding Open Arms, and in return a few, small, individual rooms were set up, and reserved for destitute men deported from the UK.

I visited Open Arms several times, sometimes to see Jason, who lived there between 2014 and 2017, but mostly in the hope of meeting other deported persons. I was always struck by how many men were just sat gazing into space. Some were heavily medicated, and some physically disabled, but many were simply afraid to leave the compound, and so they sat in the shade of the large mango tree in the main yard, doing very little. Of the roughly 60 residents, there were several people who had been deported from the UK (between 5 and 10 on average), and probably more who had been deported from North America.

One afternoon in October 2015, I wanted to record interviews with Jason and I asked the management at Open Arms if we could use a room. They unlocked the IT suite for us, and Jason immediately wanted to go on Facebook. It took me several attempts to get him away from the screen and to start talking to me, and by the time we finally began recording, a few other residents had slunk in and started using the computers. Jason felt uncomfortable telling his story in their presence and so I approached the management to see if there was a quieter room we could use. A member of staff explained that the other residents should not have been in there and followed me back to the computer room to reprimand them. The manager shouted at the four men, like children, and reminded them that the computer room was out of bounds. Heads down, the men returned to the main yard.

I researched Open Arms online later, and found one article which said that 'UK money' had gone towards the 'completion of renovation works at Open Arms Drop in Centre to provide an administrative and counselling space as well as computer lab and training area'.[13] The computer room, then, was funded by the British taxpayer, but seemingly was not available for use until a British PhD student, also funded by the British taxpayer, requested space in which to conduct a research interview.

A few weeks later, I met with a diplomat from the British High Commission in Kingston, and asked him about his perspective on Open Arms. He was the Migration Delivery Officer, responsible for liaising with Open Arms and NODM and ensuring the smooth functioning of UK immigration policy in Jamaica. When we met, I asked him several questions about the work of the British High Commission in relation to deportation. He prefaced his comments by firstly claiming that there was a broad consensus on deportation. As he saw it, in both the UK and Jamaica, people understood that those who break the rules or commit criminal offences should be deported. However, he did acknowledge that perfectly legitimate deportations sometimes had unfortunate consequences for 'deportees' themselves. What deported people needed, he thought, was assistance with 're-integration', and Open Arms offered an important part of this through the provision of emergency accommodation. Indeed, he thought that UK funding for Open Arms demonstrated the humaneness of British policy and politics, and the value of good diplomacy. His impressions from visiting Open Arms, however, clearly differed markedly from mine.

Shedding some light on this, Chris told me that whenever there was an arranged visit from the British High Commission, or any other stakeholders, the management at Open Arms would ask people like Chris to return and speak with visitors about how the Centre had helped them progress, 'success stories' now that they were housed and employed. When journalists from the *Jamaica Observer* visited, they noted that 'participants were busy doing yard work, working in the thrift shop on the premises and socialising', and the manager told journalists that some former residents had 'gone on to be doctors, lawyers and teachers', thanks to the support of Open Arms.[14]

I knew several men who were living or had lived in Open Arms, and they offered a much less flattering picture of the Centre. Some explained that the management used 'tough love', and they remained grateful for the shelter and its support. But others accused the management of taking donated resources for themselves and overmedicating residents (one man claimed that they put drugs in the food). Jason complained about rats in his room and all of the men spoke about bed bugs. There were also concerns about personal security, following several break-ins, in which armed men climbed the fence and stole phones and other electronic items from the residents. On several occasions, residents were robbed just outside the compound, and when I asked the manager about one particular incident, in which Devon, the young man featured at the beginning of the book, was violently robbed of his phone, she replied: 'Oh he gives as good as he gets'. A few weeks earlier she had kicked Devon out, and with nowhere else to go he stayed under a tree on the adjacent field until she let him return.

Most of the residents I spoke with said that the image presented to funders, stakeholders and the general public was very different to the one they knew. This became particularly clear to me when I heard the manager speaking on the Jamaican radio in March 2019 (nine months before she won an MBE for her work supporting Jamaica's 'invisibles' at Open Arms).[15] Her descriptions of Open Arms during this radio interview seemed misleading, at best. She said that homeless 'deportees' were always received with 'open arms', that they had access to good facilities and three meals a day (in fact the meals were small and the facilities basic) and that residents received training in barbering (which may have happened at some point, but there were no active training schemes during all the time I was in Kingston). She then claimed that residents were assisted with securing jobs and qualifications (which was almost wholly untrue), that they were allowed to access the computers (as noted, the computer room was locked most of the time) and that they were taken on trips outside Kingston every three months (I did not know anyone who knew anything about these trips). She then stated that residents were assisted with emergency funds when necessary (I knew no one who had accessed them) and were provided with comprehensive support to help them 'rehabilitate' (a telling word choice).

This idea that residents need to be 'rehabilitated' captures the disciplinary nature of Open Arms. For example, in one article in the *Jamaica Observer* residents were described by management as needing to 'become productive and functional through rehabilitation … until they are ready to re-enter society'.[16] As the manager put it in the same article:

> Many of them coming off the streets are battered, bruised, very anti-social, they have a lot of relationship problems, so we tend to call them our babies when they come in and we have persons working alongside them.[17]

This infantilising and 'rehabilitative' tone might explain why residents so often complained of a lack of respect. Many deported persons, in particular, viewed themselves not as 'battered, bruised, [and] very antisocial', but as competent individuals who had been banished to an unfamiliar and difficult place.

I am not relaying these accounts simply to shame the management at Open Arms. All the men I spoke to were glad the Centre existed. Open Arms is usually preferable to roughing it on the streets (although Jason took his chances after three years) and it certainly has better facilities than the other large homeless shelter in downtown Kingston (the Marie Atkins night shelter). Indeed, these reflections on Open Arms are my own, not those of the residents I knew, who might describe and evaluate the Centre in very different ways. However, I do think it is important to voice these critical observations, because the cuddly and empowering version of Open Arms is the one on public record (at least in Jamaica and to relevant stakeholders), and this curated version is unchallengeable by those who live there. The residents themselves are ignored and silenced – described as battered, bruised and very antisocial – and their destitution is blamed on their own moral and behavioural failures.

In fact, for many of the residents, Open Arms was a *site of confinement*, even if disguised as something humanitarian and enfranchising. Or perhaps more precisely, Open Arms was *both a shelter and a prison*, and we might describe the Jamaican nation-state in the same way.[18] Just as Open Arms can offer residents an important lifeline, a space of relative safety compared with rough sleeping on the streets, being a citizen of Jamaica is usually preferable to statelessness. Indeed, Open Arms, like the Jamaican state more broadly, has multiple and contradictory functions, some of them potentially furthering justice and providing care, but in the context of persistent poverty and immobility. No one is forcing the residents of Open Arms to stay put, but if they leave it is unclear where they will go – just as citizens of Jamaica more broadly have the right to leave the island, but no concomitant right to enter another state's territory. Indeed, this was Kemoy's predicament described in the previous chapter; he

Pictures 8.1 and 8.2. *Pictures inside Open Arms dormitories (2016)*

felt trapped both as a resident of Open Arms and as a citizen of Jamaica, and for him one form of confinement was lived through the other.

The National Organization of Deported Migrants – 'a "pact with the devil"'?

Open Arms is a deeply unsettling place, and the only way I know how to describe it is unsympathetically. NODM, on the other hand, was the organisation that hosted me, introduced me to deported people and thus made this book possible. I know the work of NODM intimately, in some ways I have been a part of it, and I remain deeply indebted to the organisation and its staff – particularly the President, Ossie. Despite my obvious biases, however, it was clear to me that NODM was compromised by its dependence on UK funding. When NODM met deported people after they landed, they travelled to and from Montego Bay airport in a minivan bought and insured with UK money. When NODM assisted people with acquiring national identification and clearing items through customs, the staff doing this work were paid with UK funds. Indeed, the rented office space, the computers and all the staff's wages were funded by the UK government, through the aid budget.

Like Open Arms, NODM is regularly cited in deportation decision letters, its 'support services' used to justify further removals. This fraught relationship with the British government is something NODM has always wrestled with, and it is worth turning to the words of the late Professor Bernard Headley on this question. Headley, a criminologist and sociologist who was central to establishing NODM and to facilitating my work with the organisation, challenged the demonisation of 'deportees' in Jamaica within his own research:

> Behind the British Home Office–NODM 'alliance' are the strong racial and anti-immigrant elements in Britain's politics of illegality, crime, terrorism and punishment (similar to the situation across the pond, in America).... So, in a distressing way, NODM's relationship with the British government can be called dubious, a 'pact with the devil' that it smacks of colluding with a deportation 'enemy.' 'There's not that much difference,' cynics have charged, between this arrangement and the 'treaty' British slave owners signed with the Maroons. The Maroons agreed, for the guarantee of their freedom, to return to the plantation runaway slaves seeking their freedom. In like manner, NODM signed on – also for contractual guarantees – to help take off British hands a class of like (them-selves) 'undesirables.'[19]

Clearly, NODM has been under no illusions about its relationship with the British government. However, unlike Open Arms, it does not define its work as rehabilitative, disciplinary or humanitarian, but as eminently practical and, indeed, political (note that NODM stands for the National Organization *of*, and not *for*, Deported Migrants). Of course, the main problem is that, like Open Arms, the existence of NODM is used to justify further deportations, and Ossie and I spent many hours 'reasoning' on this question. Where I was more concerned with frustrating UK immigration policy and preventing deportation in the first place, Ossie was more focused on assisting deported people once they landed. As deported migrants themselves, staff at NODM were oriented towards *post*-deportation, concerned with how they could offer people some practical support once they returned to Jamaica. The way they found to do this work was through 'collaboration' with the British government.

It remains undeniable, however, that, from the UK perspective, funding NODM is intended to facilitate deportation. Within UK immigration law, the ability of deported persons to 'reintegrate' post-deportation is an active human rights consideration, and so the existence of Open Arms and NODM strengthens Home Office arguments for deportation, by demonstrating that deported people will be supported on their return. UK funding for the 'reintegration and rehabilitation' of deported persons therefore works to bolster the legality of future deportations. However, the Reintegration and Rehabilitation Programme is also intended to encourage people facing deportation to comply with their removal, the idea being that if individuals facing deportation think that they will be safe and well supported on their return, then they are more likely to accept their deportation.

This attempt at persuasion is most apparent in the 15-minute short film *Coming Home to Jamaica*, funded and produced by the UK government, which showcases 'reintegration services' in Jamaica, focusing mostly on NODM (the video was also funded through the Reintegration and Rehabilitation Programme).[20] According to the Foreign and Commonwealth Office on its YouTube channel, the video is intended to 'give deported migrants a visual impression of what to expect upon arrival and allay any apprehension about resettling in their home country'.[21] The video is accompanied by uplifting music, but it is hard to imagine that its feel-good, hopeful spin is particularly reassuring for people facing deportation.

In fact, the video is a follow-up to the *Coming Home to Jamaica* booklet, which was intended for deported people to read either before they fly or once they land.[22] The booklet has been updated several times since its first print, but the sixth edition, from 2014, opens:

This guide has been put together through the collaboration of a group of dedicated Jamaican not-for-profit organisations with the support of the British High Commission in Kingston and the Ministry of National Security [in Jamaica]. The guide compliments the 'Coming Home to Jamaica' DVD. We hope that you find it useful as you prepare for your return to Jamaica and re-settle back on this beautiful, diverse island![23]

The booklet goes on to signpost people to key services and responds to practical questions about return to Jamaica. It explains the process once a person lands in Jamaica, and provides information on healthcare, churches, national documentation, and skills and training. It provides contact details for NODM, Open Arms and other organisations running relevant services. In fact, part of NODM's contractual obligations with the UK government involve handing out these booklets to the returnees collected from the airport.

Interestingly, when the booklet was first published online, in 2013, it received some bad press in several UK newspapers and media outlets.[24] This criticism focused mostly on the list of 'do's and 'don't's towards the back of the booklet, which included: 'Try to be "Jamaican" – use local accents and dialect (overseas accents can attract unwanted attention)'. Of course, a Foreign Office document stating that deported people should 'Try to be "Jamaican"' is remarkable and warrants criticism, but it is interesting that the document itself was primarily written by deported migrants at NODM, and was therefore based on their own post-deportation experiences.

For NODM, the advice 'try to be Jamaican', while crude, refers to a very real set of concerns about the hypervisibility and vulnerability of involuntarily returned migrants (e.g. in relation to violence, robbery and extortion, as discussed in the previous chapter). NODM's concern is with supporting deported migrants in Jamaica, and so how its advice is read in the UK is not within its primary field of vision. This captures the tension between NODM's practical approach, and its dependence on UK funding, when contrasted with the critique of the UK immigration policy emanating from anti-racists in Britain (my conversations with Ossie rehearsed a version of this). As far as Ossie and NODM are concerned, there is work to be done supporting deported migrants in Jamaica, and UK funding allows them to do it. While this might be compromising, it is better than nothing, and this was brought into sharp relief in March 2019, when the UK decided it would discontinue funding NODM.

I was in Jamaica at the time, and when Ossie explained that the organisation was losing its funding, we spent hours in the NODM office discussing how we might crowdfund or secure money from other sources. NODM was in crisis mode, and Ossie was committed to ensuring the organisation was not simply shut down. In the end, though, after the journalist Emily Dugan reported the story for BuzzFeed online, the UK reversed its decision and committed to maintaining funding for NODM – although on a much reduced and piecemeal basis.[25] NODM would now have to invoice for services rather than receiving a full grant with attached job posts. At the time of writing, it remains unclear whether the organisation will be able to work to this arrangement. For NODM, it is difficult to know how to maintain staff, arrange working hours and afford rent and utilities when income is based on invoicing for services. Perhaps just as the only thing worse than being exploited by capitalism is not being exploited by capitalism, the only thing worse than being funded by the UK government is not being funded at all.

***

I have already made clear that NODM and Open Arms were funded through the same British development programme: the Reintegration and Rehabilitation Programme (RRP). However, they were not the only organisations or initiatives funded within the RRP.[26] In fact, while NODM and Open Arms might be described as 'service providers', most of the schemes within this programme had no such humanitarian pretence. Indeed, the RRP included several schemes which were designed to 'build capacity' within Jamaican state institutions – especially within the police and immigration authorities. As such, the RRP was not only, or even primarily, about supporting 'deported persons', but about enabling the Jamaican government to better monitor, manage and police risky populations.[27]

For example, in 2015 RRP funds were used in the 'construction of an archive dome to store old passport records' – clearly to ensure Jamaican nationals would be easier to *re-document* should the UK want to deport them.[28] Funding was also provided for the Jamaican Passport, Immigration and Citizenship Agency more broadly, to improve its work identifying and documenting Jamaican nationals. Through these schemes, the UK effectively funded the Jamaican government to modernise technologies of national identification and verification, with the intention of expediting deportation and preventing people from re-migrating through irregular means.[29] The RRP also included technical assistance and funding for the Jamaican Ministry of National Security, which includes the police force, to improve its ability to monitor deportees and 'local offenders', and RRP funds were also channelled into the management of the prison population, with substantial sums allocated to the Department of Correctional Facilities – specifically for vocational training and literacy programmes, and for rehabilitative activities with local ex-offenders.[30]

At this point we might ask why 'deported persons' and 'local offenders' fall under the same development programme (its full name being the Rehabilitation and Reintegration of Local Offender and Deported Persons Programme). Why are both crime and immigration control so central to this Official Development Assistance programme? Clearly, this reveals something important about how the UK spends its aid budget, namely on bordering and securitisation programmes targeting 'risky' populations. Indeed, the RRP reveals some of the principal and most troubling meanings of contemporary development, and it is therefore worth situating the programme in broader context.[31]

Meanings of development: securitisation, bordering and trade

The UK's Reintegration and Rehabilitation Programme in Jamaica is symptomatic of a wider emphasis on security and bordering within the politics of development.[32] Within development discourse, it has long been axiomatic that security is necessary for development. That is, for development initiatives to be most effective, they need to be implemented in the absence of internal conflict, war and political instability. As Mark Duffield explains:

> Within policy discourse, the unrestrained barbarism of internal war destroys the very possibility of self-reproduction; it wrecks public infrastructures, ruins livelihood systems, fragments social solidarity and tips the dynamics of unsecured population into disequilibrium, compounding the risk of enduring cycles of violence, displacement and migration. Consequently, instead of achieving sustainable development through improving self-reliance, internal war becomes 'development in reverse'. Moreover, because it unleashes migratory flows, asylum seekers, transborder shadow economies, international criminal networks and so on, it undermines international containment and exposes mass society to potentially catastrophic forms of unsustainable global circulation.[33]

Duffield explains that concerns around security are intimately connected to fears of uncontrolled migration, transnational crime and terrorism. Insecurity is defined in terms of 'unsustainable global circulation'. Importantly, the overarching emphasis on security represents a shift in the politics of development, away from 'conceptions of state-led modernization, industrialization and the primacy of economic growth' and towards a politics of containment, securitisation and bordering. This marks an end to 'earlier modernist assumptions that the underdeveloped world would, after passing through various stages, come to resemble the developed'.[34]

This shift in development policy reflects wider shifts under late capitalism. As vast swathes of the global population are increasingly considered superfluous, and wealth and capital are concentrated in the hands of an ever smaller minority, it is unsurprising that development now needs to be *sustainable*.[35] In the context of climate disaster, and the intensification of processes of dispossession and extraction, there are diminishing opportunities for survival/subsistence either within or outside the capture of the market, and therefore the objects of development, the global poor, are increasingly required to be self-reliant and resilient.[36] Indeed, the recognition of scarcity organises the anxieties of our time, and it has become increasingly difficult to imagine that everyone will one day be included (either as producers or consumers).[37] This recognition of scarcity creates renewed concerns about surplus populations and 'waste humanity', and about the global risks emanating from the world's displaced and unproductive masses.[38] Most importantly, this 'waste humanity' is seen to produce insecurity through unruly human mobilities, what Duffield describes as 'unsustainable global circulation'.

This is the context in which development becomes a form of containment, and we witness the shift towards 'non-material development' (i.e. sustainable development and resilience) and micro-behavioural approaches to alleviating poverty.[39] In short, development policy, even on its own terms, is now less about modernisation, tackling inequality and providing aid for the world's poorest, and more about security, 'resilience' and bordering.[40] Of course, development policy has never really been about charity or challenging inequality, and has always been defined by powerful states in the interests of capitalist development; however, the move from development as aid to development as security and bordering does mark a significant change in global politics.[41]

Most relevant for my purposes is that recent development policies have centred bordering in much more explicit and expansive ways. Today, it is impossible to consider borders and development in isolation – they are fundamental to one another's operation (and perhaps it is the expansion and intensification of bordering practices everywhere that have seen borders colonise development: its networks, funding streams and policy language).[42] Most obviously, Northern states are increasingly channelling development funds towards controlling migration in so-called 'source' and 'transit' countries.[43]

The most striking example here relates to the development policies of the European Union (EU) and its individual member states. Whether formally or informally, European aid is increasingly conditioned to encourage recipient states, primarily in Africa and the Middle East, to cooperate with European migration and border control efforts. The EU has made deals with Libya, Sudan, Mali, Niger, Senegal, Morocco, Turkey and many other 'source' or 'transit' countries. The range of these EU schemes is bewildering and the funds being channelled into them staggering. There is the Integrated Border Management Fund, the Neighbourhood, Development and International Cooperation Instrument, the New Partnership Framework (building on and expanding the EU–Turkey Plan), the EU Emergency Trust Fund for Africa, and various migration compacts and readmission agreements signed with several non-EU states, in which border control objectives are linked with development objectives.[44]

These programmes involve securing borders with more police, border guards and detention centres, but they also comprise a wider set of ostensibly humanitarian programmes. Countless EU-funded schemes are designed to discourage prospective migrants from attempting the journey to Europe in the first place, often through educational and NGO-led programmes.[45] Central to these programmes is the claim that to save people you have to prevent them from moving. Bordering becomes aid because it is about saving lives. This amounts to a kind of 'compassionate repression',[46] which explains the combination of tough border security and humanitarianism at Europe's borders, especially in the Mediterranean Sea, where the deathly spectacle of migration and bordering is most horrifying.[47]

In this context, William Walters has identified the emergence of 'humanitarian borders', which he suggests offer a method of 'compensating for the social violence embodied in the regime of migration control'.[48] Put bluntly, references to saving lives, human rights and development are necessary to justify the massive architecture of containment, immobilisation and state coercion.[49] For liberal states like the UK, repressive immigration policies cannot be seen to compromise respect for fundamental rights and for life. In this way, 'compassionate repression' is actually fundamental to the liberal state.[50] This explains why the UK can fund Open Arms and the Jamaica Constabulary Force through the same development programme, without contradiction. Open Arms and NODM reflect the UK's need to aggressively enforce immigration controls, while representing that very enforcement as legal, fair and humane.

As in the UK's RRP, however, 'capacity building' has been just as central to EU development programmes as anything resembling humanitarianism. Indeed, a significant portion of EU development spending goes toward funding the police and immigration authorities in recipient states, providing money, training and expertise so that those states – weaker, 'source' and 'transit' countries – can better monitor, document and police their nationals and the migrants moving through their territories.[51]

To give an example, the EU Emergency Trust Fund (EUTF) for Africa is designed to address 'the root causes of irregular migration and displaced persons in Africa'.[52] The EUTF operates with a budget of over €4 billion, and focuses on three key regions: North Africa; Sahel/Lake Chad; and the Horn of Africa.

The priorities for the fund include return and reintegration (i.e. of deported persons), anti-trafficking measures and refugee management. In some programmes, funds are allocated to more familiar developmental schemes: helping young people find jobs and set up businesses closer to home, supporting teachers, sustainable farmers, micro-finance initiatives, and so on. However, while these schemes might be foregrounded in the factsheets and online blogs, the EUTF is also used to 'strengthen police information systems' in the West African region, 'modernise secure identity chains' in Cape Verde and Burkina Faso, and enhance 'the institutional framework of Morocco and Tunisia to protect, monitor and manage the borders'. In Niger, the EUTF supports police officers from Spain, France and Nigeria to dismantle the criminal networks of 'smugglers and traffickers'.[53] In effect, 'tackling the root causes of irregular migration' means supporting African states to better police, contain and immobilise unruly populations.

Crucially, this account of the EUTF helps situate UK–Jamaica relations in a wider, global context. In Africa, the EU allocates billions of euros a year to combating irregular migration, and this includes programmes designed to 'reintegrate' returnees and discourage their re-migration. There are hundreds of organisations like Open Arms and NODM on the African continent, recipients of European aid tasked with supporting deported people and facilitating deportation from the West (although NODM is fairly unique as an organisation *of* deported migrants). Equally, the EUTF, much like the UK's RRP, focuses on 'capacity building', so that states in receipt of development funds can more effectively monitor, document and police would-be migrants. In this light, the UK–Jamaican case is not unique, and the deportation arrangements discussed above reveal some of the principal meanings and practices of development today.

By situating the RRP in Jamaica in relation to contemporary EU development policy, I have identified some of the ways in which security and bordering are now central to the politics of development. However, it is also important to recognise that development policy is inseparable from broad attempts to secure the optimum conditions for *capitalist development*. In other words, and as Kalpana Wilson argues, development policy is concerned not only with containment and security, but also with extraction and exploitation.[54] This becomes especially clear when reading the UK's Department for International Development's (DfID) own policy statement on the Caribbean:

> Our investments in infrastructure will also help to open up opportunities for British businesses and our work to tackle corruption will allow UK firms to compete on a level playing field in the Caribbean.... There is a major opportunity to use our resources to drive growth and provide a foundation for sustainable development and eventual progression from aid. We will do this by: investing in critical infrastructure; supporting private sector development; reducing crime and corruption; and improving public finance in the poorest and most vulnerable countries in the Caribbean. Our investments will significantly contribute to UK efforts to disrupt serious and organised crime in the Caribbean and reduce the overall threat to the UK emanating from this region.... Supporting economic growth will create opportunities for UK business and British trade with the Commonwealth Caribbean will be worth over £2 billion in the next four years.[55]

The Department is investing in tackling crime and corruption, and improving security and stability, so that UK firms can 'compete on a level playing field'. Indeed, in 2016, then Secretary of State for International Development Priti Patel said that she saw 'an opportunity to forge a new role for ourselves in the world, embedding development within trade policy'.[56] Since 2015, UK development funds have been expressly designed to reduce conflict, secure borders *and* increase trade, and this has aroused some concern from within the sector that the UK's new approach to aid means ignoring some of the world's most impoverished and marginalised populations.[57]

However, as noted already, development and aid have never been about charity, and have always been inseparable from the ordering of capitalism. It is just that the characteristics of global capitalism have changed. In this way, both securitisation and bordering are levers to ensure the smooth functioning of capitalism in an increasingly unpredictable and mobile world.[58] This argument is important because it reminds us that the UK's seemingly excessive commitment to bordering is not simply an effect of nativist closure and irrational racism. There is also a materialist explanation for why the UK uses so many tools at its disposal to control mobilities. The UK is concerned with controlling human movement not only because British voters dislike immigrants, but also because processes of sorting, il-legalising and immobilising are central to the organisation of capitalist relations.[59]

After all, capitalist development relies as much on selectively mobilising labour as it does on forcibly immobilising the global poor in low-wage zones, and therefore the claim that capital moves freely while labour cannot is an oversimplification. It is the *restriction* rather than the prevention of migration which is critical: borders filter who moves, with what rights and at what speed.[60] Indeed, restrictions on migration not only stop people moving (i.e. containment) but also render the labour of those who do move especially disposable, through deportability.[61] As Gargi Bhattacharyya argues: 'the processes of sorting, rationing, slowing up, holding up, and then on entry the processes of becoming irregular, undocumented, in the informal economy, all serve as methods of differentiating populations and their entry into economic activity'.[62] Notions of containment and immobil-ity do not capture these complex relationships between mobility, bordering and markets.

Crucially, however, this overall imperative to filter, direct and govern movement does not mean that the UK, or any other state for that matter, succeeds in fully ordering human mobilities (of course not!). There is no total or fully coherent system of government in operation here, and no single business or state interest determining who can move and how.[63] The overall point, however, is that capitalism relies on the management of mobilities, as geographically and politically disparate groups are differentially incorporated into markets.[64] This management of mobilities has always been central to the production of racial distinctions and hierarchies. As a result, to understand the connection between immigration control and racism, we need to consider bordering in relation to the wider government of mobility, of both people and things. In the next section, therefore, I consider deportation practices in relation to other kinds of (im)mobility in the Caribbean.

Differential (im)mobilities

One way to describe the UK's combined interest in bordering, securitisation and trade within development policy is in terms of the wider government of mobility. Through deportation (i.e. *bordering*), unwanted migrants are expelled from the UK and then forced to stay in Jamaica – along with all the other undesirable and immobilised Jamaican citizens (see Chapter 7). Also within UK development programmes, prisons and correctional services are 'modernised', anti-corruption measures are instituted and 'local offenders' are better 'rehabilitated' – all in a bid to reduce crime in Jamaica and restrict the illicit movement of goods and people across borders (i.e. *securitisation*).[65] Conversely, the UK's *trade* interests concern the ordered movement of goods, profits and people along particular routes and in particular directions. Importantly, these processes are not distinct, and these differential (im)mobilities structure various social hierarchies in Jamaica.[66] In this section, therefore, I want to consider the wider cast of people and things moving and being moved in and out of Jamaica, and to describe the Jamaican economy and society through the lens of mobility. This helps to place deportation among other socially and politically meaningful forms of movement, and offers a different angle on the relation between race, mobility and citizenship. In my view, thinking about differential (im)mobilities allows for a more sophisticated account of race and racism, and this section argues that racial distinctions and hierarchies are produced and reproduced through the ordering of movement.

Fundamental to this argument is the broad claim that mobility helps us understand various social relations and hierarchies. As Hagar Kotef puts it:

> We cannot understand ... the formation of gender categories without understanding the history of separate spheres and the history of confining women of certain races and classes to the home. We cannot grasp poverty without thinking about a history of vagrancy, migratory work, or about homelessness (as a concrete situation or as a specter). We cannot account for racial relations in the United States without considering, on the one hand, the practice of mass incarceration and, on the other, the history of slave trade and the middle passage.... The history of movement as well as its images, the practices of controlling it as well as the fear of it, the tradition of cherishing it as a right as well as the many exclusions that are embedded into this tradition, all are crucial in understanding social and political hierarchies, practices of rule, and identities.[67]

Especially relevant for my analysis is the relationship between racialisation and mobility. As Mimi Sheller argues:

> all racial processes, racialized spaces, and racialized identities (including whiteness) are deeply contingent on differential mobilities. Racial boundaries are formed, reformed, and transformed through mobile relations of power. Race is a performance of differential mobilities. And racial projects are concerned with the management of mobilities.[68]

Sheller's work on mobilities has been particularly insightful, and much of it is focused on the Caribbean.[69]

In fact, we can usefully approach the history of Jamaica by centring differential (im)mobilities. Under slavery, the power of the Jamaican planters and the British colonial government relied on the forcible kidnapping and transportation of millions of people from Africa, and then their incarceration and subjection on the planation, so that sugar could be produced and shipped back to the metropole. Following emancipation, indentured labourers were moved from India and China to work on plantations; they were also unfree (although not permanently) and heavily restricted in their mobility once in the Caribbean. When the sugar economy faltered in the late nineteenth century, Jamaica was developed to produce and export bananas and later bauxite. Meanwhile, in the context of economic hardship during this period, many Jamaicans migrated to work in North America and other parts of the Caribbean (especially significant was the mass migration of Jamaican men to work building the Panama Canal in the 1880s).[70] More recently, of course, transnational migration and tourism have defined Jamaica's economy and society. In short, throughout Jamaica's modern history, the uneven movement of people and things have fundamentally structured economic and social relations on the island.

Across different periods, extractive industries have facilitated certain mobilities – whether of sugar, bananas, bauxite or tourists – in the context of the restricted mobility of (often unfree) labour. These unequal relations of mobility have been central to the production of racialised social distinctions and hierarchies in each historical period. Who gets to move is always a racial question, and differential (im)mobilities both reflect and constitute racial distinctions. If blackness has been defined by particularly enduring forms of unfreedom, then this unfreedom has been about the inability to move freely.[71] Indeed, black liberation struggles have been marked by a deep desire for the right to move unchained, emancipation inseparable from the right to locomotion.[72] Inversely, racism and colonialism can be described in terms of the management of mobilities, the set of logics and coercive practices through which racially subjugated groups are forced to move and forced to stay. To be white, in this context, or at least properly white (male, heterosexual, propertied and able-bodied), is to be able to exercise freedom of movement. To be black is to be in chains.[73] Race and mobility are and have always been mutually constitutive.

Today, however, no formal racial distinctions are legislated, and Jamaica is an independent nation-state. How, then, do we describe the operation of race when it does not speak its name? How do we analyse racism without 'races'? Several theorists have approached this question much more systematically than I can here,[74] but my suggestion is that thinking carefully about differential (im)mobilities helps us understand the production and reproduction of racial distinctions and hierarchies in the present.[75] To develop this analysis, it is useful first to simply describe some of the differential (im)mobilities in contemporary Jamaica.

* * *

In contemporary Jamaica, the export of bananas and bauxite no longer sustains the economy, and therefore tourism has become the major extractive industry, one which quite literally trades on differential mobilities (significantly, the transportation of bananas and bauxite carved out the tourist routes now used by cruise liners).[76] Put simply, tourism is a motor of differential mobilities which are racialised in form. As Traci-Ann Wint puts it in her excellent master's dissertation:

> Poor Jamaicans are not tourists. Poor Jamaicans do not travel. Jamaicans are smiling faces and dancing girls. Jamaicans line up at the docks, to sell their wares to those who arrive on aeroplanes and sailing ships they do not board. Jamaicans are Black. Tourists are White. *Jamaicans stay*. Americans come and go. Jamaicans are attractions. Americans are tourists.[77]

Wint's poetic description of how black Jamaicans *stay* and white tourists *move* captures the essential relation between mobility, race and citizenship in Jamaica. However, it remains an oversimplification. For example, Ricardo's favourite hang-out spots were in tourist spaces, and not only when I was around. Relatedly, not all tourists in Jamaica are white; many black Britons and Americans, of Jamaican heritage or otherwise, visit Jamaica as tourists. They stay in resorts, they party and they go to paid-entry beaches. Put differently, while tourism might be captured by the image of black servitude and white consumption – and admittedly I did not spend time in the all-inclusive resorts where these interactions are sharpest – there are other kinds of interactions and experiences within the tourist trade, all of which mobilise divisions around 'race', class, gender and nationality, but in more complex and interesting ways than is often recognised.[78]

This is not to deny that tourism is both a site and a product of racism, however. Around 9% of the Jamaican labour force is directly employed in the tourist sector (expected to rise to 12% by 2028), and it estimated that around 30% of jobs are reliant on tourism (expected to rise to 39% by 2028). The total contribution of 'travel and tourism' was estimated at 32.9% of Jamaica's GDP in 2017, and is estimated to rise to 42.8% by 2028.[79] As Ian Strachan states, and as I alluded to in the previous chapter, 'the plantations laid the economic, political, cultural and social groundwork that has enabled tourism to function so effectively in the Caribbean'.[80] Or as Wint puts it: 'the line from sugar and slavery to tourism in Jamaica is short and bold'.[81] It is also important to recognise that tourism in the Caribbean relies on images and discourses surrounding race, gender and sexuality which are saturated with empire, and we see this in the marketing of the 'wedding in paradise', for example.[82] Appreciating these lineages is essential. But while tourism at the level of representation and interaction might be racist, I am especially interested in the way tourist encounters bring differential mobilities into sharp relief.

As Jamaica Kincaid notes in her searing essay *A Small Place*: 'You [the tourist] move through customs swiftly, you move through customs with ease. Your bags are not searched.'[83] Kincaid's focus on the border is crucial for my purposes, and in this light we might contrast the tourist not only with the 'locals' – the 'smiling faces and dancing girls' of Wint's framing – but with the 'deportees' described in this book. In fact, 'deportees' and tourists often call the same place home, and they might even share the same flight from London Gatwick to Montego Bay. Indeed, if tourism is defined as an exercise of freedom, movement for the purposes of leisure and pleasure, then it is hard to imagine a journey more opposed than that taken by the 'deportee', whose mobility is totally coerced, who is expelled, and for whom the term 'charter flight' might hold very different meanings than for those on package holidays.

Perhaps the only form of mobility more unfree is that of the transferred prisoner, who is not only forcibly expelled but is also then incarcerated on arrival in Jamaica. The UK has for many years been trying to persuade the Jamaican government to sign a 'compulsory prisoner transfer agreement', so that the UK can forcibly deport Jamaican nationals to serve their British sentences in Jamaican prisons.[84] Memorably, Prime Minister David Cameron visited Jamaica in 2015 and offered £25 million to build a modern prison in Jamaica, ultimately so that Jamaican nationals in UK prisons could be deported sooner (i.e. transferred). Jamaica would get a shiny new prison in return for complying with the UK's aggressive deportation policies (although, at the time of writing, this 'prison deal' has yet to materialise).[85]

Again, the prison was to be funded through the UK's aid budget (through the Conflict, Security and Stability Fund in particular).[86] Of note, however, was that on Cameron's official visit he also announced £300 million of funding for infrastructure projects across the Caribbean, including roads, bridges and ports.[87] It is instructive that such investments to facilitate greater mobility were used to sweeten a deal around the forced transfer of undesirable 'foreign criminals'. The crucial point is that the production of mobility and immobility were intimately connected in Cameron's 'prison deal', just as they are within development policy more broadly.

Moving away from the deportation flight and the tourist beach, another site from which to consider differential (im)mobilities in Jamaica is the Montego Bay Free Zone. Jamaica's economy is now overwhelmingly service-based – agriculture and industry having been effectively destroyed through structural adjustment programmes – and in this context offshored telemarketing services have become a key employer.[88] Thousands of Jamaicans work as customer service agents in the retail, telecommunications, healthcare, loan servicing, and technology industries, and in Montego Bay these call centres are housed within Montego Bay Free Zone, which offers North American companies 100% tax and import duty exemptions, as well as convenient placement within the Eastern Time Zone.

Crucially, the sector relies on English-speaking, low-paid and disposable labour. There is a high rate of attrition in call centres, and 'most workers seldom advance past the entry-level hourly wage of just over US $1 per hour'.[89] The low wages and disposability of this workforce is an effect of there being few other options in the Jamaican labour market – indeed, work in a call centre is considered decent employment – and the comparably low wages also rely on the inability of this labour pool to easily emigrate. The relative immobility of those labouring within the Free Zone can be contrasted with the unhindered flows of capital, finance and profit heading northwards, which make free-trade zones such an attractive feature of late capitalism.[90] Of course, the Free Zone is not the plantation, but it does exhibit some shared geographies, as devalued labourers are immobilised, exploited and indeed zoned, while surplus is freely extracted and accumulated by absentee power structures.

However, while contrasting the mobility of tourists and capital with the immobility of locals, 'deportees' and transferred prisoners is instructive, the apparent immobility of Jamaican citizens should not be exaggerated. In fact, describing Jamaican citizenship as a mode of containment appears to contradict the fact that there are some 1.3 million Jamaican-born people living abroad, mostly in North America and the UK (some of whom will have naturalised). The social, economic and cultural life of Jamaica is profoundly transnational – indeed, theories of trans-nationalism emerged from the Caribbean context[91] – and 'the Caribbean claims one of the most mobile working classes in the world'.[92] However, this mobility remains heavily restricted, and thus the relationship between movement and social hierarchy is complicated by processes of transnational migration. Importantly, the distinction between those who migrate and those who stay is not the only relevant one in Jamaica. The mobility of a worker seasonally employed in the US agricultural sector, for example, is very different from the mobility of someone with permanent US residence or dual nationality,[93] just as the immobility of people who remain in Jamaica has different social meanings depending on age, social class and family.[94]

My point is that differential (im)mobility in Jamaica is not defined by a flat distinction between the mobile, wealthy, white tourists and the poor black Jamaicans who sell their wares on the beach, watching the planes and the cruise ships come and go. Many Jamaicans have been abroad, many have family abroad on whom they rely for remittances, and everyone is enmeshed in profoundly transnational social, economic and cultural relations.[95] However, it is the complex differentiations between who can move, when and how that structure social distinctions in Jamaica. In this context, the devaluing of the 'deportee' discussed in the previous chapter is one example of how social meanings are negotiated in relation to mobility.

To return to Kotef, it is 'through the production of patterns of movement (statelessness, deportability, enclosures, confinement), [that] different categories of subjectivity are produced'.[96] The meanings assigned to 'deportees', then, are inseparable from their inability to control their own movement, and there is a profound dishonour that comes with being forcibly expelled and then prevented from returning to one's family.[97] Conversely, the social value attached to tourists and uptown Jamaicans is inseparable from their freedom of movement. Indeed, these differential (im)mobilities are part of what supply racial distinctions with their meaning and social significance. Mobility, then, is central to the reproduction of racial distinctions and hierarchies.

Movement and race-making

It might be useful here to reiterate that racial difference is not reducible to skin colour. Skin colour is not the cause of racial difference but one of its markers, and skin colour difference is made meaningful, and weighed down, by the reality of material inequalities between people racialised as white, brown and black.[98] For racial difference to mean the things it does in Jamaica, it must always correspond to material differences in relation to the distribution of opportunities, resources and freedoms. These material differences are not only about wealth, but also correspond to who can move, how and with what effects. Thought this way, the government of mobility is central to the processes through which racial categories are produced and reconfigured, given life and social meaning in the present. This does not mean that race and mobility are directly correlated. It is not as if those who cannot move are necessarily black, or that those who can are necessarily white, but it does mean that racialised social relations are substantially constituted by relations of mobility.

Let me put it another way: what it means to be black, or to be from 'the ghetto', or to be a Jamaican in the world are all constituted by relations of mobility. The distinctions between black, brown and white in Jamaica, and between local and tourist, would not hold for long, or in the same ways, if the organisation of mobility shifted, and if different groups were afforded greater or lesser access to mobility. If Jamaica's economy was governed not to export single commodities or package tourism, but to nurture liveable lives and ecologies on the island, then racialised social hierarchies would be transformed along with relations of mobility. If, somehow, the majority of black Jamaicans were able to move freely around the planet, not to toil as disposable migrant labour but simply to wander and travel, then it is hard to imagine that they would describe racism and historical injustice in quite the same way. What makes slavery so resonant for so many Jamaicans today is material hardship in the context of restricted mobility and global marginality.

This sense of historical continuity underpins Jamaican narratives on 'sufferation'. As noted in the previous chapter, 'sufferation' is 'used in Jamaican society to denote a condition of being existentially and economically stuck. It is the desire for progress, while lacking the traction and momentum for its accomplishment.'[99] Being stuck, lacking momentum: evidently 'sufferation' is about a lack of movement, both literal and existential.[100] Underlying the discourse on 'sufferation' is the sense that things will not change, and that things have not changed since slavery. This sense of unchanging 'sufferation' is fundamentally about relations of mobility, where blackness still connotes the inability to move unchained.

These historical resonances and continuities are important. However, to talk about contemporary relations of mobility in terms of 'sufferation' and the afterlives of slavery should not imply that nothing has changed.[101] Of course it has. If race and mobility are mutually constitutive, then as relations of mobility change, so do racialised social relations. Throughout *Deporting Black Britons*, I have suggested that race and racism are historically specific, and thus I have been concerned with how racialised social relations get *reconfigured* in the present. The point is that 'race' is both deeply sedimented and historically emergent, both persistent and mercurial, heavy and yet slick.[102] The challenge is therefore to work out how racial distinctions and hierarchies are made and remade.[103] The relevant point here is that if racial distinctions and hierarchies are always constituted by differential (im)mobilities, then contemporary modes of governing mobility offer a window onto *historically specific configurations of race and racism*.

As such, it is not simply that the same groups are being immobilised in the same ways and for the same reasons. It remains true that blackness is constituted by particularly violent forms of enforced (im)mobility, but there is also something emergent and new about the contemporary government of mobility.[104] Bordering practices perpetuate colonial inequalities, but they also produce new forms of racial injustice – think about the refugee camp, the bordering of the seas and the implementation of enormous biometric databases, for example. As economic and ecological crises deepen, and increasing numbers of the global poor are deemed surplus to requirements, the demand for bordering everywhere intensifies. In this context, the racist world order gets reconfigured with terrifying consequences, both familiar and novel. For Achille Mbembe, the contemporary border presents a worrying sign of where the world is going,[105] and therefore anti-racism, as the struggle for liveable futures, will increasingly have to contend with bordering practices, theorising racism not only in terms of the legacies of European colonialism but also in relation to the present and future of the border.[106]

Conclusion

Deportation relies on cooperation between deporting and receiving states. As a result, deportation practices are embedded within wider bilateral and foreign policy relationships, and this chapter has attempted to situate deportation within this wider field. This allows for a much richer critique of immigration controls and citizenship, moving beneath and beyond the national framings that characterise most policy debates and academic analyses of racism and migration.

I first described how deportation is actually arranged between the UK and Jamaican governments, before discussing Open Arms and NODM, two local NGOs whose work supporting deported migrants is made possible by UK aid funds. I then explained that both Open Arms and NODM were funded as part of the Reintegration and Rehabilitation Programme, which also included funds for the Jamaican police force, prison service and Passport, Immigration and Citizenship Agency. In short, ostensibly humanitarian programmes to support deported migrants are being funded alongside security-oriented schemes focused on 'capacity building', which assist the Jamaican state to better monitor, identify and police risky populations – namely 'local offenders' and 'deported persons'.

This focus on controlling migration and reducing crime might not look like development or aid, but in fact the Reintegration and Rehabilitation Programme is symptomatic of the wider focus on bordering, security and trade within development policy. As I went on to argue, bordering, security and trade are all characterised by uneven relations of mobility, and therefore to understand what immigration controls do in the world we need to consider them in relation to the wider government of mobility. Importantly, this wider ordering of differential (im)mobilities is central to the production and reproduction of racial distinctions and hierarchies. In short, race and racism are constituted by relations of mobility, and this insight allows us to better describe racism in our times. Indeed, the struggle against racism has always been about the freedom to move and the freedom the stay – a struggle for autonomous movement, locomotion and flight. Therefore, as borders proliferate and intensify, anti-racism becomes necessarily the struggle against immigration controls and citizenship, which fix people in space and in law, and reproduce the racist world order. This is another way of saying, at the global scale, what this book has been arguing throughout: that immigration controls inevitably enact and reproduce racism, and so the struggle against borders and against racism are one and the same.

Chapter 9

Conclusion

The world does not stand still, and yet writing relies on pressing the pause button somewhere. As Les Back puts it, we are 'writing against time, trying to capture an outline of an existence that is fleeting'.[1] Pressing pause, then, is inevitable and ethnographic accounts are always incomplete and out of date. That said, I want to update the portraits here, writing as I am in autumn 2019, if only to remind the reader that life goes on, that deportation is not 'the end' and that people mostly find ways to survive. This feels important in a book-length account of deportation where there is space to capture lives *in motion*. In shorter and more politically motivated writing, it is easy to overstress the desperation, the hopelessness and the isolation faced by deported people, as though the world stops when their deportation flight lands. It does not.

When I returned to Jamaica in March 2019, after over 18 months away, much had changed in the lives of Jason, Ricardo, Chris and Denico, and mostly for the better. Chris was working at the Knutsford Express coach centre in New Kingston, loading luggage on and off the air-conditioned coaches used by middle-class Jamaicans and tourists. He was optimistic about his new job, and working full time, which meant that when I was in Jamaica we would mostly meet in New Kingston before he started his shift. One Sunday, however, on his day off, we

Pictures 9.1 and 9.2. *Chris and me at Ocho Rios Bay Beach (2019)*

travelled to Ocho Rios on the north coast, a resort town with busy beaches, hotels and a harbour for cruise ships.

We took the Knutsford Express coach from New Kingston. Chris travelled free, which put him in good spirits, and we arrived in the late morning for a full day at the beach. It was a joyful day for us both – eating, drinking and swimming – but also reflecting on this project, on how much had changed in the last few years, and discussing our hopes and plans for the future. Throughout the day we took pictures on my phone, one of which Chris would later print and frame for me to take to his daughter back in Leeds. As dusk fell, we were told to leave the beach, but we were not ready to head back to Kingston. We lingered, and took some more pictures on my phone, this time posing in front of the docked cruise ship just out from the shore.

Unfortunately, by September 2019 Chris had lost his job at the coach station in New Kingston after being threatened by a colleague. The young man – who Chris described as 'from the ghetto, ghetto' – felt that Chris had disrespected him, and he then followed Chris downtown, trailing his taxi and waiting for him at the drop-off point with two of his friends. Chris asked the driver to drop him further down the road, and decided not to take the risk of returning to work the next day. His employers ultimately agreed and he has been out of work since.

Denico, meanwhile, was still working in the same super-market as in 2017, and while the work was poorly paid and unrewarding, he was noticeably happier in general. He invited me to his family home in St Elizabeth for the first time, and I took the coaster bus from downtown Kingston one morning. Denico lived in a rural village, and I was anxious about whether the driver would remember my stop. When he pulled over to let me out, I was even more concerned that Denico had given me the wrong instructions. There were no landmarks, other than a very small rum shack, and Denico was not answering his phone. He soon picked up though, and his family house was just 200 yards up a dirt road. I dropped by bags at the house. Denico apologised for the lack of running water – 'this is some real country shit', he explained jokingly. He then took me on a walk around the village, and laughed when some local children asked me for a US dollar. Later in the afternoon, I met his 12-year-old twin brothers and his older sister, who was back from working in the Cayman Islands to have her baby. We all went for a swim in the nearby river – although only the twins and I actually did any swimming.

As well as the supermarket job, Denico was converting the shed near his house into a barbershop, painting it and rigging it with electricity during the time I was in Jamaica. He hoped it would provide some income on top of his meagre wage, and he was planning the opening party for a few days after I flew back to England. Whether the barbershop would succeed or not was unclear, but it was obvious that Denico was feeling more hopeful and more settled in this small patch of 'real country'.

The most significant change for Denico, however, was that after two years struggling to maintain his relationship with

Picture 9.3. *Me and Denico at Emancipation Park, Kingston (2019)*

Kendal, they had separated. They came to accept that Denico was not returning to the UK, and Kendal was not moving to Jamaica, and they found that maintaining their relationship through phone contact was unworkable – especially for Kendal's children Tamara and Maisy. They remain on good terms, though. Kendal now has a third child in Birmingham, while Denico is in a relationship with his family friend and neighbour, Shanice. Indeed, I got to know Shanice well during my 2019 visit, and we spent time together as a three, both in Kingston and in St Elizabeth. A few months later, once I had returned to the UK, Denico called me on WhatsApp with some good news: Shanice was pregnant and their baby was due in March 2020. They were both incredibly excited, and Denico asked me if I was 'ready to be the godfather'. By the time this book is published, then, both Denico and Ricardo will have fathered children in Jamaica.

When I returned to Jamaica in March 2019, Ricardo's daughter was six months old. He and Tinesha had separated, and so he was seeing his daughter for just a couple of days each week, but he still described her as his 'main priority'. Ricardo was working with his friend Everton, who also grew up in the West Midlands, in his business importing and selling beauty products. Ricardo was effectively Everton's right-hand man, and they rented a place in Kingston together and travelled between Mobay and the capital, where they sold products from two different stores.

During my visit in 2019, Ricardo, Everton and I spent time together as a three, visiting Jamaica's famous Dunn's River Falls, and hanging out in bars and restaurants in Kingston and Mobay. Everton was interested in this book project, and in fact when I left a copy of my PhD thesis for Ricardo, it was Everton who read it and then asked me engaging questions about it the next time we met. Despite recognising how cruel deportation was, however, both Everton and Ricardo thought that Jamaica was actually the best place to live in the world if you seized the opportunities on offer. These two young men from the West Midlands were positive about their futures as upwardly mobile businessmen in Jamaica; for them, deportation was as much a beginning as an end.

Things really had improved for Ricardo since we first met, more than for the other men in the book. Three years earlier he had been living with his uncle in a dangerous neighbourhood in the hills of Mobay, working long hours on a hotdog stand. In 2019, he was a businessman (of sorts), and it was obvious that he enjoyed the newfound feeling of mobility, both literal and social, as he and Everton drove around in their business car, attended parties to promote their products, and employed Instagram models as 'brand ambassadors'. Ricardo was also planning to travel outside Jamaica, first within the Caribbean and later to Europe. While he was still keen to emphasise that

Picture 9.4. *Ricardo and me, hanging my laundry, Mobay (2017)*

his daughter was his 'main priority' – and he reminded me several times that he paid for her clothes, food and childcare – he was also excited about his independence and freedom.

I come to Jason last because his circumstances had in fact worsened by March 2019. He was kicked out of Open Arms in 2017 and he had been sleeping rough since. By 2019, he had been living on the streets for over two years. I struggled to find him for the first few days, but I had heard he was staying in New Kingston, not far from where Chris worked. By chance, I bumped into him when I was there with Denico and Shanice. 'Luke!' he shouted, drawing the attention of everyone around. 'Mr De Ronha, waaaa!' I was relieved to see him alive, but he looked worse off than when I had last seen him. He was wearing a dirty polo shirt, scuffed pants, crocs and a soiled zip-up hoodie. His teeth were decaying, with several large chips on his front teeth and black marks on his incisors. He was still the same Jason, still asking earnestly about my partner and my family in his East London accent, still with his confused and lively way of expressing things. But he looked unwell, somehow more depleted.

I was with Denico as this scene unfolded and they spoke very briefly. 'Luke is a good guy', Jason said, 'so you must be a good guy if you're together, so nuff respect, big love', before attempting to fist-bump him. Denico offered only an arm bump in return. Like everyone else in the street, he was keen not to make physical contact with Jason (indeed, a couple of minutes later, when I gave Jason a hug, some bystanders were clearly horrified). 'Look, I see you're with your friend, but I need a two grand, yeah. I need help Luke', Jason implored. I only had a few hundred dollars on me at the time, and so I gave him 300, eager to hurry our uncomfortable and overly public reunion. 'Thank you Luke. This is my spot, yeah', Jason explained, 'here outside Island Grill, so just come find me, yeah. Good to see you'.

After leaving Jason, I explained something of his story to Denico, who was, in his own words, 'shook': 'That's knocked me for six', he said. Denico remained visibly affected throughout our lunch, clearly thinking about his own story in relation to Jason's. A few hours later, when I put Denico and Shanice in a taxi back up to the bus station, and crossed back over the road to find my own cab, Jason found me again. 'Luke! Two times in one day…. Luke, I need clothes. Do you have trainers? Maybe we can buy some shirts, and trousers…. I have not had a good wash in god knows how long.' He then explained that he owed someone 3,500 Jamaican dollars (about £20), and the person had said he would 'stab him up' if he did not get it to him this week. I said I couldn't give him anything now, but he pleaded for some money, 'just to buy water and food'. I only had 2,000 Jamaican dollars, and so gave him 1,000. I got in my taxi and told him I would come find him by Island Grill the following week.

I saw Jason twice again during this trip, but I was not sure what we could do together. In previous years, we would have gone into a fast-food restaurant, like Juici Patties or KFC, but he was no longer allowed inside anywhere. He was visibly destitute, and he smelled bad, and so all we could do was spend an hour

Pictures 9.5 and 9.6. *Jason in New Kingston (2019)*

or so in Emancipation Park. I showed Jason my PhD thesis and checked he was happy with the pictures I wanted to use in the book, but I did not leave a copy with him, as I did Ricardo, Chris and Denico. There did not seem much point, given that he was unable to hold onto any of his possessions for very long (he lost the clothes and slippers I bought him a week earlier almost immediately).

I had no means of contacting Jason as he had no phone, but I did take the number of a kind security guard, Dawn, who worked by Island Grill and had taken a shine to him. When I contacted her over WhatsApp in September 2019, she explained that he was still on the streets of New Kingston, and still getting into fights and continually losing his few possessions. Like in London, Jason was trapped in homelessness, and it was taking its toll on him. He was surviving, but, in the context of near total social abandonment and abjection, it was not clear that he would be able to for much longer.

Conclusion

Race, racism and immigration control – thinking the problem differently

I return to the four men in this Conclusion because the previous two chapters were less descriptive, focusing as they did on questions of citizenship, development and differential (im)mobilities. *Deporting Black Britons* remains, however, a book about the lives of Jason, Ricardo, Chris and Denico, and I want to re-emphasise the centrality of portraiture, description and biography here. That said, the book has not been written in a journalistic mode, and the chapters have clearly been framed by my own political and theoretical preoccupations. To be more precise, the chapters have been structured by an overarching concern with better understanding the productive character of immigration controls, as they shape various social distinctions, exclusions and hierarchies at different scales. I have been especially concerned with understanding the connection between immigration controls and racism, and in what remains of the Conclusion I want to underline the political significance of some of the arguments I have been developing.

I argued in the Introduction that racism is always historically specific and that racial distinctions and hierarchies must be made and remade. On reflection, the central argument in *Deporting Black Britons* – that borders reconfigure race and racism – is broad and fairly intuitive. The reason for working this argument through in an entire book is not simply to hammer the point home, however, but to give it some texture, detail and empirical grounding. Importantly, I have not attempted to provide a neater, fuller or better definition of what racism is or is not, but simply to convince the reader that it is impossible to understand the politics of migration without thinking substantively about the histories and dynamics of racism. Indeed, if immigration controls are central to the production of racial distinctions and hierarchies, then anti-racists need to challenge all forms of immigration control – and where better to start than with those archetypal 'bad migrants': 'foreign criminals' subject to the most extraordinary, cruel and naked form of state power.

The book's analysis has not been particularly systematic in this regard, but hopefully the various arguments scattered across the chapters open up some new lines of critique. If *Deporting Black Britons* can suggest some different ways of thinking about the problem, however subtle, then it has succeeded. Returning to the stories of Jason, Ricardo, Chris, Denico, and their friends and family, it might be possible to approach some of the following questions differently: What is racism in Britain, and where do we look for it? How should we resist it? Equally, how should we talk about immigration controls, what kinds of arguments should we be making, and who is impacted by immigration controls and how? Telling different stories can encourage us to think about these problems differently, and ultimately this can lay the ground for different kinds of political action.

Of course, for those struggling against racism and bordering, ours is a truly terrible time. Deportations have become an increasingly routine element of immigration policy, and the number of people being both detained and deported globally has increased dramatically in the past few decades.[2] Borders and walls are proliferating, even as ecological and economic crises push greater numbers of people to leave their homes and move across international borders.[3] Globally, the border is now increasingly central to foreign policy and development practice, a testing ground for new forms of state power, as technologies of surveillance and biometrics are everywhere expanded.[4] Things feel bleak, and the struggle for the right to move and the right to stay feels both more impossible and more urgent than ever. However, there is nothing profound about espousing hopelessness, and so we must end on a hopeful note. Hope is not the same as wishful thinking, but represents an attentiveness to the present, to the critical openings and alternative ways of being already perceptible in the now.[5] With this in mind, how can we draw out some hope from the stories in this book?

Hope and exile

What the deported people in this book ultimately remind us is that state definitions of belonging are always transgressed by people who are much more interesting than the racial and national categories which violently delimit them.[6] In multi-status Britain, despite the intensification of everywhere, everyday bordering, people who grow up in the same neighbourhoods, or go to the same schools, or are incarcerated in the same prisons, develop friendships that demonstrate a banal disregard for the logic of the border. This might not be revolutionary, or even political, but it is *hopeful*. As Sivamohan Valluvan argues, 'it is the realities of *everyday multiculture* that constitute a ready-made counterpoint to nationalist capture'.[7] The question, of course, is whether the radical openness of lived culture – what Paul Gilroy refers to as an outernational sensibility[8] – can be harnessed in the political struggle against racism, nationalism and bordering. An important first step, however, comes with simply appreciating the potential.

Recognising that citizens and non-citizens care for one another, often in very ordinary and unremarkable ways, allows us to transcend the argument that 'deportation is wrong because it destroys families'. I have shown that deportation does, indeed, destroy families, but I have also critiqued the state's legislation of the heteronormative nuclear family, and tried to draw attention to people's wider networks of mutual support. In each of the ethnographic portraits, friendship is a theme returned to again and again, friendships which were illegible and ir-relevant within immigration law. In this light, resistance to immigration control should rely on a deeper appreciation for the value of friendship. This builds on feminist critiques of the family as a site of violence, and chimes with queer writing on kinship, intimacy and 'the families we choose'.[9] A world without deportation, then, will also have to be one in which friendship is accorded its proper value, and family takes on very different meanings. Indeed, valuing intimacy, friendship and care beyond the nuclear family provides a challenge to the 'blood and soil' thinking of race and nation.[10]

Crucially, though, it is not only that non-citizens adapt and make friends, they also actively transform the neighbourhoods and cities where they live.[11] Politicians and social commentators might imply that British society is being assaulted from without, but the outsiders are very much within the gates, and they have been for some time. The primary concern of anti-immigrant voices seems to be that Britain will become 'unrecognisable' to itself,[12] and yet our hope must be that they are right – and that Britain's multicultural, multi-ethnic and multi-status realities will afford the country's young people a different kind of 'common sense' in the process of Britain's remaking.[13]

Of course, not all young people are at ease with difference, and Britain remains structurally racist. However, my point is that there are different constituencies emerging in the political struggle against racism and nationalism, and non-citizens are key here: their 'struggles unsettle the space of the political'.[14] The political challenge is to harness these social and demographic processes into an anti-racist programme, so that deportation comes to represent the panicked and desperate protestation of a white nation in decline, rather than a sign of what is to come. If the state fails to expel all the 'illegals' and discipline all the 'migrants', then what can be made of that failure? How best to politicise the hordes of young people and 'dark strangers' who want the world to be otherwise?

It is useful at this point to turn to the literature on the 'autonomy of migration', which gifts us the radical suggestion that borders respond to mobilities as much as the other way around.[15] In other words, states are always catching up, migration policies are incoherent and contested, and immigration controls never command total jurisdiction over people's lives. Autonomy does not imply 'pure self-legislation or un-restricted self-determination', then, but refers us to those 'moments of uncontrollability and excess that escape the capaci-ties of existing mechanisms of control'.[16] In this light, describing Britain as 'multi-status' should refer not only to the violence of immigration controls – and the separation of families, friends and neighbours – but also to the broad terrain of struggle, in which the logic of classification and separation is always con-fronted by refusal, evasion and flight.[17] Again, the immigration system ultimately fails to fully know, control, monitor and fix everyone, and there is hope in the failure. There is hope in the fact that social and cultural life is too dynamic, and people and places refuse to stand still, and new forms of resistance emerge in response to new conditions. I am not trying to romanticise things here, only to suggest that even when it feels as though everything is getting worse, there are always critical openings. 'There is a crack in everything, that's how the light gets in.'[18]

Finally, there is also hope, even if a sad kind of hope, in the recognition that most deported people survive. Most find a way to keep going, and this simple fact is hopeful.

> RICARDO: If I didn't let incarceration break me, I'm not gonna let freedom break me. Wherever you put me, I've got freedom.

For Jason, Ricardo, Chris and Denico, exile is a process and deportation is not 'the end', even if, as a new beginning, it has been marked by immeasurable suffering. The ability of deported people to survive and rebuild does not make deportation any less cruel, but there must always be hope, otherwise it really is hopeless.[19] There is always something that can be learned and something that can be done. The life stories of Jason, Ricardo, Chris and Denico testify to the violence of immigration control, reminding us of what we are up against, but they also remind us that, amid the damage of racism and nationalism, there are always connections being built, friendships being made and boundaries being crossed. Perhaps 'deportees', like all exiles, can offer some pointers on how to live together differently. As Edward Said puts in his reflections on exile:

> The exile knows that in a secular and contingent world, homes are always provisional. Borders and barriers, which enclose us within the safety of familiar territory can also become prisons, and are often defended beyond reason or necessity. Exiles cross borders, break barriers of thought and experience.[20]

* * *

For John Berger, 'the opposite of love is not to hate but to separate'.[21] Borders and deportation do their best to separate. But they fail, and fail again they must.

Afterword, *by Chris*

How can I forget what I went through?
How can I move on?
Three years back now, yet it felt like yesterday.
The guards, the cell of the condemned,
The taste of the food, the routine,
Hearing the guards' keys jingle, the still doors
Shut!
How can I forget?

Six years ago, a judge told me in an immigration hearing that I can be a father from Jamaica. My son is now 10, my daughter is nine, and I cannot remember the last time I saw them in person. They don't know each other, even though they live in the same city.

Knowing that my kids are in England creates an empty space. To know that I created two beautiful beings, and the only thing I can do is talk to them every now and then on the phone. The conversations are not the greatest either because I hardly know them, each conversation is getting to know them.

And so, it's hard to say I've got a family. I've got kids, but not a family. I live alone. I've been living by myself for so long. The only time I had a family was when I was living with my mum.

My mum is in London, and she has had depression since 2013. My brothers who I raised from birth also suffer from depression and now depend on medication to feel normal. Sometimes I find myself walking, going nowhere, just walking and thinking to myself: What if I had gotten another chance, would I mess up again? Will I see my kids again? Am I slowly going insane?

Since being back in Jamaica, I have had five different jobs in six years, and lived at 12 different addresses – sometimes with family, with friends, or in Open Arms homeless shelter.

It is possible to get work here – in a supermarket, packing shelves, or a cleaning job – but you only get enough money to take you to work and back. You can't even pay your rent, and you definitely can't save. What do you do? Do that, or try to find something better? When better means better qualifications and better links?

I've currently got a job delivering food. I spend a third of my wage renting the bike, then another chunk goes towards paying off rent arrears, and so I have about £20 a week to get around, to eat, and to buy essentials. Maybe two or three days a week I don't eat anything, I just battle through. That's how I am living right now.

Finding a safe environment for a decent rent is hard out here. I've lived in '"Dunkirk', for example. Rent there was cheap, like £40 a month, but there was gun violence every other night, gunmen used to walk through the yard, and so I had to leave that environment. I went to another place where rent was affordable, but the road was a bad road. Gunmen had captured a yard when people moved abroad, and they stole most of my stuff. I turned to family, but they said 'there's no space, you're using up the resources'.

Now I'm down by Bull Bay, Seven Mile. It's not perfect, but the rent is decent, about £60 a month, and that's what I can afford with my wage. There's no violence, but the roof is collapsing slowly.

It's rough in Jamaica, but I would say I'm getting a bit more used to it. Sometimes I still get lost in the roads, but I'm meeting people, and feeling friendlier. I'm even getting used to the roughness. I can cope on a bad day.

I've got a few close friends here that I'd call family. I keep my circle small, but I do hang out with people in Rockfort, and I like being in the community. I like laughter, or hearing some story about some funny event or encounter. Those things make me feel good.

A good day out here might be when I've helped someone or someone's helped me, or when I am cooking, chilling and laughing with friends. There's not much to do out here, but on a good day it's the simple things that really please me.

Compared to other deported Jamaicans, I feel lucky. I'm doing alright. I've got a roof over my head. I might not be as successful as some who have come and opened businesses, but I'm luckier than others who have come back and lost their sanity, who are eating out of garbage bins and living on the roadside, on the floor. There's a few Jamaicans who were deported and then got into badness and died. Some are still in Open Arms shelter right now, taking medication and crying, wanting to go back to the UK or Canada or America.

So, I feel lucky. I've still got my sanity, and my freedom, and my life. I feel lucky to say I've found a little life that I can live.

Going back in time, I would have liked to have finished school, finished college and got qualified as an electrical installation engineer, or taken football seriously and gone about my coaching.

Going back in time, I wish I had patience. As my baby mums know, I didn't need to go sell drugs to provide for them. I could have just taken my time and got a job. The kids were kids, and their mothers could provide for them as well, it wasn't just me. Going back in time I definitely would have changed that, just had a bit more patience, just thought twice and looked to other options.

My plan now is to work towards owning a house, where I can live without worrying about rent. I've been moving up and down, and I don't want to experience that as an old man.

The next thing I hope for, in the next three to five years, is to see my kids again. That's the main thing. Hopefully I can achieve a certain status in life where I can say 'Here kids, I can book your holiday, every summer holiday, or Christmas holiday. I've got a house where you can come and stay.' Hopefully by then I can even take a trip to England, and visit them on a holiday. To see them at least, just experience something with them, instead of a phone call. That's what I hope for.

Deportation has torn my family apart and changed my life forever. My past haunts me, and reminds me of what have I lost. My future is uncertain but I believe that Allah has a plan for me, so I leave my faith in God's hands.

Chris
8 January 2020

Acknowledgements

This book is not as sad, infuriating or as stirring as it should be. It is about a set of state practices which are unimaginably cruel, and yet it remains quite sober, perhaps too prosaic. I don't have the words or the skill to properly convey what deported people taught me, but this book is my attempt to place their stories meaningfully, to ensure their meaning is not 'disappeared', as the logic of deportation might dictate. My first and final thanks, then, go to the deported people I met in Jamaica – to Jason, Ricardo, Chris, Denico and others – as well as their friends and family in the UK, who took a risk and followed me with this. Thank you.

It is a platitude, but a necessary one, to acknowledge that I am not the sole author of this book – far from it (and why would such a thing be desirable?). I have been graced with many friends who have taught me so much: friends who have read and commented on draft chapters, or who have talked aloud with me about the politics and the ideas that frame it. There are too many for me to be able to name them all, but in no particular order, thanks to: Lucy Mort, Tanzil Chowdhury, Sam Kidel, Adam Elliott-Cooper, Malcolm James, Helen Kim, Nisha Kapoor, Daniel Trilling, Leon Sealey-Huggins, Nadine El-Enany, Musab Younis, Gracie Mae Bradley, Becky Clarke, Patrick Williams, Kerem Nisancioglu, Monish Bhatia, Karis Campion, Eilat Maoz, Hicham Yezza, Alexandra Wanjiku Kelbert, Joshua

Virasami, William Tantam, Anish Chhibber, Tom Cowan, Amit Singh, Ikamara Larasi, Andonis Marden, Melanie Griffiths, Alpa Parmar, Scarlet Harris, Halimo Hussein, Joel Sharples, Timesh Pillay, Cecil Sagoe, Jess Costar, Mike Etienne and Remi Joseph-Salisbury. Further thanks must go to the RICE crew, Rosa May Fan Klub, E5 Massive, Chantelle, Tissot and George at Surviving Society, everyone at Bail for Immigration Detainees, my three legal expert friends called Tom – Southerden, Nunn and Giles – friends at the Unity Centre/Roots to Return, especially Jasmine, Lucy, Lotte and Yvonne, and folks at Haringey Anti Raids.

It is of course only proper to recognise and thank one's elders, my mentors and supervisors throughout the PhD process and beyond. Most notably, Bridget Anderson has been a constant guide and inspiration for as long as I can remember (anyone familiar with her work will recognise how fundamentally it shapes this book). Special thanks must also go to Les Back and Claire Alexander for their encouragement, kindness and invaluable comments on my PhD thesis, as well as to Satnam Virdee and Vron Ware for their incredibly generous and helpful remarks on earlier drafts of this book. Yasmeen Narayan, Julia O'Connell Davidson and Mette Berg have also provided so much wisdom and support over the years.

Extra special thanks must go to Sivamohan Valluvan (Vallu) for his tireless enthusiasm and backing, and for heartily responding to every muddled WhatsApp message hurled his way. To Thandi Loewenson and Miranda Critchley, for taking deportation stories and putting them into space, opening up and sharing this research in new and remarkable ways. To Sita Balani, for reading and discussing drafts, and for always opening up space in my head, where things can be thought and said more clearly. Finally to Gargi Bhattacharyya, my comrade and 'auntie', who warrants so much credit, beyond and against accreditation, not only for her intellectual work, but for her inexhaustible politics of doing and caring (it really is quite a remarkable thing).

Acknowledgements

The Sociological Review Fellowship allowed me to write for a year, and I am grateful to everyone at the journal, but most importantly to Michaela Benson for her support. Tom Dark has been a brilliant editor and friend, allaying my nerves about putting something as weighty as a book out into the world. So much love to Maureen Gillespie for hosting me in Dublin while I finalised the manuscript, and to Matt Davies and Becky Neal for sharing space and making me dinner during much of this writing. Gratitude too to new colleagues at Manchester, especially those comrades from the cold, wet picket line (Wendy, Luke, Bridget, Remi, Simin, Elisa, Meghan, Leah and Dharmi).

Thanks must always go to my Manchester family. To friends old and dear: Zussman, Matt, Slev, Andy, Sam, Rick, Loz, Kassim, Mish and the rest. To my siblings Clare, Adam and Joel (and Lars); my nieces Charday, Suranne and Isla, and my nephew Dominic (Charday deserves special thanks here: for taking particular interest in this project, for suggesting pseudonyms, for making me laugh and occasionally trying – and failing – to teach me to dance). Also thanks to Julia, Peter and Hannah, who are family too. And to Marvin and friends at the barbershop in Old Trafford, who shared invaluable insights into deportation with me. The biggest thanks must of course go to my Mum and Dad, Rhonna and Nigel de Noronha, for getting me interested in and angry about the world in the first place, for reading everything I've published, and for being there, always.

It is impossible to imagine writing this book without Georgia, who collaborated in the life lived around it, who travelled to Jamaica twice and made such an impression on the men written here, and who has supported, inspired and nurtured me for the duration, I am so grateful. Thank you for the laughter and the light.

Finally, again, I want to thank the deported people in Jamaica who let me into their lives. To Ossie for taking me under your wing and making this all possible; to Glen and Bernard Headley

('Prof'), who I hope rest peacefully; and to everyone else at NODM for their support. To all the people who shared their stories with me, even if they are not featured in this book, I am grateful for your time and trust. This book is dedicated to Jason, Chris, Ricardo and Denico – as well as to John, Kemoy, Shana, Michael, Tyson, Omari, Winston and Youan. It has been amazing getting to know you, and I hope that we remain friends. In the struggle for anti-racist and liveable futures, your stories offer the most urgent reminder of just how much work there is to do. Thanks for deciding to talk to me. I hope it was worth it, and that it's not too weird to read about yourselves.

Notes

Notes to Chapter 1. Introduction

1 Bernard Headley and Dragan Milovanovic, 'Rights and reintegrating deported migrants for national development: the Jamaican model', *Social Justice* 43 no. 1 (2016): 68–69.

2 At this point, the UK was deporting 'foreign criminals' under a policy called 'deport first, appeal later', which meant that individuals like Devon were denied an 'in-country right of appeal', and instead had to appeal immigration decisions once they had been removed. Unsurprisingly, out-of-country appeals were difficult, if not impossible, to lodge from thousands of miles away and in the context of deportation. There was not a single case of a non-EU national winning an out-of-country appeal in the first three years of this policy's operation (2014–2017) – which was perhaps precisely the intention. The 'deport first, appeal later' policy was found unlawful by the UK Supreme Court in June 2017, but thousands like Devon had already been deported under the system. Devon is a pseudonym – see 'A note on format' at the end of this chapter.

3 Mary Bosworth, 'Penal humanitarianism? Sovereign power in an era of mass migration', *New Criminal Law Review* 20 no. 1 (2017): 39–65.

4 See also Amnesty International, *Waiting in Vain – Jamaica: Unlawful Police Killings and Relatives' Long Struggle for Justice* (London: Amnesty International, 2016).

5 Amelia Gentleman, '"My life is in ruins": wrongly deported Windrush people facing fresh indignity', *The Guardian*, 10 September 2018, https://www.theguardian.com/uk-news/2018/sep/10/windrush-people-wrongly-deported-jamaica-criminal-offence, accessed 18 December 2019.

6 Amelia Gentleman, *The Windrush Betrayal: Exposing the Hostile*

Environment (London: Guardian Faber Publishing, 2019); Maya Goodfellow, *Hostile Environment: How Immigrants Became Scapegoats* (London: Verso, 2019).

7 Damien Gayle, Diane Taylor and Amelia Gentleman, 'Jamaican deportations "must be halted until Windrush report published"', *The Guardian*, 7 February 2020, https://www.theguardian.com/uk-news/2020/feb/07/jamaica-deportations-must-be-halted-until-windrush-report-published, accessed 28 February 2020.

8 Luke de Noronha, *Unpacking the Figure of the 'Foreign Criminal': Race, Gender and the Victim–Villain Binary'*, COMPAS Working Paper 121 (Oxford: COMPAS, University of Oxford, 2015).

9 Jenna Loyd, Matt Mitchelson and Andrew Burridge, eds, *Beyond Walls and Cages: Prisons, Borders, and Global Crisis* (Athens, GA: University of Georgia Press, 2012).

10 For post-deportation studies see: Shahram Khosravi, ed., *After Deportation: Ethnographic Perspectives* (Cham: Palgrave Macmillan, 2017); Nathalie Peutz, 'Embarking on an anthropology of removal', *Current Anthropology* 47 no. 2 (2006): 217–241; Tanya Golash-Boza, *Deported: Immigrant Policing, Disposable Labor, and Global Capitalism* (New York: New York University Press, 2015); Daniel Kanstroom, *Aftermath: Deportation Law and the New American Diaspora* (Oxford: Oxford University Press, 2012); Susan B. Coutin, *Exiled Home: Salvadoran Transnational Youth in the Aftermath of Violence* (Durham, NC: Duke University Press, 2016); David Brotherton and Luis Barrios, *Banished to the Homeland: Dominican Deportees and Their Stories of Exile* (New York: Columbia University Press, 2011); Elena Zilberg, *Space of Detention: The Making of a Transnational Gang Crisis Between Los Angeles and San Salvador* (Durham, NC: Duke University Press, 2011); Heike Drotbohm, 'The reversal of migratory family lives: a Cape Verdean perspective on gender and sociality pre- and post-deportation', *Journal of Ethnic and Migration Studies* 41 no. 4 (2015): 653–670; Liza Schuster and Nassim Majidi, 'Deportation stigma and re-migration', *Journal of Ethnic and Migration Studies* 41 no. 4 (2015): 635–652; Clara Lecadet, 'From migration destitution to self-organization into transitory national communities: the revival of citizenship in post-deportation experience in Mali', in *The Social, Political and Historical Contours of Deportation*, eds B. Anderson, M. J. Gibney and E. Paoletti (New York: Springer, 2015).

11 Daniel Kanstroom, *Deportation Nation: Outsiders in American History* (Cambridge, MA: Harvard University Press, 2010); Imogen Tyler, 'Deportation nation: Theresa May's hostile environment', *Journal for the Study of British Cultures* 25 no. 1 (2018).

12 Stephanie Silverman, '"Regrettable but necessary?" A historical and theoretical study of the rise of the UK immigration detention estate and its opposition', *Politics and Policy* 40 no. 6 (2012): 1131–1157.

13 Paul Gilroy, *After Empire: Melancholia or Convivial Culture?* (London: Routledge, 2004).

14 Matthew Gibney, 'Asylum and the expansion of deportation in the United Kingdom', *Government and Opposition* 43 no. 2 (2008): 146–167.

15 Ibid.

16 Don Flynn, 'New borders, new management: the dilemmas of modern immigration policies', *Ethnic and Racial Studies* 28 no. 3 (2005): 463–490; Alice Bloch and Liza Schuster, 'At the extremes of exclusion: deportation, detention and dispersal', *Ethnic and Racial Studies* 28 no. 3 (2005): 491–512.

17 This is not meant to deny that these migrants had compelling claims to protection under the refugee convention, but my concern here is not with defending any notion of the 'genuine refugee'. From my perspective, an 'asylum seeker' – or indeed a 'labour migrant' or a 'spouse' – is a juridical or legal category, and a not human type.

18 Bridget Anderson, *Us and Them? The Dangerous Politics of Immigration Control* (Oxford: Oxford University Press, 2013), chs 3 and 4.

19 Ibid.

20 Reece Jones, *Violent Borders: Refugees and the Right to Move* (London: Verso, 2016).

21 Nicholas De Genova, 'Migrant "illegality" and deportability in everyday life', *Annual Review of Anthropology* 31 (2002): 419–447.

22 Catherine Dauvergne, *Making People Illegal: What Globalization Means for Migration and Law* (Cambridge: Cambridge University Press, 2008).

23 Anderson, *Us and Them?*

24 Nicholas De Genova and Nathalie Peutz, eds, *The Deportation Regime: Sovereignty, Space, and the Freedom of Movement* (Durham, NC: Duke University Press, 2010).

25 Bridget Anderson, Matthew Gibney and Emanuela Paoletti, 'Citizenship, deportation and the boundaries of belonging', *Citizenship Studies* 15 no. 5 (2011): 547–563.

26 Nicholas De Genova, 'Spectacles of migrant "illegality": the scene of exclusion, the obscene of inclusion', *Ethnic and Racial Studies* 36 no. 7 (2013): 1180–1198.

27 De Genova, 'Migrant "illegality" and deportability in everyday life'.

28 Golash-Boza, *Deported*, 5.

29 Gargi Bhattacharyya, *Rethinking Racial Capitalism: Questions of*

Reproduction and Survival (London: Rowman & Littlefield International, 2018), ix.

30 My own thinking on the contradictions, the conjuncture and the relationship between racist culture, authoritarianism and neoliberal statecraft has been profoundly shaped by the work of Stuart Hall. See, for example, Stuart Hall, *The Hard Road to Renewal: Thatcherism and the Crisis of the Left* (London: Verso, 1988).

31 Gargi Bhattacharyya, *Crisis, Austerity, and Everyday Life: Living in a Time of Diminishing Expectations* (Basingstoke: Palgrave Macmillan, 2015); Imogen Tyler, *Revolting Subjects: Social Abjection and Resistance in Neoliberal Britain* (London: Zed Books, 2013).

32 While this law-and-order 'moral authoritarianism' is most closely associated with Thatcherism, these political rationalities were only extended under New Labour (indeed, the UK's prison population went from 61,000 to over 80,000 under Tony Blair).

33 Hall, *The Hard Road to Renewal*; Bhattacharyya, *Crisis, Austerity, and Everyday Life*.

34 On Brexit, see: Satnam Virdee and Brendan McGeever, 'Racism, crisis, Brexit', *Ethnic and Racial Studies* 48 no. 10 (2018); Sivamohan Valluvan, *The Clamour of Nationalism: Race and Nation in Twenty-First Century Britain* (Manchester: Manchester University Press, 2019); Gurminder Bhambra, 'Brexit, Trump, and "methodological whiteness": on the misrecognition of race and class', *British Journal of Sociology* 68 no. 1 (2017): 214–232.

35 Didier Bigo, 'Security and immigration: toward a critique of the politics of unease', *Alternatives* 27 (2002): 63–92.

36 Nisha Kapoor, *Deport, Deprive, Extradite: 21st Century State Extremism* (London: Verso, 2018).

37 Stuart Hall and Les Back, 'At home and not at home: Stuart Hall in conversation with Les Back', *Cultural Studies* 23 no. 4 (2009): 658–687.

38 Wendy Brown, *Walled States, Waning Sovereignty* (New York: Zone, 2010).

39 Saskia Sassen, *Expulsions: Brutality and Complexity in the Global Economy* (Cambridge, MA: Harvard University Press, 2014), 1.

40 De Genova and Peutz, *The Deportation Regime*.

41 Anderson, Gibney and Paoletti, 'Citizenship, deportation and the boundaries of belonging', 549.

42 Scott Blinder, *Deportations, Removals and Voluntary Departures from the UK: A Briefing* (Oxford: Migration Observatory, 2017), 3.

43 Bridget Anderson and Martin Ruhs, 'Semi-compliance and illegality in migrant labour markets: an analysis of migrants, employers and the state in the UK', *Population, Space, Place* 16 no. 3 (2010): 195–211.

44 Corporate Watch, Deportation charter flights: updated report 2018 (2 July 2018), https://corporatewatch.org/deportation-charter-flights-updated-report-2018, accessed 4 January 2020.

45 Nosheen Iqbal, 'Stansted 15: "We are not terrorists, no lives were at risk. We have no regrets"', *The Guardian*, 16 December 2018, https://www.theguardian.com/world/2018/dec/16/migrants-deportation-stansted-actvists, accessed 22 December 2019.

46 Table 1 shows the total number of 'enforced returns' from the UK, and the number of 'enforced returns' from the UK to Jamaica between 2004 and 2018 (beginning in 2004 because this is where current Home Office statistics begin). From Table 1, the first question worth asking is why did the total number of 'enforced returns' peak in 2004? In the early 2000s, immigration was fast becoming one of the primary political concerns among voters, specifically in relation to the issue of asylum. Asylum became perhaps the defining issue of Tony Blair's rule (overshadowed only by the Iraq War), so that by 2004 he had announced that, every month, more 'failed asylum seekers' would be removed than new claims made – the so-called 'tipping point' approach – an aim which proved impossible to meet. Between 2000 and 2004, the Labour government was desperately trying to 'assert control' over migration, and it repeatedly set aggressive removal targets. This explains the marked

Table 1. *Numbers of enforced returns (total and to Jamaica) from the UK, 2004–2018*

Year	Total	To Jamaica
2004	21,425	1,645
2005	20,808	1,373
2006	19,372	1,045
2007	17,770	906
2008	17,239	980
2009	15,252	686
2010	14,854	495
2011	15,063	332
2012	14,647	310
2013	13,311	288
2014	14,395	291
2015	13,690	310
2016	12,469	250
2017	12,049	142
2018	9,474	62

increase in the overall number of removals during this time. The demand for greater control was also intensified with the accession of 10 new countries to the European Union in 2004, whose citizens would now be able to meet the demand for 'unskilled labour'. In this context, 'unproductive', asylum-seeking, non-European migrants, especially Muslims, were wholly unwanted.

The focus on 'asylum seekers', however, was not exclusive, and the government was ultimately committed to removing as many people as possible. Jamaican nationals were targeted in this broader context: only 25% of the 1,645 Jamaicans removed in 2004 had claimed asylum, but Jamaican nationals more broadly found themselves easy targets in this drive to deport by any possible means (relevant here is the fact that the Jamaican government was more obliging in receiving 'deportees' than many of the other states to which unwanted migrants were to be deported).

As we can see in Table 1, the total number of 'enforced returns' has been falling since 2004, but the number of 'enforced returns' specifically to Jamaica has been falling at an even greater rate. It is impossible to say with certainty exactly why the number has fallen so sharply, although several explanations are worth forwarding. Firstly, there have been significantly fewer Jamaican nationals arriving since 2003, when pre-entry visa controls were introduced (pre-entry visa controls were introduced much earlier, in the 1980s, for former Commonwealth subjects from Sri Lanka, Bangladesh, India, Pakistan, Ghana and Nigeria). Before 2003, Jamaican nationals did not need visas before flying to the UK, and so in the 1990s and early 2000s many travelled to the UK as visitors, received a six-month visa and then simply overstayed. Indeed, this is the migration history of the four men featured in this book, and of many of the other deported people I met in Jamaica (I only met one deported person in Jamaica who had moved to the UK after 2003). Visa controls do much of the dirty work of immigration control, and fewer Jamaican nationals have been able to move to the UK since 2003, which has reduced the pool of migrants liable to deportation.

There has also been a reduction in the number of Jamaican nationals in UK prisons – from 1,516 in 2006 to 467 in 2019 – and given that most 'foreign offenders' are now deported, this has implications for the number of 'enforced returns' each year. Although the overall number of 'foreign offenders' deported increased markedly from 2006 onwards, and has hovered between 5,000 and 6,000 since then, in recent years the number of EU nationals has increased as a proportion of the total – from under 14% in 2009 to 68% in 2017.

Finally, following the 'Windrush scandal' in the spring of 2017, removals to Jamaica dipped significantly, not least because Virgin Atlantic stopped deporting individuals on its commercial flights, including that from Gatwick Airport to Montego Bay.

Despite the recent decline in the number of deportations to Jamaica, the numbers remain significant and, importantly for this study, any Jamaican nationals with a criminal record is still likely to be facing deportation, regardless of their ties to the UK, even if their deportation is occurring less speedily in the wake of the 'Windrush scandal'. Given that Home Office statistics are slippery and incomplete, and methods of collection and categorisation change over time, these explanations offer some possible reasons for the spike in deportations in 2004, and the sharp decline in removals to Jamaica since then.

47 Liberty, 'A guide to the hostile environment', May 2019, https://www. libertyhumanrights.org.uk/policy/policy-reports-briefings/guide-hostile-environment-border-controls-dividing-our-communities-%E2%80%93, accessed 3 January 2020.

48 For an excellent account of everyday bordering, see the film *Everyday Bordering* produced by the Centre for Research on Migration, Refugees and Belonging and available on Vimeo at https://vimeo. com/126315982, accessed 4 January 2020.

49 Hannah Jones, et al., *Go Home? The Politics of Immigration Controversies* (Manchester: Manchester University Press, 2017); Tyler, 'Deportation nation'.

50 Gentleman, *The Windrush Betrayal*.

51 David Lammy, 'Don't led Rudd's departure distract from a toxic policy that needs to die', *The Guardian*, 30 April 2018, https://www. theguardian.com/commentisfree/2018/apr/30/amber-rudd-departure-toxic-policy-windrush-generation-home-secretary-david-lammy, accessed 24 November 2019.

52 See note 46 to this chapter (above).

53 Luke de Noronha, 'Sajid Javid's deportation flight shows the hostile environment in action', *The Guardian*, 6 February 2019, https:// www.theguardian.com/commentisfree/2019/feb/06/sajid-javid-windrush-deportation-criminal-jamaica, accessed 17 September 2019.

54 Gayle et al., 'Jamaican deportations'.

55 Cited in de Noronha, *Unpacking the Figure of the 'Foreign Criminal'*, 13.

56 BBC, 'How the deportation story emerged', 9 October 2006, http:// news.bbc.co.uk/2/hi/uk_news/politics/4945922.stm, accessed 11 September 2019.

57 de Noronha, *Unpacking the Figure of the 'Foreign Criminal'*.

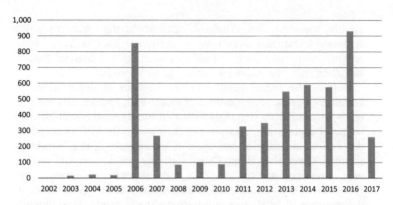

Graph 1. *Numbers of articles featuring the terms 'foreign criminal' and 'foreign prisoner' in UK national newspapers, 2002–2017*

58 Graph 1 shows the number of stories in UK national newspapers featuring the terms 'foreign criminal' and 'foreign prisoner' over time (author's own graph – based on a Nexis search).

59 Emma Kaufman, *Punish and Expel: Border Control, Nationalism, and the New Purpose of the Prison* (Oxford: Oxford University Press, 2015).

60 Emma Kaufman, 'Hubs and spokes: the transformation of the British prison', in *The Borders of Punishment: Migration, Citizenship, and Social Exclusion,* eds Katja Aas and Mary Bosworth (Oxford: Oxford University Press, 2013), 169.

61 Liz Fekete and Frances Webber, 'Foreign nationals, enemy penology and the criminal justice system', *Race and Class* 51 no. 4 (2010): 1–25.

62 John Vine, *A Thematic Inspection of How the UK Border Agency Manages Foreign National Prisoners* (London: Independent Chief Inspector of UK Border Agency, 2011); Blinder, *Deportations, Removals and Voluntary Departures from the UK.*

63 Kaufman, *Punish and Expel.*

64 See Graph 1 at note 58. Importantly, the figure of the 'foreign criminal' remains a central trope in British politics. For example, a few days after Boris Johnson became the Prime Minister, his special adviser, Dominic Cummings, vowed to 'clamp down on dangerous foreign criminals and paedophiles', a promise that was reported favourably in the *Daily Mail.* See https://www.dailymail.co.uk/news/article-7345043/Dominic-Cummings-slams-f-mad-justice-system.html, accessed 23 March 2020.

65 Luqmani Thompson & Partners, 'Operation Nexus: briefing

paper', 2014, https://www.luqmanithompson.com/operation-nexus, accessed 30 August 2019; Frances Webber, 'Deportation on suspicion', Institute for Race Relations, 20 June 2013, http://www.irr.org.uk/news/deportation-on-suspicion, accessed 11 June 2019; Melanie Griffiths, 'Foreign, criminal: a doubly damned modern British folk-devil', *Citizenship Studies* 21 no. 5 (2017): 527–546.

66 The police are not only working with the Home Office to build deportation cases against *suspected* criminals but are also now using on-the-spot fingerprint scanning to check if individuals are wanted by the Home Office. See Remi Joseph-Salisbury, 'Stop the scan: turning police into border guards', *Red Pepper Magazine,* 7 July 2019.

67 R (on the application of Kiarie) (Appellant) *v.* Secretary of State for the Home Department (Respondent), [2017] UKSC 42, 14 June 2017.

68 Melanie Griffiths, '"My passport is just my way out of here". Mixed-immigration status families, immigration enforcement and the citizenship implications', *Identities* [published online 18 July 2019], DOI: 10.1080/1070289X.2019.1625568.

69 Home Office, Immigration Rules: Section 13, https://www.gov.uk/guidance/immigration-rules, accessed 1 September 2018.

70 Bloch and Schuster, 'At the extremes of exclusion'.

71 For a more detailed account of legal journeys in relation to deportation, see Ines Hasselberg, *Enduring Uncertainty: Deportation, Punishment and Everyday Life* (New York: Berghahn Books, 2016).

72 Benjamin Bowling and Coretta Phillips, *Racism, Crime and Justice* (Harlow: Longman, 2002).

73 Claire Alexander, 'Breaking black: the death of ethnic and racial studies in Britain', *Ethnic and Racial Studies* 41 no. 6 (2018): 1034–1054.

74 Paul Gilroy, *There Ain't No Black in the Union Jack: The Cultural Politics of Race and Nation* (London: Routledge, 2002); Centre for Contemporary Cultural Studies (CCCS), *The Empire Strikes Back: Race and Racism in 70s Britain* (London: Hutchinson, 1982); John Solomos, *Black Youth, Racism and the State: The Politics of Ideology and Policy* (Cambridge: Cambridge University Press, 1988); Michael Keith, *Race Riots and Policing: Lore and Disorder in a Multi-racist Society* (London: UCL Press, 1993).

75 Patrick Williams and Becky Clarke, *Dangerous Associations: Joint Enterprise, Gangs and Racism* (London: Centre for Crime and Justice Studies, 2016).

76 Niamh Eastwood, Michael Shiner and Daniel Bear, *The Numbers in Black and White: Ethnic Disparities in the Policing and Prosecution of Drug Offences in England and Wales* (London: Release, 2013).

77 Mike Phillips and Trevor Phillips, *Windrush: The Irresistible Rise of Multi-racial Britain* (London: Harper Collins, 1998).

78 Kathleen Paul, *Whitewashing Britain: Race and Citizenship in the Postwar Era* (Ithaca, NY: Cornell University Press, 1997); John Solomos, *Race and Racism in Britain*, 3rd edition (Basingstoke: Palgrave Macmillan, 2003); Ian Spencer, *British Immigration Policy Since 1939: The Making of Multi-racial Britain* (London: Routledge, 1997); Ann Dummett and Andrew Nicol, *Subjects, Citizens, Aliens, and Others: Nationality and Immigration Law* (London: George Weidenfeld & Nicholson, 1990); Steve Cohen, *Deportation Is Freedom: The Orwellian World of Immigration Controls* (London: Jessica Kingsley, 2005).

79 For a compelling and more recently published account of this history, see Nadine El-Enany, *Bordering Britain: Law, Race and Empire* (Manchester: Manchester University Press, 2020).

80 Ibid.

81 Stuart Hall, *Familiar Stranger: A Life Between Two Islands* (London: Allen Lane, 2017); Obika Gray, *Demeaned but Empowered: The Social Power of the Urban Poor in Jamaica* (Kingston: University of the West Indies Press, 2004).

82 See, for example: Laurie Gunst, *Born Fi' Dead: A Journey Through the Yardie Underworld* (Edinburgh: Cannongate Books, 2003); Ian Thomson, *The Dead Yard: Tales of Modern Jamaica* (London: Faber & Faber, 2009).

83 See the documentary *Life and Debt* for a compelling account of this history (directed by Stephanie Black, 2001).

84 Rivke Jaffe, 'The hybrid state: crime and citizenship in urban Jamaica', *American Ethnologist* 40 no. 4 (2013): 734–748.

85 Iain Chambers, 'Method: ways of seeing migration, ways of narrating ... the world', in *A Jar of Wild Flowers: Essays in Celebration of John Berger*, eds Yasmin Gunaratnam and Amarjit Chandan (London: Zed Books, 2016).

86 Deborah Thomas, *Exceptional Violence: Embodied Citizenship in Transnational Jamaica* (Durham, NC: Duke University Press, 2011); Mimi Sheller, *Consuming the Caribbean: From Arawaks to Zombies* (New York: Routledge, 2003); Michel-Rolph Trouillot, *Silencing the Past: Power and the Production of History* (Boston, MA: Beacon Press, 2015).

87 Brown, *Walled States, Waning Sovereignty*, 21.

88 For an excellent critique of this liberal (non-racial) framing of migration and borders within the academy, see Alana Lentin, 'Postracial silences: the othering of race in Europe', in *Racism and Sociology*, eds Wulf Hund and Alana Lentin (Berlin: Lit Verlag, 2014).

89 On the links between race and nation, see: Étienne Balibar and Immanuel Wallerstein, *Race, Nation, Class: Ambiguous Identities* (London: Verso, 1991); Valluvan, *The Clamour of Nationalism*.

90 Nicholas De Genova, 'The "migrant crisis" as racial crisis: do black lives matter in Europe?', *Ethnic and Racial Studies* 41 no. 10 (2017) 1769. See also Nicholas De Genova, 'Migration and race in Europe: the trans-Atlantic Metastases of a post-colonial cancer', *European Journal of Social Theory* 13 no. 3 (2010): 405–419.

91 David Moffette and William Walters, 'Flickering presence: theorizing race and racism in the governmentality of borders and migration', *Studies in Social Justice* 12 no. 1 (2018): 96.

92 Anderson, *Us and Them?*

93 David Goldberg, *The Threat of Race: Reflections of Racial Neoliberalism* (Malden, MA: Wiley-Blackwell, 2009).

94 Stuart Hall, 'Race, articulation and societies structured in dominance', in *Black British Cultural Studies: A Reader*, eds Houston Baker, Manthia Diawara and Ruth Lindeborg (Chicago, IL: University of Chicago Press, 1996).

95 Mae Ngai, *Impossible Subjects: Illegal Aliens and the Making of Modern America* (Princeton, NJ: Princeton University Press, 2004).

96 Jon Fox, Laura Moroşanu and Eszter Szilassy, 'The racialization of the new European migration to the UK', *Sociology* 46 no. 4 (2012): 692.

97 Les Back and Shamser Sinha, with Charlynne Bryan, 'New hierarchies of belonging', *European Journal of Cultural Studies* 15 no. 2 (2012): 139–154.

98 A short vignette can demonstrate how borders actively produce racial categories. In Croydon, south London, in the shadow of the Home Office's immigration headquarters, Rekar Ahmed, a Kurdish-Iranian asylum seeker, was attacked by six young men in March 2017, and suffered a fractured spine and bleeding in the brain. One of the young men who attacked Ahmed first shouted: 'You are asylum seekers ... you have to go back to your own country'. The connection here between immigration law and racist violence is difficult to deny. The 'asylum seeker' is a juridical category, a product of the law, and yet the juridical category becomes so saturated with social and cultural meaning that it can motivate acts of murderous mob violence. When individuals are subjected to racist attacks on the street, *while being hailed as 'asylum seekers'*, we can see quite clearly the relationship between the law, racial meaning and racist violence (interestingly or, rather, painfully, one of Ahmed's six attackers was black, which raises difficult and complex questions about 'new hierarchies of belonging' in multi-status Britain). In subsequent chapters, I am interested in further tracing some of these connections between the law and racist culture.

99 Nicholas De Genova, *Working the Boundaries: Race, Space, and 'Illegality' in Mexican Chicago* (Durham, NC: Duke University Press, 2005).

100 Nira Yuval-Davis, Georgie Wemyss and Kathryn Cassidy, *Bordering* (Oxford: Polity, 2019).

101 Étienne Balibar, *We, the People of Europe? Reflections on Transnational Citizenship* (Princeton, NJ: Princeton University Press, 2004), 104.

102 Nandita Sharma, *Home Economics: Nationalism and the Making of 'Migrant Workers'* (Toronto: University of Toronto Press, 2006).

103 Luke de Noronha, 'Deportation, racism and multi-status Britain: immigration control and the production of race in the present', *Ethnic and Racial Studies* 42 no. 14 (2019): 2413–2430.

104 Cinzia Rienzo and Carlos Vargas-Silva, *Migrants in the UK: An Overview*, Migration Observatory Briefing (Oxford: COMPAS, University of Oxford, 2017).

105 Back and Sinha, 'New hierarchies of belonging'.

106 Bridget Anderson, Nandita Sharma and Cynthia Wright, 'Editorial. Why no borders?', *Refuge: Canada's Journal on Refugees* 26 no. 2 (2009): 6.

107 Anderson, *Us and Them?*

108 Eithne Luibhéid, *Entry Denied: Controlling Sexuality at the Border* (Minneapolis, MN: University of Minnesota Press, 2002).

109 Griffiths, '"My passport is just my way out of here"'.

110 Headley and Milanovic, 'Rights and reintegrating deported migrants'.

111 See Stuart Hall's work on identity, in particular: Stuart Hall, 'Cultural identity and diaspora', in *Identity, Community, Culture, Difference*, ed. Jonathan Rutherford (London: Lawrence & Wishart, 1990); Stuart Hall, 'Minimal selves', in *Black British Cultural Studies: A Reader*, eds Houston A. Baker, Manthia Diawara and Ruth H. Lindeborg (Chicago, IL: University of Chicago Press, 1996).

112 Rebecca Hanson and Patricia Richards, *Harassed: Gender, Bodies and Ethnographic Research* (Berkeley, CA: University of California Press, 2019).

113 Raewyn Connell, *Masculinities*, 2nd edition (Cambridge: Polity Press, 2005).

114 Gail Lewis, 'Unsafe travel: experiencing intersectionality and feminist displacements', *Signs* 38 no. 4 (2013): 877.

115 Akhil Gupta and James Ferguson, 'Beyond "culture": space, identity and the politics of difference', in *Culture, Power, Place:*

Explorations in Critical Anthropology, eds Akhil Gupta and James Ferguson (Durham, NC: Duke University Press, 1997), 25.

116 Clifford Geertz, 'Deep hanging out', *New York Review of Books* 45 no. 16 (1998).

117 De Genova, *Working the Boundaries*.

118 Brotherton and Barrios, *Banished to the Homeland*; Coutin, *Exiled Home*; Golash-Boza, *Deported*.

119 Mitch Duneier and Les Back, 'Voices from the sidewalk: ethnography and writing race', *Ethnic and Racial Studies* 29 no. 3 (2006): 554.

120 For an excellent example of life-story portraiture in a study of racism and immigration control, see Les Back and Shamser Sinha, *Migrant City* (Oxford: Routledge, 2018).

Notes to Chapter 2. Jason

1 For a critical overview of the UK's immigration regime, see Corporate Watch, *The UK Border Regime: A Critical Guide* (London: Corporate Watch, 2018), https://corporatewatch.org/wp-content/uploads/2018/10/UK_border_regime.pdf, accessed 4 January 2020; and see also the 'Right to Remain Toolkit', available at https://right-toremain.org.uk/toolkit/, accessed 5 January 2020.

2 In discussing 'damage' and 'vitality', I am indebted to Les Back, *The Art of Listening* (Oxford: Berg, 2007).

3 C. Wright Mills, *The Sociological Imagination* (New York: Oxford University Press, 1959).

4 In Jamaica, route taxis are cars that run a specified route, collecting single passengers who share their journey with others going along the same route. In this case, I am referring to the 'Half Way Tree to Campus' route.

5 João Biehl, *Vita: Life in a Zone of Social Abandonment* (Berkeley, CA: University of California Press, 2005).

6 Jason's grandmother moved to the UK to join her sister, who had been living there since the late 1950s. This is important because it reminds us that newer migrants from Jamaica often migrate via networks formed through post-war mass migration. See Luke de Noronha, 'The "Windrush generation" and "illegal immigrants" are both our kin', Verso Books Blogs, https://www.versobooks.com/blogs/3771-the-windrush-generation-and-illegal-immigrants-are-both-our-kin, accessed 13 June 2019.

7 As with the other men in this book, Jason arrived on a visitor visa and overstayed.

8 Although I cannot verify the details of the fight, it is worth noting that black boys are disproportionately excluded from British schools. According to government statistics published in September 2018, Black Caribbean pupils were excluded at nearly three times the rate of White British pupils (from 'Ethnicity Facts and Figures' online, https://www.ethnicity-facts-figures.service.gov.uk/education-skills-and-training/absence-and-exclusions/pupil-exclusions/latest, accessed 25 March 2020), while a government-commissioned literature review of the available evidence published in May 2019 found that even when controlling for other factors, Black Caribbean children are more likely to be excluded from schools, both temporarily and permanently: Berni Graham et al., *School Exclusion: A Literature Review on the Continued Disproportionate Exclusion of Certain Children* (London: Department of Education, 2019).

9 It is not uncommon for homeless people to sleep on buses in London, because it is safer and warmer than sleeping rough on the street. In fact, one London charity for young homeless people resorted to handing out bus tickets in 2015: see Amelia Gentleman, 'Charity gives London's young homeless tickets to sleep on night buses', *The Guardian*, 24 September 2015.

10 Prison Reform Trust, *Prison: The Facts – Bromley Briefings Summer 2019* (London: Prison Reform Trust, 2019), http://www.prisonreformtrust.org.uk/Portals/0/Documents/Bromley%20Briefings/Prison%20the%20facts%20Summer%202019.pdf, accessed 4 January 2020.

11 Vickie Cooper and Joe Sim, 'Punishing the detritus and the damned: penal and semi-penal institutions in Liverpool and the North West', in *Why Prison?*, ed. David Scott (Cambridge: Cambridge University Press, 2013), 189–210.

12 On the criminalisation of migration, see Katja Aas and Mary Bosworth, eds, *The Borders of Punishment: Migration, Citizenship, and Social Exclusion* (Oxford: Oxford University Press, 2013); Mary Bosworth and Mhairi Guild, 'Governing through migration control: security and citizenship in Britain', *British Journal of Criminology* 48 no. 6 (2008): 703–719; Juliet Stumpf, 'The crimmigration crisis: immigrants, crime, and sovereign power', *American University Law Review* 56 no. 2 (2006): 367–419.

13 Luqmani Thompson & Partners, 'Operation Nexus: briefing paper'.

14 On detention, see Mary Bosworth, *Inside Immigration Detention* (Oxford: Oxford University Press, 2014).

15 On charter flights, see Corporate Watch, 'Deportation charter flights'.

16 Back and Sinha, *Migrant City*.

17 Hasselberg, *Enduring Uncertainty*.

18 Anderson, *Us and Them?*
19 Bhattacharyya, *Crisis, Austerity, and Everyday Life*.
20 May Bulman, 'Number of homeless people sleeping on streets in England hits highest level on record', *The Independent*, 25 January 2018, https://www.independent.co.uk/news/uk/home-news/homelessness-rough-sleepers-record-england-stats-homeless-people-2017-increase-a8177086.html, accessed 14 September 2019.
21 Loïc Wacquant, *Punishing the Poor: The Neoliberal Government of Social Insecurity* (Durham, NC: Duke University Press, 2009), 287–314.
22 Lauren Wroe, Rachel Larkin and Reima Ana Maglajlic, eds, *Social Work with Refugees, Asylum Seekers and Migrants: Theory and Skills for Practice* (London: Jessica Kingsley, 2019).
23 I borrow the concept of disentitlement from Gargi Bhattacharyya in *Crisis, Austerity, and Everyday Life*.
24 Tyler, *Revolting Subjects*.
25 Bridget Anderson, '"Heads I win. Tails you lose". Migration and the worker citizen', *Current Legal Problems* 68 no. 1 (2015): 179–196.
26 Anderson, *Us and Them?*
27 Ibid.
28 Vickie Cooper and David Whyte, *The Violence of Austerity* (London: Pluto Press, 2017).
29 Anderson, '"Heads I win. Tails you lose"', 181.
30 Ibid., 196.
31 For a historical account of the relationship between race, class and deservingness in Britain, see Robbie Shilliam, *Race and the Undeserving Poor* (Newcastle-Upon-Tyne: Agenda Publishing, 2018).
32 Valluvan, *The Clamour of Nationalism*, 155–183; Virdee and McGeever, 'Racism, crisis, Brexit'.
33 Ambalavaner Sivanandan, *A Different Hunger* (London: Pluto, 1982); Satnam Virdee, *Racism, Class and the Racialized Outsider* (London: Routledge, 2014).
34 De Genova, 'Migrant "illegality" and deportability in everyday life'.
35 On the role of racism in dividing the working class see: W. E. B. Du Bois, *Darkwater: Voices from Within the Veil* (London: Verso, 2016); Theodore Allen, *The Invention of the White Race, Volume 1* (London: Verso, 1994); David Roediger, *Class, Race, and Marxism* (London: Verso, 2017); Virdee, *Racism, Class and the Racialized Outsider*.
36 For an excellent ethnographic study of how racism gets into young people's lives, see Les Back, *New Ethnicities and Urban Culture: Racisms and Multiculture in Young Lives* (London: UCL Press, 1996).

37 Anderson, *Us and Them?*, 70.
38 Biehl, *Vita*, 5.

Notes to Chapter 3. Ricardo

1 Famously in that election, the Conservative MP Peter Griffiths was elected on the slogan 'If you want a nigger for a neighbour, vote Labour'. While Griffiths did not officially campaign on that slogan, he refused to disown it, instead stating: 'I would not condemn any man who said that.... I regard it as a manifestation of popular feeling'. See Stuart Jeffries, 'Britain's most racist election: the story of Smethwick, 50 years on', *The Guardian*, 15 October, 2014; Elizabeth Buettner, '"This is Staffordshire not Alabama": racial geographies of Commonwealth immigration in early 1960s Britain', *Journal of Imperial and Commonwealth History* 42 no. 4 (2014): 710–740.

2 Sheller, *Consuming the Caribbean*.

3 Ian G. Strachan, *Paradise and Plantation: Tourism and Culture in the Anglophone Caribbean* (Charlottesville, VA: University of Virginia Press, 2002).

4 Adrian Frater, 'St James closing in on 250 murders – five people killed in less than 72 hours', *Jamaica Gleaner*, 16 December 2016.

5 '2017 murders by divisions ... St James leads with 335 homicides', *Jamaica Gleaner*, 5 January 2018.

6 Tinesha worked at a call centre in Montego Bay Free Zone, calling people in the US to collect repayments for medical fees. See Jovan Scott Lewis, 'Structural readjustment: crime, development, and repair in the Jamaican lottery scam', *Anthropological Quarterly* 91 no. 3 (2018): 1029–1048.

7 On ASBOs, see Phil Scraton, *Power, Conflict and Criminalisation* (Oxford: Routledge, 2007), 126–147.

8 See Liberty, 'ASBOs and civil orders', https://www.libertyhuman rights.org.uk/human-rights/justice-and-fair-trials/asbos-and-civil-orders, accessed 17 September 2019.

9 On the use of pre-criminal punishment within immigration control, see Lucia Zedner, 'Is the criminal law only for citizens? A problem at the borders of punishment', in *The Borders of Punishment: Migration, Citizenship, and Social Exclusion*, eds Katja Aas and Mary Bosworth (Oxford: Oxford University Press, 2013).

10 David Lammy, *The Lammy Review: An Independent Review into the Treatment of, and Outcomes for, Black, Asian and Minority Ethnic Individuals in the Criminal Justice System* (London: Ministry of Justice, 2017); Bowling and Phillips, *Racism, Crime and Justice*.

11 See, for example, Williams and Clarke, *Dangerous Associations'*.

12 In this context, police racism is not merely an effect of some hard-wired anti-black impulse deep within the minds of offending officers (even if it is partly that), but also a reflection of historically specific racist cultures – within particular police forces, in particular parts of the country, at particular historical moments. See Keith, *Race Riots and Policing*.

13 For an excellent account of racial dynamics in the context of local specificity and identity, see Jacqueline Nassy-Brown, *Dropping Anchor, Setting Sail: Geographies of Race in Black Liverpool* (Princeton, NJ: Princeton University Press, 2005).

14 De Genova, 'The "migrant crisis" as racial crisis'; Fox, Moroşanu and Szilassy, 'The racialization of new European migration'.

15 See footnote 97, Chapter 1.

16 Caroline Knowles, 'Theorizing race and ethnicity: contemporary paradigms and perspectives', in *The Sage Handbook of Race and Ethnic Studies*, eds Patricia Hill Collins and John Solomos (London: Sage, 2010).

17 de Noronha, 'Deportation, racism and multi-status Britain'.

18 James Ferguson, *Global Shadows: Africa in the Neoliberal World Order* (Durham, NC: Duke University Press, 2006), 110.

19 For Nicholas De Genova, this can lead to 'a mere politics of anti-discrimination, which in its refusal to interrogate the sociopolitical production of racialized distinctions, re-stabilizes the notion that racism is little more than a discriminatory hostility towards pheno-typic and anatomical differences, and thus re-naturalizes race as "biology"'. De Genova, 'The "migrant crisis" as racial crisis', 1769.

20 As De Genova puts it again: 'race is not a fact of nature; it is a sociopolitical fact of domination'. Ibid., 1770.

21 de Noronha, 'Deportation, racism and multi-status Britain'; Knowles, 'Theorizing race and ethnicity'; Fox, Moroşanu and Szilassy, 'The racialization of the new European migration'.

22 In fact, the police have long been involved in immigration enforce-ment in the UK, particularly in relation to immigration raids. Most notably, a Jamaican national named Joy Gardner was killed in 1993 by both police and immigration officers, during an immigration raid at her house. See Nick Cohen, 'Why did Joy Gardner die?', *The Independent*, 8 August 1993. More precisely, then, I am referring to the involvement of police in new kinds of bordering practices: sharing police intelligence in support of deportation cases, checking the nationality of arrestees against computerised databases and working with immigration officers embedded within police stations and prisons.

23 Alpa Parmar, 'Policing belonging: race and nation in the UK', in *Race, Criminal Justice and Migration Control: Enforcing the Boundaries of Belonging*, eds Mary Bosworth, Alpa Parmar and Yolanda Vazquez (Oxford: University of Oxford Press, 2018).

24 Vikram Dodd, 'Police to stop passing on immigration status of crime victims', *The Guardian*, 7 December 2018.

25 Joseph-Salisbury, 'Stop the scan'.

26 Luqmani Thompson & Partners, 'Operation Nexus: briefing paper'.

27 Williams and Clarke, *Dangerous Associations*.

28 Amnesty International UK, *Trapped in the Matrix: Secrecy, Stigma, and Bias in the Met's Gangs Database* (London: Amnesty, 2018).

29 Ferguson, *Global Shadows*, 110.

30 Emma Kaufman, 'Finding foreigners: race and the politics of memory in British prisons', *Population, Space and Place* 18 no. 6 (2012): 701–714.

31 Coretta Phillips, *The Multicultural Prison: Ethnicity, Masculinity, and Social Relations Among Prisoners* (Oxford: Oxford University Press, 2012).

32 Back, *The Art of Listening*, 75.

33 Ibid., 76–77.

34 Back and Sinha, *Migrant City*.

Notes to Chapter 4. Chris

1 Section 13 of the Immigration Rules states that an individual can appeal 'his' (in the gendered language of the Rules) deportation on the grounds that he has 'been lawfully resident in the UK for most of his life', and is 'socially and culturally integrated in the UK'. As a result, part of the Home Office determination involves questioning whether a person is integrated, and removals are often partly justified on the grounds that the individual is not.

2 Susan Coutin makes a similar point in relation to El Salvadorans who move to the US as children: 'Like other 1.5-generation children, these deportees became part of the U.S. neighborhoods, and in fact the crimes of which some of them were convicted are evidence of the degree to which they joined in local youth culture.' Coutin, *Exiled Home*, 133.

3 On the broader causes of social harm and a critique of dominant accounts of 'crime', see Paddy Hillyard and Steve Tombs, 'From "crime" to social harm?', *Crime, Law and Social Change* 48 no. 1–2 (2007): 9–25; Steven Box, *Power, Crime and Mystification* (London: Routledge, 1983).

4 Sivamohan Valluvan, 'Racial entanglements and sociological confusions: repudiating the rehabilitation of integration', *British Journal of Sociology* 69 no. 2 (2018): 436–458.

5 Lentin, "Postracial silences.

6 Valluvan, *The Clamour of Nationalism.*

7 Anderson, *Us and Them?*

8 Home Office, 'Criminality – Article 8 ECHR cases', 33, published for Home Office staff on 13 May 2019, https://www.gov.uk/government/publications/criminality-guidance-in-article-8-echr-cases, accessed 6 January 2020.

9 Home Office 2007, quoted in Anderson, *Us and Them?*, 155.

10 Back, *New Ethnicities and Urban Culture.*

11 Lee Bridges, 'Lammy Review: will it change outcomes in the criminal justice system?', *Race and Class* 59 no. 3 (2018): 80–90.

12 Stuart Hall et al., *Policing the Crisis: Mugging, the State and Law and Order* (London: Macmillan, 1978); Solomos, *Black Youth, Racism and the State*; Keith, *Race Riots and Policing.*

13 Adam Elliott-Cooper, 'The struggle that cannot be named: violence, space and the re-articulation of racism in post-Duggan Britain', *Ethnic and Racial Studies* 41 no. 14 (2018): 2445–2463; Hall et al., *Policing the Crisis.*

14 Centre for Contemporary Cultural Studies, *The Empire Strikes Back*; Gilroy, *There Ain't No Black.*

15 Claire Alexander, *(Re)thinking 'Gangs'* (London: Runnymede Trust, 2008).

16 Paul Gilroy, 'The myth of black criminality', *Socialist Register*, 19 (1982), 52.

17 Simon Hallsworth, *Street Crime* (Exeter, Willan Publishing, 2005).

18 Hall et al., *Policing the Crisis.*

19 See for example Rod Liddle, 'Half of black children do not live with their father. And we wonder why they're dying', *The Times*, 13 January 2019.

20 Vikram Dodd, 'Met police "disproportionately" use stop and search powers on black people', *The Guardian*, 26 January 2019.

21 Matthew Tempest, 'Black communities must speak out, says Blair', *The Guardian*, 11 April 2007.

22 For more on the history of 'the gang' in UK politics and policing, see Hannah Smithson, Rob Ralphs and Patrick Williams, "Used and Abused: The Problematic Usage of Gang Terminology in the United Kingdom and its Implications for Ethnic Minority Youth', *British Journal of Criminology* 53 no. 1 (2013): 113–128.

23 Jamie Grierson, 'Sajid Javid introduces knife crime prevention orders', *The Guardian*, 31 January 2019.

24 Roger Grimshaw and Matt Ford, *Young People, Violence and Knives – Revisiting the Evidence and Policy Discussions*, UK Justice Policy Review (issue 3) (London: Centre for Crime and Justice Studies, November 2018).

25 Back, *New Ethnicities and Urban Culture*; see also Malcolm James, *Urban Multiculture: Youth Politics and Cultural Transformation in a Global City* (Basingstoke: Palgrave Macmillan, 2015).

26 Robin D. G. Kelley, *Yo' Mama's Disfunktional! Fighting the Culture Wars in Urban America* (Boston, MA: Beacon Press, 1997).

27 Ben Quinn, 'David Starkey claims "the whites have become black"', *The Guardian*, 13 August 2011.

28 Gilroy, *After Empire*.

29 Les Back and Shamser Sinha, 'Multicultural conviviality in the midst of racism's ruins', *Journal of Intercultural Studies* 37 no. 5 (2016): 522.

30 Gilroy, *There Ain't No Black*.

31 Ibid.; see also Gail Lewis, 'Stuart Hall and social policy: an encounter of strangers?', in *Without Guarantees: In Honour of Stuart Hall*, eds Paul Gilroy, Lawrence Grossberg and Angela McRobbie (London: Verso, 2000), 193–202.

32 Gilroy, *After Empire*, 131–132.

33 Valluvan, *The Clamour of Nationalism*, 202, 205.

34 Arun Kundnani, *The Muslims Are Coming! Islamophobia, Extremism, and the Domestic War on Terror* (London: Verso, 2014).

35 Back and Sinha, 'Multicultural conviviality in the midst of racism's ruins', 523

36 On benefit sanctions and austerity, see Cooper and White, *The Violence of Austerity*.

37 TUC, 'Youth unemployment and ethnicity – TUC report', 2012, https://www.tuc.org.uk/news/young-black-men-have-experienced-sharpest-unemployment-rise-2010, accessed 15 September 2019.

38 As several scholars have shown, welfare and criminal justice policies represent a shared system of governance over marginalised groups, always connected to the wider organisation of economic relations and labour markets (see e.g. Wacquant, *Punishing the Poor*). In the last few decades, the retrenchment of the welfare state has been accompanied by the expansion of penal institutions and logics, and this has particularly racialised implications in the context of structural racism within education, employment, housing, social provision and the criminal justice system.

39 Planning Institute of Jamaica, *Economic and Social Survey 2013* (Kingston: Planning Institute of Jamaica, 2014).

40 G. Mosse, *Nationalism and Sexuality: Middle-Class Morality and*

Sexual Norms in Modern Europe (Madison, WI: University of Wisconsin Press, 1985).

41 Hazel Carby, 'White woman listen! Black feminism and the boundaries of sisterhood', in *The Empire Strikes Back: Race and Racism in 70s Britain*, Centre for Contemporary Cultural Studies (London: Hutchinson, 1982); Angela Davis, *Women, Race and Class* (London: Women's Press, 1982); Hortense Spillers, '"Mama's baby, papa's maybe: an American grammar book', *Diacritics* 17 no. 2 (1987): 64–81.

42 Tracey Reynolds, 'Exploring the absent/present dilemma: black fathers, family relationships and social capital in Britain', *Annals of the American Academy of Political and Social Science* 624 no. 12 (2009).

43 Ibid.

44 Griffiths, '"My passport is just my way out of here"'. See also Betty de Hart, 'Superdads: migrant fathers' right to family life before the European Court of Human Rights', *Men and Masculinities* 18 no. 4 (2015).

45 Peter Wade, 'Racial identity and nationalism: a theoretical view from Latin America', *Ethnic and Racial Studies* 24 no. 5 (2001): 847.

46 On 'hegemonic masculinity', see Connell, *Masculinities*.

47 Luibhéid, *Entry Denied*.

48 For example, exceptional circumstances might be when a parent or sibling is dependent on the individual facing removal for essential care, and they would not be able to receive that same care by other means.

49 Angela Davis, *Are Prisons Obsolete?* (New York: Seven Stories Press, 2011).

50 Here I am paraphrasing Stuart Hall when he says, in relation to young black people living in London in the 1990s, 'in spite of everything [they] are centred, in place ... they occupy a new kind of space at the centre'. Hall, 'Minimal selves', 116.

Notes to Chapter 5. Denico

1 Luibhéid, *Entry Denied*; Griffiths, '"My passport is just my way out of here"'.

2 Anderson, *Us and Them?*

3 According to *The Independent*, just 1% of seasonal farm workers are British. See William Booth and Karla Adam, 'Brits don't want to work on farms – so who will pick fruit after Brexit?', *The Independent*, 4 August 2018.

4 In fact, on the night before his flight, when Denico was taken to a detention centre from prison, Tracy wrote a heartfelt letter about the injustice of his removal to the *Daily Mail*, hoping it would be published (she later reflected that she should have sent it to a different newspaper).

5 de Noronha, *Unpacking the Figure of the 'Foreign Criminal'*; Hasselberg, *Enduring Uncertainty*.

6 Michele Barrett and Mary McIntosh, *The Anti-social Family*, 2nd edition (London: Verso, 2015), 19; see also Sophie Lewis, *Full Surrogacy Now: Feminism Against Family* (London: Verso, 2019).

7 Indeed, Marx and Engels called for the abolition of the family in the *Communist Manifesto*. See also Lewis, *Full Surrogacy Now*.

8 Jyoti Puri, *Sexual States: Governance and the Struggle over the Antisodomy Law in India* (Durham, NC: Duke University Press, 2016); Gayle Rubin, *Deviations: A Gayle Rubin Reader* (Durham, NC: Duke University Press, 2011); Lewis, *Full Surrogacy Now*.

9 Home Office, Immigration Rules: Section 13.

10 Reynolds, 'Exploring the absent/present dilemma'.

11 Griffiths, '"My passport is just my way out of here"'.

12 Helena Wray, *Regulating Marriage Migration into the UK: A Stranger in the Home* (London: Ashgate, 2012); Georgie Wemyss, Nira Yuval-Davis and Kathryn Cassidy, '"Beauty and the beast": everyday bordering and "sham marriage"', *Political Geography* 66 (2018): 151–160.

13 Luke de Noronha, 'No tears left to cry: being deported is a distressing nightmare', *VICE News*, 1 December 2016.

14 Silvia Federici, *Wages Against Housework* (Bristol: Falling Wall Press, 1975); de Hart, 'Superdads'.

15 I was able to verify the details of his immigration history and the reasons for his deportation when Darel sent me some of his legal documents, including the Home Office 'decision to deport' letter. On Operation Nexus, see Griffiths, 'Foreign, criminal'; Luqmani Thompson & Partners, 'Operation Nexus: briefing paper'.

16 Luibhéid, *Entry Denied*, xxi.

17 George Greenwood, 'Homeless families rehoused out of London "up five-fold"', BBC News, https://www.bbc.co.uk/news/uk-england-london-39386587, accessed 5 January 2020.

18 Planning Institute of Jamaica, *Economic and Social Survey 2013'*.

19 Michelle wrote a comment piece about her deportation in *The Guardian*: Michelle Blake, '"Act Jamaican", they said when they deported me. But I'm British', *The Guardian*, 18 April 2018, https://www.theguardian.com/commentisfree/2018/apr/18/act-jamaica-deported-british-england-home-office, accessed 5 January 2020.

20 Sarah Keenan, *Subversive Property: Law and the Production of Spaces of Belonging* (Abingdon: Routledge, 2015), 131–134.

21 Ibid.

22 Nicholas De Genova, 'The queer politics of migration: reflections on "illegality" and incorrigibility', *Studies in Social Justice* 4 no. 2 (2010): 101–126.

23 Caroline Sawyer, 'Not every child matters: the UK's expulsion of British citizens', *International Journal of Children's Rights* 14 (2006): 157–185; Anderson, *Us and Them?*, 129.

24 Jonathon Price and Sarah Spencer, *Safeguarding Children from Destitution: Local Authority Responses to Families with 'No Recourse to Public Funds'* (Oxford: COMPAS, 2015).

25 Eithne Luibhéid, *Pregnant on Arrival: Making the Illegal Immigrant* (Minneapolis, MN: University of Minnesota Press, 2013).

26 Laura Hughes, 'Up to three in four babies born last year in parts of the UK had foreign mothers, official figures have disclosed', *The Telegraph*, 25 August 2016.

27 Michael Hamilton, 'Migrant baby boom: Third of babies born in England and Wales in 2015 have at least one foreign parent', *The Sun*, 14 January 2017.

28 Luibhéid, *Pregnant on Arrival*.

29 Pei-Chia Lan, 'Migrant women's bodies as boundary markers: reproductive crisis and sexual control in the ethnic frontiers of Taiwan', *Signs: Journal of Women in Culture and Society* 33 no. 4 (2008): 833–861.

30 Luibhéid, *Entry Denied*, 75.

31 Michel Foucault, 'Friendship as a way of life', in *Foucault Live (Interviews, 1961–1984)*, ed. Sylvere Lotringer (New York: Semiotext(e), 1989).

32 Anderson, *Us and Them?*, 180–1, emphasis added.

33 Sophie Lewis, 'The satanic death-cult is real', *Commune Magazine* issue 3 (2019), https://communemag.com/the-satanic-death-cult-is-real, accessed 6 January 2020.

34 UN Declaration of Human Rights, Article 16(3).

Notes to Chapter 6. Family and friends

1 Melanie Griffiths, in her important article '"My passport is just my way out of here"', makes several cognate arguments to the ones developed here. Griffiths interviews the British-citizen partners of deportable men, and examines 'the impact of their partners' immigration battles on the women's own sense of stability and

belonging in the UK'. Like me, she argues that immigration controls reveal the differentiated nature of citizenship. Griffiths's paper and this chapter share the same critical thrust, both building heavily on the work of Bridget Anderson. However, my focus is not only on British-citizen partners, but on a broader cast of multi-status friends and family. Moreover, Griffiths does not centre racism analytically in the same way that I do.

2 For a critique of the abstract view of citizenship see: Elizabeth Cohen, *Semi-citizenship in Democratic Politics* (Cambridge: Cambridge University Press, 2014); Barbara Welke, *Law and the Borders of Belonging in the Long Nineteenth Century United States* (Cambridge: Cambridge University Press, 2010); Laura Brace, *The Politics of Property: Labour, Freedom and Belonging* (Edinburgh: Edinburgh University Press, 2004).

3 Benedict Anderson, *Imagined Communities: Reflections on the Origin and Spread of Nationalism* (London: Verso, 1983).

4 On citizenship deprivation, see Kapoor, *Deport, Deprive, Extradite*. On 'neoliberal statecraft', see Wacquant, *Punishing the Poor*; Tyler, *Revolting Subjects*.

5 Cohen, *Semi-citizenship in Democratic Politics*.

6 Anoop Nayak, 'Purging the nation: race, conviviality and embodied encounters in the lives of British Bangladeshi Muslim young women', *Transactions of the Institute of British Geographers* 42 no. 2 (2017).

7 Leah Bassel and Akwugo Emejulu, *Minority Women and Austerity: Survival and Resistance in France and Britain* (Bristol: Policy Press, 2017); Frances Ryan, *Crippled: Austerity and the Demonization of Disabled People* (London: Verso, 2019); Welke, *Law and the Borders of Belonging*.

8 Linda Bosniak, *The Citizen and the Alien: Dilemmas of Contemporary Membership* (Princeton, NJ: Princeton University Press, 2006), 10.

9 Ngai, *Impossible Subjects*.

10 The academic work that does analyse the impact of immigration controls on citizens tends to focus on partners and children, and not on siblings, friends and neighbours. Following on from the arguments raised in the previous chapter, my intention here is to transcend the argument that deportation is wrong because it 'destroys families', and this means talking to a wider range of people who witness deportation.

11 See Hasselberg, *Enduring Uncertainty*.

12 Claire Fitzpatrick and Patrick Williams, 'The neglected needs of care leavers in the criminal justice system: practitioners' perspectives

and the persistence of problem (corporate) parenting', *Criminology and Criminal Justice* 17 no. 2 (2017): 175–191.

13 Achille Mbembe, *Critique of Black Reason* (Durham, NC: Duke University Press, 2017); Paul Gilroy, *The Black Atlantic: Modernity and Double Consciousness* (London: Verso, 1993).

14 Yuval-Davis, Wemyss and Cassidy, *Bordering*.

15 Anderson, Gibney and Paoletti, 'Citizenship, deportation and the boundaries of belonging', 548.

16 Ngai, *Impossible Subjects*, 6.

17 See David Pegg, 'The "golden visa" deal: "We have in effect been selling off British citizenship to the rich"', *The Guardian*, 7 July 2017.

18 Kapoor, *Deport, Deprive, Extradite*; Matthew Gibney, 'Should citizenship be conditional? The ethics of denationalization', *Journal of Politics* 75 no. 3 (2013): 646–658.

19 Lizzie Dearden, 'Shamima Begum: number of people stripped of UK citizenship soars by 600% in a year', *The Independent*, 20 February 2019.

20 Kapoor, *Deport, Deprive, Extradite*.

21 Frances Perraudin, 'Judges uphold decision to strip grooming gang members of citizenship', *The Guardian*, 8 August 2018.

22 Matthew Gibney, 'Denationalisation and discrimination', *Journal of Ethnic and Migration Studies* [published online 13 February 2019], DOI: 10.1080/1369183X.2018.1561065.

23 Ibid. The UK government has also in fact attempted to deport people who have no other nationality, on the basis that the individual can reasonably be expected to apply for and secure the citizenship of another state. For important case law, see: Secretary of State for the Home Department (Appellant) *v.* Al-Jedda (Respondent), [2013] UKSC62; Pham (Appellant) *v.* Secretary of State for the Home Department (Respondent), [2015] UKSC 19, 25 March 2015. Moreover, in the case of Shamima Begum – the young woman who left the UK to join ISIS when she was just 15 – the UK government argued that she would be able to secure Bangladeshi citizenship based on its particular reading of Bangladeshi nationality law. See Dearden, 'Shamima Begum'.

24 Bobbie Mills, 'Citizenship deprivation: how Britain took the lead on dismantling citizenship', European Network on Statelessness Blog, 3 March 2016, https://www.statelessness.eu/blog/citizenship-deprivation-how-britain-took-lead-dismantling-citizenship, accessed 25 November 2019.

25 Griffiths, '"My passport is just my way out of here"'.

26 Ali Sirreyeh, 'All you need is love and £18,600: class and the new

UK family migration rules', *Critical Social Policy* 35 no. 2 (2015): 228–247.

27 Katharine Charsley, 'Vulnerable brides and transnational ghar damads', *Indian Journal of Gender Studies* 12 no. 2–3 (2005): 381–406.

28 Anderson, *Us and Them?*, 66; Bassel and Emejulu, *Minority Women and Austerity*.

29 Wray, *Regulating Marriage Migration*.

30 Valluvan, *The Clamour of Nationalism*, 52.

31 When an individual facing deportation appeals on the grounds of 'genuine and subsisting' relationships with children, part of the legal consideration concerns whether it would be 'unduly harsh' for the children to move with them. This applies to British-citizen children, and while the Home Office usually argues that the 'best interests of the child' can be observed by remaining in the UK, either with family members or in the care of the state, some deported people decide to take their children with them (unsurprisingly). In these cases, British-citizen children are effectively deported (although of course legally they can return). See Sawyer, 'Not every child matters'.

32 Yuval-Davis, Wemyss and Cassidy, *Bordering*.

33 Valluvan, *The Clamour of Nationalism*.

34 Bridget Anderson and Vanessa Hughes, 'Introduction', in *Citizenship and Its Others*, eds Bridget Anderson and Vanessa Hughes (London: Palgrave Macmillan, 2015), 2.

35 Ibid., 2.

36 Anderson, '"Heads I win. Tails you lose"'.

37 Back and Sinha, *Migrant City*.

Notes to Chapter 7. Post-deportation

1 Headley and Milanovic, 'Rights and reintegrating deported migrants', 68–69.

2 Radhika Mongia, *Indian Migration and Empire: A Colonial Geneaology of the Modern State* (Durham, NC: Duke University Press, 2018); Marilyn Lake and Henry Reynolds, *Drawing the Global Colour Line: White Men's Countries and the International Challenge of Racial Equality* (Cambridge: Cambridge University Press, 2008).

3 Huon Wardle, 'The boy who knew how to fly', *Anthropology Today* 20 no. 6 (2004): 20–21.

4 See Thomas, *Exceptional Violence*, for a historically grounded and

theoretically rich account of the substance of Jamaican citizenship. My intervention in this chapter involves very little engagement with the specificities of Jamaican citizenship, and instead offers a broader account of how citizenship functions as an international regime which fixes people in space and in law (i.e. my focus is more on borders and bordering in global perspective, and less on the deep history of Jamaican politics and society). For studies of citizenship in Jamaica and the Caribbean, see Deborah Thomas, *Modern Blackness: Nationalism, Globalization, and the Politics of Culture in Jamaica* (Jamaica: University of West Indies Press, 2004); Gray, *Demeaned but Empowered*; Diane Austin-Broos, *Jamaica Genesis: Religion and the Politics of Moral Orders* (Chicago, IL: University of Chicago Press, 1997); Mimi Sheller, *Citizenship from Below: Erotic Agency and Caribbean Freedom* (Durham, NC: Duke University Press, 2012); Aaron Kamugisha, 'The coloniality of citizenship in the contemporary Anglophone Caribbean', *Race and Class* 49 no. 2 (2007): 20–40; Brian Meeks, *Radical Caribbean: From Black Power to Abu Bakr* (Kingston: University of the West Indies Press, 1993); Anthony Bogues, 'Politics, nation and postcolony', *Small Axe* 6 no. 1 (2002): 1–30.

5 Barry Hindess, 'Citizenship in the international management of populations', *American Behavioural Scientist* 43 no. 9 (2000): 1486–1497; William Walters, 'Deportation, expulsion, and the international police of aliens', *Citizenship Studies* 6 no. 3 (2002): 265–292; De Genova and Peutz, *The Deportation Regime*.

6 In 2010, it was estimated that 10% of street homeless persons in Jamaica were deportees, and this is likely based on a significant underestimation of rates of homelessness. See Wendel Abel, 'I am what I think: there is no home to go back to – the cries of deportees', *Jamaica Gleaner*, 28 March 2007.

7 Sidney Mintz, *Sweetness and Power: The Place of Sugar in Modern History* (New York: Penguin Books, 1986).

8 On race, class and colour in Jamaica see: Hall, *Familiar Stranger*; Thomas, *Modern Blackness*.

9 Mimi Sheller, *Mobility Justice: The Politics of Movement in an Age of Extremes* (London: Verso, 2018).

10 Tanya Golash-Boza, 'Forced transnationalism: transnational coping strategies and gendered stigma among Jamaican deportees', *Global Networks: A Journal of Transnational Affairs* 14 no. 1 (2014): 63–79.

11 International Organization for Migration, *Migration in Jamaica: A Country Profile 2018* (Kingston: International Organization for Migration, 2018), 44–46.

12 Planning Institute of Jamaica, *Economic and Social Survey 2013*.

13 On 'the garrison' see Beverley Mullings, 'Garrison communities', in *Keywords in Radical Geography: Antipode at 50*, Antipode Editorial Collective (Oxford: Wiley Blackwell, 2019).

14 Buju Banton makes this point in his 1993 song, 'Deportees (Things Change)'.

15 'Foreign nuh easy' is a song by reggae artist Brimstone.

16 Golash-Boza, 'Forced transnationalism'.

17 Eilat Maoz, 'The meaning of police', PhD thesis, Department of Anthropology, University of Chicago (forthcoming); Jaffe, 'The hybrid state'.

18 Amnesty International, *Waiting in Vain*.

19 Importantly, it is likely that other deported people were killed in that period, without any media reportage of their deaths or migration histories. Diane Taylor, 'Revealed: five men killed in past year after being deported from UK to Jamaica', *The Guardian*, 9 May 2019.

20 On the culture of disbelief, see Jessica Anderson, *The Culture of Disbelief: An Ethnographic Approach to Understanding an Undertheorised Concept in the UK Asylum System*, Refugee Studies Centre Working Paper 102 (Oxford: Refugee Studies Centre, University of Oxford, 2014). On post-deportation deaths more broadly, see the website of the Post-Deportation Monitoring Network, part of the Rights in Exile Programme, http://www.refugeelegalaidinformation. org/post-deportation-monitoring-network-suggested-reading-list, accessed 5 January 2020.

21 For an account of similar working conditions, see Katie Cruz, Julia O'Connell Davidson and Jacqueline Sanchez Taylor, 'Tourism and sexual violence and exploitation in Jamaica: contesting the "trafficking and modern slavery" frame', *Journal of the British Academy* 7 no. 1 (2019): 191–216.

22 Bank of Jamaica, *Remittances Bulletin: June 2019*; Beverley Mullings, 'Neoliberalization, social reproduction and the limits to labour in Jamaica', *Singapore Journal of Tropical Geography* 30 (2009): 174–188.

23 World Population Review, 'Unemployment by country population', September 2019, http://worldpopulationreview.com/countries/ unemployment-by-country, accessed 18 September 2019. On youth unemployment see Jamaica Information Service, 'Youth unemployment falls', 15 February 2018, https://jis.gov.jm/youth-unemployment-falls, accessed 19 September 2019.

24 International Organization for Migration, *Migration in Jamaica*.

25 William Tantam, 'Higgler tactics: techniques of intermediary market traders in Jamaica', *Journal of Latin American and Caribbean Anthropology* 24 no. 1 (2018): 70–87.

26 Kalyan Sanyal, *Rethinking Capitalist Development: Primitive Accumulation, Governmentality and Post-colonial Capitalism* (London: Routledge, 2014).

27 Ibid.; see also International Labour Organization, 'More than 60 per cent of the world's employed population are in the informal economy', ILO press release, 30 April 2018, https://www.ilo.org/global/about-the-ilo/newsroom/news/WCMS_627189/lang--en/index.htm, accessed 15 September 2019.

28 Bhattacharyya, *Rethinking Racial Capitalism*.

29 On 'lotto scamming' see Lewis, 'Structural readjustment'.

30 Bhattacharyya, *Rethinking Racial Capitalism*.

31 Mullings, 'Neoliberalization, social reproduction and the limits to labour'.

32 Kei Miller, *Augustown* (New York: Pantheon Books, 2016), 3.

33 Hall, *Familiar Stranger*, 65.

34 Jovan Scott Lewis, 'Sufferer's market: sufferation and economic ethics in Jamaica', PhD thesis, Department of Anthropology, London School of Economics and Political Science (2014), 13.

35 Ibid., 12–13, original emphasis.

36 Hall, *Familiar Stranger*; Maoz, 'The meaning of police'.

37 Ahmed Reid, 'Sugar, slavery and productivity in Jamaica, 1750–1807', *Slavery and Abolition* 37 no. 1 (2016): 160.

38 Sheller, *Consuming the Caribbean*.

39 George Beckford, *Persistent Poverty: Underdevelopment in Plantation Economies of the Third World* (New York: Oxford University Press, 1972).

40 Derek Walcott, *What the Twilight Says: Essays* (New York: Farrar, Straus & Giroux, 1998), 56–57.

41 Michael Manley, *Up the Down Escalator: Development and the International Economy – A Jamaican Case Study* (Washington, DC: Howard University Press, 1987), 4.

42 Sheller, *Consuming the Caribbean*.

43 Don Robotham, 'The third crisis: Jamaica in the neoliberal era', in *African Caribbean Worldview and the Making of Caribbean Society*, ed. Horace Levy (Kingston: University of West Indies Press, 2009); Mullings, 'Neoliberalization, social reproduction and the limits to labour'. See also Stephanie Black's *Life and Debt* documentary.

44 Mullings, 'Neoliberalization, social reproduction and the limits to labour'.

45 Jake Johnston, *Partners in Austerity: Jamaica, the United States and the International Monetary Fund* (Washington, DC: Center for Economic and Policy Research, 2015).

46 Shalman Scott, '2018 marks 41 years of IMF "rescue" of Jamaica', *Jamaica Observer*, 13 May 2018; Jeremy Dear, Paula Dear and Tim Jones, *Life and Debt: Global Studies of Debt and Resistance* (London: Jubilee Debt Campaign, October 2013), https://www.jubileedebt.org.uk/wp-content/uploads/2013/10/Life-and-debt_Final-version_10.13.pdf, accessed 18 September 2019; Johnston, *Partners in Austerity*.

47 Mullings, 'Neoliberalization, social reproduction and the limits to labour'; Sheller, *Consuming the Caribbean*.

48 Carl Stone, *Democracy and Clientelism in Jamaica* (New Brunswick, NJ: Transaction Publishers, 1980); Gray, *Demeaned but Empowered*; Mullings, 'Neoliberalization, social reproduction and the limits to labour'.

49 Stone, *Democracy and Clientelism in Jamaica*.

50 Colin Clarke, *Decolonizing the Colonial City: Urbanization and Social Stratification in Kingston, Jamaica* (Oxford: Oxford University Press, 2006).

51 Mullings, 'Neoliberalization, social reproduction and the limits to labour', 179–180.

52 Jamaica Constabulary Force Crime Statistics, http://www.jcf.gov.jm/crime-stats, accessed 4 November 2018; Jamie Grierson, 'Homicide rate in England and Wales highest since 2008', *The Guardian*, 18 October 2018.

53 Patrick Wolfe, *Traces of History: Elementary Structures of Race* (London: Verso, 2016).

54 Coutin, *Exiled Home*, 154.

55 John Torpey, *The Invention of the Passport: Surveillance, Citizenship and the State* (Cambridge: Cambridge University Press, 2000); Btihaj Ajana, 'Biometric citizenship', *Citizenship Studies* 16 no. 7 (2012): 851–870.

56 Stephanie Camp, *Closer to Freedom: Enslaved Women and Everyday Resistance in the Plantation South* (Chapel Hill, NC: University of North Carolina Press, 2004).

57 Hindess, 'Citizenship in the international management of populations', 1487; Barry Hindess, 'Neo-liberal citizenship', *Citizenship Studies* 6 no. 2 (2002): 127–143; Barry Hindess, 'Citizenship and empire', in *Sovereign Bodies: Citizens, Migrants, and States in the Postcolonial World*, eds Thomas Blom Hansen and Finn Stepputat (Princeton, NJ: Princeton University Press, 2005).

58 Walters, 'Deportation, expulsion, and the international police of aliens', 288.

59 Hindess, 'Citizenship in the international management of populations'; Sheller, *Consuming the Caribbean*; Sheller, *Citizenship from Below*.

60 Hindess, 'Citizenship in the international management of populations'; Hindess, 'Neo-liberal citizenship'.

61 James Hampshire, *The Politics of Immigration* (Cambridge: Polity, 2013), 107–130; Randall Hansen, 'The poverty of postnationalism: citizenship, immigration, and the new Europe', *Theory and Society* 38 no. 1 (2009): 1–24.

62 Hindess, 'Citizenship in the international management of populations'; De Genova, *Working the Boundaries*.

63 Hindess, 'Citizenship and empire'.

64 Hindess, 'Neo-liberal citizenship'.

65 Kerem Nisancioglu, 'Racial sovereignty', *European Journal of International Relations* (published online 5 November 2019), DOI: 10.1177/1354066119882991.

66 Ferguson, *Global Shadows*, 50–68.

67 Roxanne Doty, *Imperial Encounters: The Politics of Representation in North–South Relations* (Minnesota, MN: University of Minnesota Press, 1996); Branwen Gruffydd-Jones, 'Race in the ontology of international order', *Political Studies* 56 no. 4 (2008): 907–927.

68 Merav Amir, 'The making of a void sovereignty: political implications of the military checkpoints in the West Bank', *Environment and Planning D: Society and Space* 31 no. 2 (2013): 227–244.

69 Achille Mbembe, 'The society of enmity', *Radical Philosophy* 200 (2016).

70 Ferguson, *Global Shadows*, 50–68.

71 Ibid.

72 Balibar and Wallerstein, *Race, Nation, Class*.

73 Sheller, *Consuming the Caribbean*.

74 Robert Young, *Colonial Desire: Hybridity in Theory, Culture and Race* (London: Routledge, 1995), 173.

75 Ann Stoler, *Duress: Imperial Durabilities in Our Times* (Durham, NC: Duke University Press, 2016), 117, original emphasis.

76 Anderson, *Us and Them?*

77 Sheller, *Mobility Justice*.

78 Frantz Fanon, *Toward the African Revolution* (New York: Grove Press, 1964), 29–44.

79 Anderson, *Us and Them?*, ch. 3.

80 Mark Duffield, 'Racism, migration and development: the foundations of planetary order', *Progress in Development Studies* 6 no. 1 (2006): 68–79.

81 Catherine Besteman, 'Militarized global apartheid', *Current Anthropology* 60 no. 19 (2019): 26–38.

82 Nicholas De Genova, 'The deportation regime: sovereignty, space and

the freedom of movement', in *The Deportation Regime: Sovereignty, Space, and the Freedom of Movement*, eds Nicholas De Genova and Nathalie Peutz (Durham, NC: Duke University Press, 2010), 33–65.

83 De Genova, 'The "migrant crisis" as racial crisis'.

Notes to Chapter 8. Deportation as foreign policy

1 Walters, 'Deportation, expulsion, and the international police of aliens'.

2 William Walters, 'The flight of the deported: aircraft, deportation, and politics', *Geopolitics* 21 no. 2 (2016): 435–458; Diane Taylor, 'Shackles and restraints used on hundreds of deportees from UK', *The Guardian*, 11 August 2019.

3 Lorena Gazzotti, 'From irregular migration to radicalisation? Fragile borders, securitised development and the government of Moroccan youth', *Journal of Ethnic and Migration Studies* 45 no. 15 (2019): 2888–2909.

4 Bosworth, 'Penal humanitarianism?'

5 Biehl, *Vita*.

6 William Walters, 'Foucault and frontiers: notes on the birth of the humanitarian border', in *Governmentality: Current Issues and Future Challenges*, eds U. Bröckling, S. Krasmann and T. Lemke (New York: Routledge, 2011).

7 Ruben Andersson, *Illegality, Inc.: Clandestine Migration and the Business of Bordering Europe* (Oakland, CA: University of California Press, 2014); Bosworth, 'Penal humanitarianism?'

8 Hindess, 'Citizenship in the international management of populations'; Walters, 'Deportation, expulsion, and the international police of aliens'; De Genova and Peutz, *The Deportation Regime*.

9 In 2019, there was some controversy over similar interviews conducted with Zimbabwean nationals, raising questions about the legality of the Home Office allowing Zimbabwean officials to interview people seeking asylum in the UK – see Frances Perraudin, 'Home Office faces legal cases over Zimbabwean asylum seekers', *The Guardian*, 5 January 2020, https://www.theguardian.com/uk-news/2020/jan/05/home-office-faces-legal-cases-over-zimbabwean-asylum-seekers, accessed 6 January 2020.

10 Jamie Grierson, 'Windrush row: 63 people could have been wrongly removed, says Javid', *The Guardian*, 15 May 2018; Jacqueline Stevens, 'U.S. government unlawfully detaining and deporting U.S. citizens as aliens', *Virginia Journal of Social Policy and the Law* 18 no. 3 (2011): 606.

11 Frances Perraudin, 'Home Office criticised for accelerating removals to Zimbabwe', *The Guardian*, 12 February 2019.

12 On 'garrison towns', see Mullings, 'Garrison communities'.

13 'Deportee programme gets $7 million', *Jamaica Observer*, 25 February 2015, http://www.jamaicaobserver.com/news/Deportee-programme-gets--7-million, accessed 10 June 2019.

14 'Open Arms Centre – rehabilitating and reintegrating', *Jamaica Observer*, 25 December 2017, http://www.jamaicaobserver.com/news/open-arms-centre-8212-_120429?profile=1373, accessed 19 September 2019.

15 Paul Clarke, '"Taking care of invisibles" – Jamaican MBE awardee says she was called to care for homeless', *Jamaica Gleaner*, 30 December 2019, http://jamaica-gleaner.com/article/lead-stories/20191230/taking-care-invisibles-jamaican-mbe-awardee-says-she-was-called-care, accessed 12 January 2020.

16 'Open Arms Centre', *Jamaica Observer*.

17 Ibid.

18 Credit must go to Eilat Maoz for suggesting this line of argument to me.

19 Headley and Milanovic, 'Rights and reintegrating deported migrants', 74–76.

20 Foreign and Commonwealth Office, *Coming Home to Jamaica*, 11 November 2014, YouTube video, https://www.youtube.com/watch?v=AXNWbe7_bpo, accessed 22 December 2019.

21 Ibid.

22 'Coming Home to Jamaica', *Foreign and Commonwealth Office* (London: FCO, 2016) – in 2019 the booklet was taken down from the UK's government website.

23 *Coming Home to Jamaica*, 6th edition, February 2014, author's copy.

24 See, for example, Kevin Rawlinson, 'British residents deported to Jamaica told to "put on accent"', *The Guardian*, 17 April 2018.

25 Emily Dugan, 'The Home Office pulled funding for a charity helping people it deported to Jamaica, days before announcing Windrush compensation', BuzzFeed News, 8 April 2019, https://www.buzzfeed.com/emilydugan/home-office-nodm-jamaica-funding, accessed 22 December 2019; Emily Dugan, 'The Home Office says it will continue funding a charity that helps people the UK deported to Jamaica', BuzzFeed News, 9 April 2019, https://www.buzzfeed.com/emilydugan/the-home-office-says-it-will-continue-funding-a-charity, accessed 22 December 2019.

26 In fact, the UK operated a Returns and Reintegration Fund globally between 2008 and 2016 – see Bosworth, 'Penal humanitarianism?'

27 See Gazzotti, 'From irregular migration to radicalisation?'
28 'Deportee programme gets $7 million', *Jamaica Observer*.
29 Bosworth, 'Penal humanitarianism?'
30 Ibid.
31 In fact, in 2016 the tasks formerly undertaken by the Reintegration and Rehabilitation Fund were absorbed into the Conflict, Security and Stability Fund (CSSF). The CSSF now accounts for around 11% of the UK's aid budget, and is designed to provide development and increase security in countries at risk of conflict or instability. Importantly, the CSSF's strategic direction is set by the National Security Council, and while not all the funds for CSSF programmes come from the aid budget (about half do), the CSSF has been central to the shift in which Official Development Assistance funds are allocated to bodies other than the Department for International Development (DfID) – most critically the Ministry of Defence and the Foreign Office (which are now allocated over a quarter of the UK's aid budget). The CSSF has been criticised for its lack of transparency – most notably when it emerged that the UK had covered up its use to train the Bahraini security services in crowd control techniques (there were similar concerns about links to Ethiopian security services) – as well as for how it reflects the broader move within development policy from poverty alleviation towards more militarised concerns.
32 Mark Duffield, *Development, Security and Unending War* (Cambridge: Polity, 2007).
33 Duffield, 'Racism, migration and development', 75.
34 Mark Duffield, 'Getting savages to fight barbarians: development, security and the colonial present', *Conflict, Security and Development* 5 no. 2 (2005): 152.
35 Ibid.; see also Bhattacharyya, *Rethinking Racial Capitalism*.
36 Duffield, 'Getting savages to fight barbarians'.
37 Bhattacharyya, *Rethinking Racial Capitalism*.
38 Zygmunt Bauman, *Wasted Lives: Modernity and Its Outcasts* (Cambridge: Polity, 2003).
39 Vanessa Pupavac, 'Human security and the rise of global therapeutic governance', *Conflict, Security and Development* 5 no. 2 (2005): 161–181.
40 Mark Duffield, 'Resilience and abandonment', *International Policies, Practices and Discourses* 3 no. 2 (2015): 137–140.
41 Duffield, 'Getting savages to fight barbarians'.
42 Paolo Novak, 'Placing borders in development', *Geopolitics* 21 no. 3 (2016): 483–512; Brad Evans and Julian Reid, *Resilient Life: The Art of Living Dangerously* (Cambridge: Polity, 2014).

43 Nick Vaughan-Williams, *Europe's Border Crisis: Biopolitical Security and Beyond* (Oxford: Oxford University Press, 2015).

44 Ruben Andersson, *No Go World: How Fear Is Redrawing Our Maps and Infecting Our Politics* (Berkeley, CA: University of California Press, 2019).

45 Importantly, externalised European bordering practices are now also increasingly justified through reference to threats of Islamic fundamentalism – see Gazzotti, 'From irregular migration to radicalisation?'

46 Didier Fassin, *Humanitarian Reason: A Moral History of the Present* (Berkeley, CA: University of California Press, 2012). See also Miriam Ticktin, *Casualties of Care: Immigration and Politics of Humanitarianism in France* (Berkeley, CA: University of California Press, 2011).

47 Adrian Little and Nick Vaughan-Williams, 'Stopping boats, saving lives, securing subjects: humanitarian borders in Europe and Australia', *European Journal of International Relations* 23 no. 3 (2017): 11.

48 Walters, 'Foucault and frontiers', 137.

49 This combination of humanitarian and securitising logics is also evident in discourses on trafficking (with the US State Department's Office to Monitor and Combat Trafficking in Persons the most significant incarnation of this global anti-trafficking infrastructure). To be saved, the 'victim of trafficking', who is without agency, must be prevented from moving. The idea that a significant number of irregular migrants might be being trafficked licenses tougher border security on humanitarian grounds. This humanitarian reasoning is particularly effective because it recasts aggressive bordering practices in terms of 'saving lives'. When states are criticised for their coercive and violent bordering practices, they reply that their intention is to protect both their own citizens *and* vulnerable people who are being trafficked, or at the very least swindled by smugglers. In this way, European states attempt to outmanoeuvre humanitarians at their own game. See Julia O'Connell Davidson, *Modern Slavery: The Margins of Freedom* (Basingstoke: Palgrave Macmillan, 2015).

50 As Nick Vaughan-Williams, drawing on the work of Didier Fassin, puts it: 'humanitarianism and securitisation, compassion and re-pression, hospitality and hostility are not ... straightforwardly in contradiction with each other'. Vaughan-Williams, *Europe's Border Crisis*, 41.

51 Andersson, *No Go World*.

52 Elise Kervyn and Raphael Shilhav, 'An emergency for whom? The EU Emergency Trust Fund for Africa – migratory routes and

development aid in Africa', Oxfam briefing note, 15 November 2017, https://oxf.am/2zG8aau, accessed 19 September 2019.

53 These examples were all taken from the European Commission website: https://ec.europa.eu/trustfundforafrica/index_en, accessed 20 September 2019.

54 Kalpana Wilson, *Race, Racism and Development: Interrogating History, Discourse and Practice* (London: Zed Books, 2012).

55 Department for International Development, 'DFID Caribbean profile: July 2017', https://www.gov.uk/government/publications/dfid-caribbean-profile-july-2017, accessed 2 September 2019.

56 Quoted in Ben Quinn and Karen McVeigh, 'Plan to align UK aid with trade policy could sideline poor countries', *The Guardian*, 1 December 2016.

57 Ibid.

58 Wilson, *Race, Racism and Development*.

59 Sandro Mezzadra and Brett Neilson, *Border as Method, Or, the Multiplication of Labor* (Durham, NC: Duke University Press, 2013); Stephan Scheel, *Autonomy of Migration? Appropriating Mobility Within Biometric Border Regimes* (London: Routledge, 2019); Dimitris Papadopoulos, Niamh Stephenson and Vassilis Tsianos *Escape Routes: Control and Subversion in the Twenty-First Century* (London: Pluto Press, 2008).

60 Mezzadra and Neilson, *Border as Method*.

61 De Genova, *Working the Boundaries*.

62 Bhattacharyya, *Rethinking Racial Capitalism*, 127.

63 Brown, *Walled States, Waning Sovereignty*, 99.

64 Bhattacharyya, *Rethinking Racial Capitalism*, 125–150.

65 See Benjamin Bowling, *Policing the Caribbean: Transnational Security Cooperation in Practice* (Oxford: Oxford University Press, 2010).

66 Sheller, *Consuming the Caribbean*.

67 Hagar Kotef, *Movement and the Ordering of Freedom: On Liberal Governances of Mobility* (Durham, NC: Duke University Press, 2015), 3.

68 Sheller, *Mobility Justice*, 57.

69 Sheller, *Consuming the Caribbean*; Sheller, *Citizenship from Below*; Sheller, *Mobility Justice*; Mimi Sheller, *Aluminium Dreams: The Making of Light Modernity* (London: MIT Press, 2014). See also the work of John Urry, for example *Mobilities* (Cambridge: Polity Press, 2007).

70 Sheller, *Consuming the Caribbean*.

71 Camp, *Closer to Freedom*; O'Connell Davidson, *Modern Slavery*, 81–108.

72 Edlie Wong, *Neither Fugitive Nor Free* (New York: New York University Press, 2009).

73 Mbembe, *Critique of Black Reason*.

74 Goldberg, *The Threat of Race*.

75 Genevieve Carpio, *Collisions at the Crossroads: How Place and Mobility Make Race* (Berkeley, CA: University of California Press, 2019).

76 Sheller, *Consuming the Caribbean*.

77 Traci-Ann Wint, '"Once you go you know": tourism, colonial nostalgia and national lies in Jamaica', Master's thesis, Graduate School – University of Texas at Austin (2012), 25.

78 For a fascinating and challenging account of the production of racial difference within tourist spaces, beyond skin colour difference, see Arun Saldanha, *Psychedelic White: Goa Trance and the Viscosity of Race* (Minneapolis, MN: University of Minnesota Press, 2007).

79 World Travel and Tourism Council, *Travel and Tourism: Economic Impact 2018 – Jamaica* (London: WTTC, 2018), https://www.wttc.org/economic-impact/country-analysis/country-reports, accessed 19 September 2018; Edmund Bartlett, 'Tourism: a strong pillar for economic growth', *Jamaica Observer*, 18 February 2018.

80 Strachan, *Paradise and Plantation*, 9.

81 Wint, '"Once you go you know"', 11.

82 Karen Wilkes, *Whiteness, Weddings, and Tourism in the Caribbean: Paradise for Sale* (New York: Palgrave Macmillan, 2016).

83 Jamaica Kincaid, *A Small Place* (London: Virago, 1988), 5.

84 Bosworth, 'Penal humanitarianism?'

85 Luke de Noronha, 'David Cameron's prison: a show of ignorance, cruelty and historical amnesia', *Ceasefire Magazine*, 1 October 2015, https://ceasefiremagazine.co.uk/david-camerons-jamaican-prison-show-ignorance-cruelty-historical-amnesia, accessed 23 September 2019.

86 See note 31 to this chapter.

87 'UK to build £25m Jamaican prison', BBC News, 30 September 2015, https://www.bbc.co.uk/news/uk-34398014, accessed 3 September 2019.

88 Scott Lewis, 'Structural readjustment'.

89 Ibid., 1032.

90 Keller Easterling, *Extrastatecraft: The Power of Infrastructure Space* (London: Verso, 2016).

91 Linda Basch, Nina Glick Schiller and Cristina Szanton Blanc, *Nations Unbound: Transnational Projects, Postcolonial Predicaments, and Deterritorialized Nation-States* (London: Routledge, 1993).

92 Sheller, *Aluminium Dreams*, 164.

93 Cindy Hahamovitch, *No Man's Land: Jamaican Guestworkers in America and the Global History of Deportable Labor* (Princeton, NJ: Princeton University Press, 2013).

94 Wardle, 'The boy who knew how to fly'.

95 Mullings, 'Neoliberalization, social reproduction and the limits to labour'.

96 Kotef, *Movement and the Ordering of Freedom*, 15.

97 On dishonour in the context of slavery, see Orlando Patterson, *Slavery and Social Death: A Comparative Study* (London: Harvard University Press, 1982).

98 On colour distinctions in Jamaica see Hall, *Familiar Stranger*.

99 Scott Lewis, 'Sufferer's market', 13

100 On migration and existential mobility, see Ghassan Hage, 'A not so multi-sited ethnography of a not so imagined community', *Anthropological Theory* 5 no. 4 (2005): 463–475.

101 I borrow 'afterlives of slavery' from Saidiya Hartman, *Lose Your Mother: A Journey Along the Atlantic Slave Route* (New York: Farrar, Straus & Giroux, 2007).

102 Cedric Robinson, *Forgeries of Memory and Meaning: Blacks and the Regimes of Race in American Theater and Film Before World War II* (Chapel Hill, NC: University of North Carolina Press, 2007), 4.

103 Knowles, 'Theorizing race and ethnicity'.

104 De Genova, 'The "migrant crisis" as racial crisis'.

105 Mbembe, 'The society of enmity'.

106 On anti-racism see Alana Lentin, *Racism and Anti-racism in Europe* (London: Pluto Press, 2004).

Notes to Chapter 9. Conclusion

1 Back, *The Art of Listening*, 204.

2 De Genova and Peutz, *The Deportation Regime*.

3 Jones, *Violent Borders*.

4 Todd Miller, *Empire of Borders: The Expansion of the U.S. Border Around the World* (London: Verso, 2019); Dennis Broeders, 'The new digital borders of Europe: EU databases and the surveillance of irregular migrants', *International Sociology* 22 no. 1 (2007): 71–92.

5 Les Back, 'Blind pessimism and worldly hopes', 2019 Antipode RGS IBS Lecture, London, 27 August 2019, https://www.youtube.com/watch?v=m2z6qxYfULM, accessed 19 September 2019.

6 For an excellent edited collection on the relationship between

culture, power and place, see Akhil Gupta and James Ferguson, eds, *Culture, Power, Place: Explorations in Critical Anthropology* (Durham, NC: Duke University Press, 1997). On the politics of nativism and autochthony, see: Mahmood Mamdani, *Define and Rule: Native as Political Identity* (Cambridge, Mass: Harvard University Press, 2012); Peter Geschiere, *The Perils of Belonging: Autochthony, Citizenship and Exclusion in Africa and Europe* (Chicago: The University of Chicago Press, 2009); Nandita Sharma, *Home Rule: National Sovereignty and the Separation of Natives and Migrants* (Durham, NC: Duke University Press, 2020).

7 Valluvan, *The Clamour of Nationalism*, 202, original emphasis.

8 Gilroy, *After Empire*, xi.

9 Kath Weston, *Families We Choose: Lesbians, Gays, Kinship* (New York: Columbia University Press, 1991); Elizabeth Povinelli, *The Empire of Love: Toward a Theory of Intimacy, Genealogy, and Carnality* (New York: Columbia University Press, 2006); David L. Eng, *The Feeling of Kinship: Queer Liberalism and the Racialization of Intimacy* (Durham, NC: Duke University Press, 2010); Lewis, *Full Surrogacy Now*.

10 Judith Butler, 'Is kinship always already heterosexual?', *Differences: A Journal of Feminist Cultural Studies* 13 no. 1 (2002); Lewis, *Full Surrogacy Now*.

11 Coutin, *Exiled Home*, 58.

12 Eric Kaufmann, *Whiteshift: Populism, Immigration and the Future of White Majorities* (London: Allen Lane, 2018).

13 On 'common sense' see Centre for Contemporary Cultural Studies, *The Empire Strikes Back*, 45–92; Antonio Gramsci, *Prison Notebooks* (London: Lawrence & Wishart, 1971).

14 Maribel Casas-Cortes et al., 'New keywords: migration and borders', *Cultural Studies* 29 no. 1 (2015): 83.

15 Mezzadra and Neilson, *Border as Method*; Martina Tazzioli, *Spaces of Governmentality: Autonomous Migration and the Arab Uprisings* (London: Rowman & Littlefield, 2014).

16 Stephan Scheel, 'Recuperation through crisis talk: apprehending the European border regime as a parasitic apparatus of capture', *South Atlantic Quarterly* 117 no. 2 (2018): 274. While I find the 'autonomy of migration' (AoM) approach very generative, most of the literature tends to focus on clandestine movement, unruly mobility, evasion and escape. Studies are often located at the borders of Europe, in those hotspots where people are moving and bordering practices are often most conspicuous, even spectacular. Arguably, there is a certain romance surrounding the figure of the irregular migrant, whose autonomy grants them a kind of revolutionary potential (this

body of literature develops out of autonomist Marxism). There is nothing wrong with this *per se*, but it cannot be so easily transposed to this book, given that, for the men in this study, having migrated was not the most significant aspect of their biographies. In light of this, I have found it helpful to engage with Gilroy's reflections on the 'radical openness of lived culture' (*After Empire*), and to replace the romance of movement and evasion with the romance of conviviality and lived culture. Put another way, what happens if the uncontrollability, the excess and indeed the autonomy are made to refer to culture as much as to border crossing?

17 See the 'Migrant struggles' entry in Maribel Casas-Cortes et al., 'New keywords: migration and borders'.

18 This line is taken from Leonard Cohen's song 'Anthem'.

19 Bridget Anderson, 'Interview: Bridget Anderson on Europe's "violent humanitarianism" in the Mediterranean', *Ceasefire Magazine*, 27 May 2015, https://ceasefiremagazine.co.uk/interview-bridget-anderson, accessed 19 September 2019.

20 Edward Said, *Reflections on Exile and Other Literary and Cultural Essays* (London: Granta, 2001), 185.

21 John Berger, *and our faces, my heart, brief as photos* (London: Bloomsbury, 1984), 9.

Index